Introduction to Existential–Phenomenological Psychology

Methodology and Perspective in the Science of Living-Experience

Eugene Mario DeRobertis

Colorado Springs, CO
www.universityprofessorspress.com

Introduction to Existential–Phenomenological Psychology: Methodology and Perspective in the Science of Living-Experience
By Eugene DeRobertis

First Published in 2026, University Professors Press.

Hardcover ISBN:	978-1-955737-69-2
Paperback ISBN:	978-1-955737-68-5
ebook ISBN:	978-1-955737-70-8

University Professors Press
Colorado Springs, CO
www.universityprofessorspress.com

Cover Design by Laura Ross
Cover Image Designed by Violet Void of True Poison Art & Graphics

Eugene DeRobertis's introductory book should be mandatory reading for any student of existential phenomenological psychology or qualitative psychological research. In his pedagogically illuminating style, DeRobertis takes the reader through the landscape of phenomenological and existential thought and how it applies to a psychology envisioned as a human science. Content ranges from research methodology to concrete studies of anxiety, to the unconscious, and includes both theoretical controversies and future challenges.

Magnus Englander, PhD, Associate Professor
of Health and Society Studies at Malmö University

DeRobertis's latest book is a tour de force that brings together in one place his decades-long dedication and personal edification within the existential phenomenological tradition in psychology. The book as a whole is nothing short of a masterclass in how to take an audience by the hand through the history, philosophical underpinnings, institutional developments, and individual contributions from a myriad of sources that together constitute the state-of-the-art in the field of existential phenomenological psychology today. Drawing generously from both European and American primary sources, DeRobertis offers clear exposition with painstaking attention to detail, providing readers with authoritative and trustworthy characterizations of a tradition that holds the promise not only of filling gaps in current psychological theory but also of offering a viable pathway forward. The prose is readable and engaging throughout, and the included demonstration of an actual existential phenomenological research investigation provides compelling testimony to the value of this approach in grasping at the meanings that lie just below the surface within human experience. This book is a must-read not only for graduate students and advanced undergraduates but for professors and qualitative research mentors looking for a reliable guide in the classroom.

Scott Churchill, PhD
Author, *Essentials of Existential Phenomenological Research*

Table of Contents

Acknowledgments

I would like to thank Heather A. DeRobertis for transcribing the original form of this manuscript in total and for her patient support throughout the process of developing this text. I would also like to thank Violet Void of True Poison (https://www.instagram.com/violet_void/) for graciously offering me cover art for this text.

Foreword

Existential-phenomenological psychology is an approach to psychology and a large body of knowledge that has been building since the early 20th century. With deep roots in the critical and expansive work of philosophers and psychologists in the 19th century, this is a movement that continues to grow and make crucial contributions to psychology in the 21st century. This volume, by eminently qualified Professor DeRobertis, is a welcome new contribution that promises to ensure the continued growth of existential-phenomenological psychology by offering new generations a broad and sorely needed orientation in the history, methods, and theory of this distinctive approach. The book explains, in accessible ways, why existential-phenomenological knowledge is still needed in the field of psychology, how existential-phenomenological philosophy informs psychological theory and research methods, and what difference it makes in the science of psychology as a whole as well as in the clinical world. This volume aims to assure that the existential-phenomenological approach remains capable not only of introducing new psychological knowledge but of providing a framework that sets psychology on an authentic scientific foundation.

Phenomenology was founded by the philosopher Edmund Husserl, a philosopher and mathematician who wrote more about psychology than any other discipline outside of philosophy. He introduced a new way of thinking that crystallized and offered a rigorous method for investigating consciousness and lived experience at a time when other great thinkers such as Franz Brentano and Wilhelm Dilthey in Europe and William James in America were insisting that psychology requires a distinctive approach, one fundamentally different from the physical sciences, to investigate psychological subject matter. Husserl's work educated and inspired some of the greatest thinkers of the 20th century, many of whom actually conducted philosophically informed psychological research as well as research across other social sciences. Lester Embree documented the significant employment of phenomenology in more than 50 countries and three dozen sciences, including not only psychology but sociology, theology, and art history (Embree, 2010). The astonishing growth of phenomenology was carried forward by followers of Husserl and original thinkers in their own right, including Martin Heidegger, who drew on the earlier work of psychologically minded existential philosophers Søren Kierkegaard and Friedrich Nietzsche, as well as others too numerous to exhaustively name, including Jean-Paul Sartre, Maurice Merleau-Ponty, Simone de Beauvoir, Gabriel Marcel, Alfred Schutz, Aron Gurwitsch, Emmanuel Levinas, Paul Ricoeur, Franz Fanon, Hannah Arendt, Hans-Georg Gadamer, and Jacques Derrida (Wertz, 2025a).

This unique existential–phenomenological point of view could only have generated such diverse and fruitful scholarship through the 20th century if it addressed issues and introduced insights that resonated with the needs of humanity in a century that was fraught with calamitous wars, political turmoil, poverty, economic upheavals, and personal challenges that could not be addressed exclusively by the natural sciences. Even as successful as natural sciences were in providing knowledge of the material world and offering new and valuable technologies, they required supplementation by a more comprehensive rationality and methods that addressed the lived experiences and deepest needs of humanity (Husserl, 1970). Mainstream psychology based itself on natural science, prioritizing measurement, quantitative methods, and experiments that failed to incorporate the phenomena of lived, personal experience or to employ procedures capable of producing knowledge of it.

Meanwhile, lesser known research enacted by the above-mentioned existential phenomenologists remained marginal in psychology. For instance, works by Otto on human spirituality, by Sartre on the imagination and emotions, by Simone de Beauvoir on the oppression and potential liberation of women, by Fanon on racism, by Merleau-Ponty on key subject matters of psychology (e.g., behavior and perception), by Bachelard on the physical world, by Buytendijk on the human meanings of physiological processes, by van den Berg on psychopathology and the changes of human nature over history, and by Laing on schizophrenia as a social phenomenon were advanced by existential–phenomenological psychology. Although this mostly European scholarship finally entered the English-speaking world when May, Angel, and Ellenberger (1958) published *Existence*, this approach still lacked a clearly defined method capable of transforming academic psychology (Wertz, 2025b). It was not until Adrian Van Kaam established a doctoral program and full faculty at Duquesne University entirely dedicated to existential–phenomenological psychology that Giorgi articulated the distinctive phenomenological approach as a foundation for the entire field of psychology (1970) and developed specific research procedures (1985) with other seminal Duquesne Circle scholars such as William Fischer, Rolf Von Eckartsberg, Constance Fischer, Edward Murray, Frank Buckley, and others. They extended this approach to the full spectrum of psychological subject matter, introduced it in American psychology, established journals, and assumed leadership positions in the American Psychological Association (Wertz, 2025a, 2025b). Although the successes of this movement had some impact on psychology (and continues more broadly as the "human science" approach to this day at Duquesne) most 20th century psychology continued for the most part to employ a natural science model that remained largely incapable of addressing human experience with methods particularly suited to it.

Partly in response to the "replication crisis" of psychology—the failure to re-verify established results in research—criticisms that Giorgi (1970) documented throughout the 20th century have continued to be voiced even today. Recently the lack of an adequate approach within psychology, with significant consequences, has continued to be voiced in the new century. For instance, Devine (2020) claimed that psychology is a discipline in crisis, identifying the "four horsemen" of the crisis in the problems of replication, measurement, generalizability, and practicality. He argued that the replication crisis is an outcome of three other deeper problems—the lack of methods to know what we are measuring, the inability to generalize beyond research to real-life situations, and the ineptness to effectively address society's practical and social problems. Devine suggested that psychology radically rethink its place among the sciences and in society; address the issue of values, which requires philosophical reflection; converse with thinkers in other fields to reunite psychology and the humanities; and transcend the limits of psychology in a collective search for truth in science.

The huge body of existential-phenomenological psychology that has been developing resolutions for the foundational problems of psychology remains largely unknown among contemporary psychologists. It has been integrated into the curriculum only in a very limited number of universities and is largely carried forth by isolated researchers often in undergraduate institutions. The crisis of existential-phenomenological psychology is that it has not been successful in reaching the emerging generation of psychologists. The most difficult challenge of doing so is the movement's difficult philosophy and enormous body of literature, which is beyond the scope and capability of students and even the most open established scholars in psychology. It is this possibly even fatal problem in the movement that Professor DeRobertis's volume addresses. The volume is a third, revised, and updated edition of his previous books that address the tremendous challenge of introducing unfamiliar readers to the approach, methods, and achievements of existential–phenomenological psychology in a manner that promises to bring this movement home to psychology. It is hoped that these invaluable resources might shape the future of psychology in the hands of emerging generations of psychologists.

The book begins from a simple but profound question: Given the extraordinary success of psychology's existing traditions—sense-empiricism and cognitive psychology—what remains unaccounted for in our understanding of human existence? The opening chapters argue that something essential is missing when psychology models itself exclusively on the natural sciences: the rigorous study of lived experience, which implicates meaning and intentionality. Thus, existential-phenomenological psychology is not merely an alternative viewpoint operating alongside various traditions in psychology but is required to enable this science to research its own subject matter in a valid way.

From this starting point, the book seeks to show how psychology can draw on phenomenological and existential philosophy accurately and productively. It traces the historical tensions involved in the appropriation of philosophy by psychology, clarifies the conceptual and methodological challenges that accompany it, and demonstrates that phenomenological psychology is methodologically disciplined, systematic, reflexive, and therefore scientifically conscientious. Drawing on both this generative modern philosophy and established psychological research, the text shows how existential–phenomenological insights address and clarify core problems in psychological science.

Finally, the book informs readers about the fruitful contributions existential–humanistic psychology has already made in psychology, including phenomenological considerations of clinically relevant topic areas such as anxiety and "the unconscious." The book invites a new generation of psychologists who might be interested in existential phenomenology to participate in a living tradition that addresses what psychology has always sought to understand but has not theoretically and methodologically secured: the elucidation of human experience in its living forms.

This volume has numerous virtues that promise to meet the challenge of psychology's crisis exemplified by Devine's (2020) clarion call (noted above). It is written specifically for contemporary psychologists and corrects the many misunderstandings of other introductions to existential-phenomenological psychology. It is philosophically sound, clarifies the distinctive approach, emphasizes method, covers not only clinical but all areas of psychology, and reflects the many changes that have taken place in psychology through the present. *Phenomenological Psychology: A Text for Beginners* (DeRobertis, 1996) is currently out of print, and psychology has evolved significantly in the last 30 years. One of the most confusing challenges for the uninitiated is that there are many meanings of "phenomenology," and this volume clarifies the distinctiveness of *existential* phenomenology, specifies the European philosophical tradition, discusses Giorgi's contributions within the existential–humanistic camp of phenomenology, and refers throughout to the great existential thinkers and their profound insights. Moreover, key challenges of mainstream psychology, such as the problem of securing a philosophically grounded method (to which a whole chapter is dedicated), are placed front and center in this book. It contains a list of key terms and themes (e.g., intuition, the phenomenological epoché, intentionality, the lifeworld), makes no apologies about utilizing insights of philosophy (e.g., clarifying the epistemological problems with the empiricism–rationalism binary and overcoming mind–body ontological dualism), and contains abundant references to historical (e.g., William James) and contemporary (e.g., developmental, cognitive) psychology. This book shows that existential-phenomenological psychology is neither dead nor even close to finished but is still alive and moving into the future, a future that this book promises to secure.

Many readers of this volume will not have had the benefit of an extensive and rigorous philosophical education and consequently may have difficulty understanding the philosophical foundations of psychology. The author recognizes that even those who are attracted to existential-phenomenological psychology may be confused when approaching its literature. They are likely to be unclear about the distinctiveness of phenomenological philosophy, how it differs from all other philosophies and its unique, unparalleled relationship to psychology. Indeed, not only do professional philosophers broadly debate the nature and value of phenomenology and existentialism, but even the pioneers and leaders of these philosophies differ in their understandings and interpretations. Philosophy has numerous variants of phenomenology that have been called realistic, descriptive, transcendental, hermeneutic, narrative, critical, and ethical as well as existential. Although these variants are often contrasted with each other and even held to be incompatible with each other, all these developments have made extremely relevant and important contributions to psychology. The greatest challenge for students of existential–phenomenological psychology is to sort out these differences, understand their interrelations, and put the entire field in perspective with secure understanding.

Even as Professor DeRobertis highlights existential phenomenology in this volume, he views and places it within the phenomenological movement as a whole. Rather than promoting one variant in contrast to others, as many introductory texts do, this one views the variants of phenomenology as compatible with one another, clearly articulates phenomenology's essential core, and integrates variations within existential phenomenology for the benefit of psychology. This book systematically and rigorously addresses the need for a common phenomenological foundation and cohesive method that helps bring unity to the field of phenomenological research in psychology and even to psychology as a whole. Far from presenting "old wine in a new bottle," this book honors the entire dynamic history of the phenomenological movement. Readers of this volume will thereby be prepared to likewise integrate extant variations in their further study and as they invent and develop their own, original research and theorizing within a well-understood movement whose complexities and continuing variegations are far greater than any of its specific contributions. What psychology needs most is students who learn and engage new problems and their own innovations in an evolving field far greater than themselves. This book is an invitation and preparation for members of a new generation to become capable participants in the phenomenological movement, the most powerful and rich basis for fruitful and generative historical progress in psychology.

Fred Wertz

Preface

In 1994, as a graduate student, I began writing what was intended to be a paper on misinterpretations of existential-phenomenological psychology. The would-be paper was inspired by a chapter from Medard Boss's *Psychoanalysis and Daseinsanalysis* (1963) entitled "The Most Common Misunderstandings about Analysis of Dasein." As a student of existential-phenomenological psychology, I found that chapter to be helpful in trying to understand how the existential-phenomenological perspective was different from other viewpoints in philosophy and psychology. I wondered why more authors did not write along these foundational lines, so I decided to take it upon myself to try my hand at it. What began as a paper soon ballooned into a small text: *Phenomenological Psychology: A Text for Beginners* (DeRobertis, 1996). My intention was to create an introduction to existential-phenomenological psychology by fashioning the contents of the book according to the issues that most frequently arose in my discussions with fellow students. I wanted the text to be as brief and to the point as possible without sacrificing depth and rigor.

A decade later, long after the text was out of print, I looked back on it and sensed that there might still be a need for an introductory phenomenology text for psychology. I looked around and found that my feeling was quite warranted. The situation regarding introductory phenomenology texts had not changed since 1996. I feel the same today. High-quality introductions to phenomenology are more likely to be written by philosophers for philosophy students. But psychologists need something different, something custom tailored to the work they would be doing in their disciplinary context. There are many good articles and chapters in edited volumes that could be pieced together, but there is no substitute for a single text dedicated to providing a general, broad-based introduction to phenomenological psychology. As Kruger (1979) once noted, the lack of a properly designed introductory text when trying to teach phenomenology to a new generation of psychology students is a "handicap" (p. vii).

While there are a few introductory texts available, the general stockpile of choices, I submit, are not optimal. Perhaps the most popular introductory phenomenology text is Spinelli's (1989) *The Interpreted*

World: An Introduction to Phenomenological Psychology. This is unfortunate because it is also likely the least reliable when it comes to providing students with a clear understanding of the distinctive characteristics of phenomenological psychology. As its title suggests, it advocates a hermeneutic universalism (see Giorgi, 2018) that papers over the important distinction between description and interpretation. Moreover, the text regularly presents topics in a manner that confusedly intermingles natural science and phenomenological, human science views and concepts. Indeed, many of its chapters discuss psychological topics at length using traditional psychological terms, research, and theories, offering but a few words from a well-known phenomenological author before concluding. Opportunities to discuss the topics at length from a specifically phenomenological viewpoint are missed throughout the book. Conceptually, Keen's (1975) *A Primer in Phenomenological Psychology* fares somewhat better, but the same basic criticisms apply. Keen not only fuses description to interpretation, but he blurs the distinction between description and explanation as well (see p. 139). His chapters also often speak in such general terms that they offer little of substance concerning a specifically phenomenological articulation of the issues. Sometimes a phenomenological perspective is merely approximated by citing the views of individuals like Carl Rogers or George Kelly.

McCall's (1983) *Phenomenological Psychology: An Introduction with a Glossary of Some Key Heideggerian Terms* provides stimulating and insightful discussions concerning the historical context of phenomenological philosophy and phenomenological psychology. It is more conceptually rigorous than the texts just mentioned. But it is methodologically mute, and (as its subtitle indicates) it is exclusively Heideggerian in nature with a general emphasis on clinical application. It also makes a straw man of Husserl, citing only ideas that pertain to the period of his static phenomenology. This is typical of introductory texts and, in McCall's defense, many advanced texts as well. Husserl scholarship has come a long way, and a quality introductory text in today's world cannot continue the trend of pigeonholing Husserl.

One of the highest quality introductory texts is van den Berg's (1972) *A Different Existence*, and I cite it numerous times in the chapters that follow. But, as good as it is, it is very terse, and it says little about methodological issues. It is also unabashedly clinical, tightly focused on (re)conceptualizing the problems of the therapist from an existential–phenomenological perspective. Of all the introductory texts that I have seen, the one that comes the closest to my own in terms of the overall selection of content areas is Dreyer Kruger's (1979) *An Introduction to Phenomenological Psychology*. Above all other authors, I think Kruger had the right idea in envisioning an introductory phenomenological psychology text. But the book is long out of print and would have to be revised to reflect the changes that have taken place in the field since 1979. Sadly, Kruger is no longer with us to do so.

After my own text went out of print, I became too busy with other projects to return to it. Still, a sense of urgency remained. I felt I had to revise the text one day. The original was saved on the already long-outmoded floppy disk, so I would have to retype the whole thing. I casually noted as much to my wife and she surprised me that Christmas by retyping the original book in its entirety. This provided an opportunity to make a few changes and refinements. The result was the release of a second version with the revised title, *Existential–Phenomenological Psychology: A Brief Introduction* (DeRobertis, 2012a). The original characterization of the book as a text for beginners was dropped. The reasons for this alteration were twofold. On the one hand, the title suddenly seemed unclear to me. What exactly is a "beginner" reader in phenomenological psychology? Is it someone with no background at all in psychology or philosophy? Is it someone with a background in psychology or philosophy who wants to start learning about phenomenological psychology? I remembered speaking to "beginners" who had little or no background in one or the other discipline who found the content too difficult at various points. On the other hand, all phenomenologists, even experts, are perpetual beginners. So, in this light, "beginner" suddenly appeared tautological to me.

It goes without saying that the title of the current volume has been altered again. The word "brief" was deemed superfluous, so it was dropped. Introductions are briefer than advanced texts by their very nature. Also, this attempt at an introductory text is more robust than the previous works. Last time around, "phenomenological psychology" was changed to "existential–phenomenological psychology." This alteration has been retained for three reasons. First, there is a long tradition in psychology, especially American psychology, of misunderstanding phenomenology as a term for "subjective experience," where subjectivity is interpreted within the context of the subject–object dichotomy (e.g., see Churchill, 1988; Spiegelberg, 1972). Thus, I felt that the title ought to make it clear that the content of this text is rooted in the European current of phenomenology, which is often referred to as existential–phenomenological psychology. Second, phenomenology emerged, and has always operated, within the existential–humanistic camp in psychology (e.g., Giorgi, 1970; Kuenzli, 1959; van Kaam, 1966).

Third and finally, existential thinkers, issues, and insights are peppered throughout the text and have been since its inception. Thus, it only makes sense to be more precise in the title. There is no question that the text takes advantage of existential thought for psychological purposes. For me, the term existential phenomenology best captures the paradoxical nature of the kind of phenomenological psychology represented herein. Existential–phenomenological psychology seeks an alternative to all-out objectivism, whether founded upon sense-empirical and/or rationalistic principles.[1] At the same time, it does not altogether disavow nomothetic (generalizable) science in favor of an exclusive focus on the unique experience of the situated existential subject. Von Eckartsberg (1998) referred to this as the existential–phenomenological paradox, citing Natanson (1970) as follows:

> If Phenomenology depicts the typical, Existentialism shows the unique; if Phenomenology deals with essence, Existentialism handles concreteness; if Phenomenology is interested in the structure of consciousness, Existentialism, is concerned with the reality of the individual. It would seem these philosophies represent divergent standpoints rather than complementary approaches to human reality. That they are congenial, indeed intimately inter-sustaining and supporting views . . . is the methodological thesis on which we have proceeded. What appears to be a paradox is a metaphysical duality which affects all . . . reality . . . . In classical and traditional terms the duality has been called the Universal and the Particular, or Thought and Life. The question is how the truth of the world in general is related to the truth of individual experience and how a theoretical system can understand the immediacy of the person. (p. 66)

Existential–phenomenological psychology is about conducting psychological science in a manner is that is both traditional and revisionist. Science has always been about rendering reality more

---

[1] Objectivism in this context does not refer to the philosophy of Ayn Rand. It refers to the way that natural science psychology greatly reduces and misunderstands subjectivity's necessary role in the constitution of objectivity (see Moran, 2013).

comprehensible by exposing the underlying themes that undergird its complexity. Of course, this leads to still more riddles, but it is nonetheless an attempt to find some degree of intelligible regularity nascent within the flux of human experience. The phenomenological method makes this possible by allowing psychologists to explicate generalizable structural descriptions from human experience. In the practice of phenomenology in psychology, the researcher performs scientific reductions. These include turning one's attention toward the object of study precisely as it is experienced (rather than as it is hypothesized) and, later, distinguishing essential from incidental meanings (Wertz, 2023). But these "phenomenological" and "eidetic" reductions do not commit reduction*ism*. Rather, they are used to render human psychology more comprehensible without attempting to explain it away, such that there is little or nothing recognizably human left in one's findings. It is in this sense that existential–phenomenological psychology deviates from what has become tradition in psychology. Existential–phenomenological psychology is psychological science, not a mere reversion to philosophy, but it is a human science that is not content with what Frankl referred to as the *scientistic* tendency toward nothing-but-ness[2] (Frankl, 1967, 1969). Edmund Husserl famously spoke of this tendency as a manifestation of *psychologism* (see Moran, 2013). William James, before him, spoke of reductionism in terms of *the psychologist's fallacy*, the unreflective assumption that the research participant's experience matches the researcher's abstract natural scientific concepts and categories (see Ashworth, 2009; Wilshire, 1968). From William James and the tradition of existential phenomenology comes an approach to psychology that insists on respecting the indeterminant, ambiguous aspects of psychological phenomena, protecting them from forced (artificial) clarity. Exactitude is not privileged over fidelity to the "object" of study. Existential–phenomenological psychology involves a delicate balancing act between abstraction and concretion.

For the reader who is familiar with my previous efforts (DeRobertis, 1996, 2012a), I note various structural changes specific to the content of the current volume. The chapter that began the project, *What Phenomenology is Not*, is gone. It no longer seemed useful to dedicate a

---

[2] Frankl spoke of scientism to refer to the way scientists, under the influence of naturalism, "rationalize away" the distinctly human aspects of existence, thereby leveling the depth and breadth of psychological life in advance of study (e.g., see Frankl, 1967, p. 88).

chapter to brief comparisons and contrasts with other schools of thought. Some comparisons and contrasts remain, but they are spread out across the chapters in connection to relevant content. The chapter on the nature/nurture debate is gone, as that material has taken its place in my works on developmental psychology (e.g., DeRobertis, 2008, 2012b, 2017). What began as a methodology chapter has been expanded to an entire methodology section. This coverage now features a concentrated focus on controversial topics within phenomenological psychology and comparisons with conventional psychological methods. This is the first of the book's two sections since phenomenology is considered above all a method, a systematic way of explicating structural meaning that supports its broader metapsychological perspective. The second of the two sections features new chapters as well. There are now two chapters revolving around the theme of living-experience. These chapters have absorbed much of the material from the old chapter on the human way of being. Finally, the chapters on anxiety and the unconscious have been significantly expanded.

Key Terms, Concepts, and Themes

- Existential–phenomenological psychology
- Objectivism
- Nomothetic science
- The existential–phenomenological paradox
- Phenomenological reduction
- Eidetic reduction
- Reductionism
- Scientism
- Psychologism
- The psychologist's fallacy

Chapter 1

Philosophical Background: The "Third Way" of Existential–phenomenological Psychology

> Psychology began with a concept of soul which was not at all formulated in an original way but which stemmed from . . . dualism, a concept furnished by a prior constructive idea of a corporeal nature and of a mathematical natural science. Thus psychology was burdened in advance with the task of being a science parallel [to physics] and with the conception that the soul—its subject matter—was something real in a sense similar to corporeal nature, the subject matter of natural science. As long as the absurdity of this century-old prejudice is not revealed, there can be no psychology which is the science of the truly psychic . . . . (Husserl, 1970, p. 212)

> *Existentialism, in short, is the endeavor to understand . . . by cutting below the cleavage between subject and object which has bedeviled Western thought and science since shortly after the Renaissance.* This cleavage Binswanger calls "the cancer of all psychology up to now . . . the cancer of the doctrine of subject-object cleavage of the world." (May, 1958b, p. 11, emphasis in original)

Psychology has been dominated by the underlying philosophy of sense-empiricism since the days of its formal founding. For sense-empiricists, knowledge and truth are derived from the electrical impulses transmitted to the brain by the sense organs. The roots of sense-empiricism extend back to the pre-Socratic philosophies of Leucippus and Democritus, who held that all of reality was made of atoms. This *atomism*, as it is commonly known, has exerted a powerful influence on the discipline of psychology since the era of its founding. Thus, William James (1961) observed:

> Most books adopt the so-called synthetic method. Starting with "simple ideas of sensation," and regarding these as so many atoms, they proceed to build up the higher states of mind out of their "association," "integration," or "fusion," as houses are built by the agglutination of bricks. (p.18)

With respect to method, sense-empiricism has given rise to the dominant trend of explaining human psychology in reified mechanistic terms (Woody & Viney, 2017). The *APA Dictionary of Psychology* entry for mechanistic theory provides an illustrative definition:

> [Mechanistic theory is] the assumption that psychological processes and behaviors ultimately can be understood in the same way that mechanical or physiological processes are understood. Its explanations of human behavior are based on the model or metaphor of a machine and invoke mechanical causality, reducing complex psychological phenomena to simpler physical phenomena. Also called mechanistic approach. See reductionism. (American Psychological Association, n.d.-a)

Following Edmund Husserl, phenomenological philosophers and psychologists often refer to sense-empiricism as an all-embracing *naturalism* because it studies human experience as it would any other material thing in the natural world. In its specifically psychological form, this viewpoint is referred to by the terms *natural scientific psychology* or *natural science psychology* (Dilthey, 1988; Giorgi, 1970).

The second most influential underlying philosophy in the history of psychology is rationalism. Rationalism finds sense-empiricism's reduction of knowledge and truth to the yield of the sense organs to be indefensible. As an alternative, rationalists insist that truth claims must instead be founded upon the human subject's structuration of reality in accord with the principles of reason. In other words, truth must operate according to an internal logic, an abstract system of noncontradictory ideas. This way of thinking has roots that extend back to the philosophy of Plato. As Peters (1965) observed:

> [For rationalists,] to start from observations, to check our assumptions by experiment could never take us out of the

> realm of mere opinion; knowledge proper could only come to those who used the peerless instrument of reason rather than the shoddy tool of sense. Like Descartes, who followed him, [Plato] saw in the procedure of mathematics the key to knowledge. (p. 69)

Rationalistic psychology emphasizes the calculative abilities inherent in the human intellect and their power to bring constancy and order to the ever-changing empirical world. Thus, Merleau-Ponty dubbed rationalism in psychology *intellectualism*, the most famous example of which is the work of Jean Piaget (see DeRobertis, 2021a). Piaget's contributions come to psychology through the area of human development, where descriptions such as the following illustrate his influence: With respect to knowledge acquisition, "Structure [is] created by the human mind and evaluated according to rational criteria, such as coherence, consistency, and parsimony" (Bergen 2008, p. 11); with respect to learning, "[Learning] processes . . . take place when the mind applies an existing structure to new experience to understand it" (p. 11); and with respect to development itself, "Long-term, transformational change . . . takes place in the structures into which new experience is assimilated" (p. 11).

Perhaps nothing speaks louder to the relative influence that empiricism and rationalism have exerted on psychology than Haggbloom and colleagues' (2002) analyses, arriving at a list of the 100 most eminent psychologists of the 20th century, with B. F. Skinner and Jean Piaget first and second, respectively. Skinner is commonly associated with sense-empiricism, while Piaget represents the rationalistic (intellectualist) countermovement in psychology.

Existential–phenomenological psychology is one of many nonconforming viewpoints that offer a third alternative or third way of approaching psychology. As Giorgi (1970) noted, phenomenological psychology emerged alongside and in partnership with what used to be called *third-force psychology*, otherwise known as *humanistic psychology* (which encompasses a mosaic of perspectives; e.g., see DeRobertis, 2023). This chapter provides an overview of sense-empiricism and rationalism as requisite context for understanding the rationale of existential phenomenology's "third way" approach to psychology. But to understand this rationale, one must first understand why anyone would seek out an alternative to sense-empiricism and rationalism in the first place. In what way do these perspectives leave something to be desired? To answer these questions, one must get a sense of how sense-empiricism and rationalism deviated from what preceded their rise to prominence around the 17th century. No one would dispute that sense-empiricism and rationalism made advancements that led to new discoveries and that both traditions contributed to the development of philosophy and science. But for the purposes of the current discussion, one needs to appreciate how the upsurge of sense-empiricism and rationalism also gave rise to the conviction (common among existential–phenomenological psychologists and the wider community of humanistic psychologists) that something essential had been lost or left behind in the history of Western thought. An exemplary way to get this sense of appreciation is to consider the hylomorphic philosophy that was developed by Aristotle and later expanded upon by St. Thomas Aquinas.

Hylomorphism and the Human *Unitas Multiplex*

From a hylomorphic perspective, human beings are seen as composites, amalgams, or blends of matter (*hylê*) and form (*morphê*). The human body is made of matter, but this matter is neither amorphous (it has a unique functional architecture) nor self-sufficient (it is more than the mass of biomechanical causes and effects of traditional anatomy and physiology). The human body acquires its functional form by its interdependent relationship to the human soul (i.e., the body is "besouled" or "ensouled"). The soul is the body's principle of animation (i.e., the basic orientation of its lifestyle). Ensoulment demands an operational design of the body to serve its way of life, which cannot be reduced to the mere sum of its parts. Because it is ensouled, the human body is a total world-relating configuration that makes a distinctively human lifestyle possible. The soul of any living being (human or non-human) is defined by its characteristic activities, which convey the essence of its way of living in the world. These characteristic activities render the organism's distinctive physical characteristics comprehensible (Aristotle, 1985).

In the case of a human being, human life extends beyond (without excluding) the sensorimotor and vital activities of non-human animal existence. As Craig (1988) put it:

> The question of the essence of human nature has been a central concern of philosophy and psychology from the very beginning of . . . human endeavors. Lying at the center of this question . . . has been the fundamentally immaterial nature of human existence. Freud himself, of course, had his own difficulties with conveying his understanding of the fundament of human existence and ultimately "called on" the Greek word Psyche . . . to designate this immaterial foundation of human existence. (pp. 62–63)

The goals and aims of human living transcend vegetative functioning and the gratification of animal appetites. Humans display an openness to the world that allows them to cooperatively actualize a more profoundly meaning-bestowing relationship with it than what is found in all other creatures. Accordingly, human biology is both similar to and different from the biology of other primates (see DeRobertis, 2012b, 2015a; Straus, 1966). Its upright posture, facial musculature, opposable thumbs, skin, and neurology support an extraordinarily cultural way of life in comparison to the rest of the animal kingdom. In the hylomorphic view, human beings are conspicuously social and political animals.

The sociopolitical nature of human existence is due, in part, to its distinctive repertoire of cognitive abilities, which are characterized as "rational" in hylomorphism. This needs some explaining. The word *rational* was presented in quotes because that word tends to be misunderstood when used in this context. Contemporary readers sometimes misinterpret the hylomorphic view as implying that human beings are just like non-human animals, but with the ability to perform logical operations added on as a mere cognitive overlay (see DeRobertis, 2015a). This misinterpretation mistakenly takes hylomorphism to be little more than a combination of modern empiricism and rationalism.

This is erroneous on two accounts. First, the rationality attributed to human beings in hylomorphic theory is not narrowly associated with logic; it is far broader and includes the imaginative powers involved in cooperative culture creation (human beings are conspicuously sociopolitical, not conspicuously "logical"). The co-creative interpersonal relatedness that is found among humans makes them, in essence, *dialogal* (sometimes dubbed dialogical) beings par excellence (Strasser, 1969, 1977). Second, misinterpreting hylomorphism as a combination of empiricism and rationalism disavows the primacy afforded to the composite nature of the total human being.

Hylomorphism founds its viewpoint in the direct experience of human beings prior to abstract reflection. What we always first encounter in concrete experience is the unitary human person with their various sensuous and non-sensuous characteristics appearing in integrated form. The ability to then glean the different constituents of the human and reflect upon each individually presupposes the prior, self-evident experience of unity. In the hylomorphic view, body and soul are first and foremost interpenetrated dimensions of one and the same existence. As Aristotle noted in his *De Anima* (2017), to question whether the body and soul are one would be akin to asking if a piece of wax and an impression in it were one. The distinctive biological and psycho–social–spiritual aspects of the person together form a Gestalt or differentiated whole that cannot be reduced to standalone matter or rational mind tacked on to standalone matter. Viktor Frankl (1969) refers to this view as representing a *dimensional ontology*, perhaps better stated as a *multi*dimensional ontology. In Frankl's words, "As Thomas Aquinas put it, man [*sic*] is a '*unitas multiplex*.' Art has been defined as unity in diversity. I would define man [*sic*] as unity in spite of multiplicity!" (p. 22). With this in mind, let us now take a closer look at sense-empiricism and rationalism to see what changed.

The Legacy of Sense-Empiricism

Sense-empiricism's rise to prominence was due in no small measure to the philosophical movement called positivism. While the name *positivism* was coined by Auguste Comte in the 19th century, positivism can be said to have Francis Bacon (1591–1626) as its originator (Urmson & Rée, 1991). In his *De Principiis atque Originibus* (first appearing around 1623–1624), Bacon (2011) tried to revive a materialistic way of thinking like that of the atomists. Positivism is the belief that all knowledge is based on sensory experiences. Thus, genuine knowledge or truth can only be achieved via the inductive methods of the physical sciences, wherein generalizations are made from repeated structured observations (Urmson & Rée, 1991). Though criticized by many, Bacon's positivism greatly influenced the thought of the British Empiricist philosophers. This is best seen in the thought of John Locke. For Locke also, all knowledge comes from sense experience. Quantifiable physical sensations, by some mysterious process, are assumed to be the cause of even our qualitatively meaningful ideas, concepts, and theories. To be clear, the claim is a radical one. Sensations are not merely deemed a precursor to knowledge but its very cause.

With this epistemological move, Locke turned the philosophical study of human knowledge into a kind of physiological psychology. Locke (1996) attempted to explain the workings of the human mind mechanistically (i.e., by cause and effect) in his *Essay Concerning Human Understanding* (first appearing in 1689 but dated to 1690; Willis, 1987). Solomon (1989) described this character of Locke's thought quite succinctly:

> Epistemology (and philosophy in general) now became . . . a study of the history of our common experiences in order to discover where we get our ideas. The question, then, is how physical objects cause us to have sensations and ideas. Locke's answer . . . is, by [chemical–electrical] impulse. (pp. 138, 141)

Once the philosophy of sense-empiricism made its way to psychology, it became a hydra of sorts. It has taken many forms in the history of psychology, and its presence can be felt when terms such as the following are used:

- *Materialistic monism*: The belief that mental events are governed by the same laws that govern and explain physical events.
- *Epiphenomenalism*: The thesis that mental events are the side effects of physical processes in the brain, such that matter determines mind, while mind has no power to affect matter.
- *Physicalism*: The view that all reality is composed of matter; thus, "mind" is ultimately reducible to matter.

All these views maintain a naive realism, a belief that reality exists fully formed, independent of human subjectivity. Human beings play no formative (i.e., integrational, organizational, meaning-making) role in the structuration of reality; they merely conform to it. Objects, assumed to exist "in themselves" in an "outside world," simply produce raw bits of sense data and ideas "inside" human minds.

To be sure, this way of thinking is not devoid of truth or value. Things in the world are not the mere projections of minds, of course. But that this viewpoint has some undeniable difficulties becomes increasingly evident the deeper we probe into its theoretical foundations. To begin with, these thinkers only pay serious attention to matter and physical laws. When it comes to human beings, this viewpoint sees parts (material parts) to the detriment of the whole, the unitas multiplex. In the process, it mistakes the forest for the trees, so to speak. If something like a soul is to be recognized at all (e.g., subjectivity, mind, consciousness, etc.), it can only be understood as some vapid side effect of certain physical causes, whatever they may be. The human being is thereby held to be understandable in the very same way we understand all of nature. As van Kaam (1966) observed, positivists do not distinguish fundamentally between human beings and the things that surround them. Ultimately, all human behavior is understood as the mere reaction of a mechanistic body to various material causes.

Since it is assumed that all knowledge can be simply reduced to the physiological activity that preceded it, the possibility of discovering any "necessary" truths is precluded. All supposedly generalizable truth claims (even scientific ones) are assumed to be nothing more than the residual side effects of neurological happenstance. If we were to maintain this reductionism, we would be doomed to absurdity and science would no longer be possible. For sense-empiricists, human experience results strictly from the incidental byproducts of physiological events occurring in a particular time and place. If this is so, then their own scientific judgments must adhere to the same criteria. A truth claim, when viewed from a sense-empiricist perspective, is really just the biochemical reaction of a given nervous system to a collection of localized material causes. Remember, any truth claim supposedly rests purely on the neurological activity of the being "receiving" its particular conglomeration of sensory input. Every truth claim thus becomes purely relative to the total set of material contingencies that preceded it, which can vary greatly. On this view, each and every scientist's "effort" to explain away all that we experience in terms of causal relationships would be nothing more than the mere side effect of some accidental material eventuality. Arguments of all kinds fall apart at the seams from a kind of reasoning that repeatedly undercuts the viability of its own stances. In phenomenology, this self-refuting, self-defeating relativism is generally referred to as *psychologism*, though its various manifestations are sometimes given more specific names, like *neurologism*, *sociologism*, *anthropologism*, and *historicism*, for example.[1]

---

[1] Psychologism undercuts the ability to make generalizable (much less necessary or universal) truth claims by conceiving them to be the byproducts of psychological states (which are by their very nature unstable and sometimes quite vague). All of these

As Moran (2013) observed, Edmund Husserl's critique of psychologism was inherently connected to his broader critique of *naturalism*:

> The critique of psychologism is extended into the critique of naturalism. Naturalism betrays the very essence of science. It misunderstands the world because it misunderstands the subject's necessary role in the project of knowledge, and in the very constitution of objectivity. One cannot subtract the knowing subject from the process of knowledge, and treat the desiccated product as if it were the real world. The real world, for Husserl, as for Kant, always involves a necessary intertwining of subject and object. This is an essential transcendental point of view and it has been present in European philosophy at least since the eighteenth century, and – if we are to believe Husserl – it is in fact inaugurated with Descartes' breakthrough discovery of the cogito ergo sum, which unfortunately he then went on to misconstrue in a naturalist manner. (pp. 92–93)

A similarly problematic consequence of the sense-empirical worldview results from its theory of sensation. According to the theory of sensation, objects in an external world are transduced into electrical impulses that reside in the internal world of the cranium. These impulses must then be translated into properties of consciousness and then projected back out to somehow form what the mind perceives as the identifiable "things" that caused the sensorial impulses in the first place. As Erwin Straus (1958) described it:

> Physiology and the psychology of the senses took over from philosophy the doctrine . . . that the original, proper, and initial content of sensory experience is an aggregate of wordless sensory data. Receptors aroused by stimuli send impulses to the central organ, whose stimulation is "accompanied" by processes of consciousness. These data, supposedly without any extrinsic meaning, are then "projected outward" by a

---

"isms" commit the same error, reducing truth to nothing more than a mere statement of probability relating to any of the various contingencies of human existence, which can be articulated in neurological terms, sociological terms, and so forth.

> process X which is as incomprehensible as it is unproven. (p. 144)

But when first-person perspectivity is duly taken into consideration (rather than minimized or ignored), we find that there is nothing in experience to indicate that perception is merely the transformation of worldless "sense bits" channeled into one's brain. Thus, Merleau-Ponty (1962) once noted, "Pure sensation would amount to no sensation" (p. 5). Any given experience already has a certain meaningfulness with respect to the context (the total experiential world) of its emergence, even if the exact meaning is uncertain and the form is in a process of unfolding. The concept of sensation in sense-empiricism is an abstraction created by scientists. It frames the origins of firsthand human experience in formless, meaningless, contextless terms. Again, William James (1961):

> Most books . . . start with "simple ideas of sensation," and regarding these as so many atoms, they proceed to build up the higher states of mind out of their "association" . . . . Instead of starting with what the reader directly knows, namely . . . total concrete states of mind, it starts with a set of supposed "simple ideas" with which [one] has no immediate acquaintance at all, and concerning whose alleged interactions . . . is much at the mercy of any plausible phrase. (p. 18)

By its adoption of the theory of sensation, psychology's progress as a science has been further hobbled since its earliest days.

Worse still, once we assume that things exist in themselves in an "external world," it becomes impossible to explain by the theory of sensation how it is that we humans could ever encounter them. To quote Solomon (1989):

> Locke had argued that our experiences were caused by . . . physical objects; but how could this claim be justified by experience? . . . [For] we [could] have no experience of either objects themselves or their causation, but only of their effects. . . . (p. 148)

If the world exists in itself, then there is an irreparable chasm between mind and world. The most we can say of our perception of the world is that it is a mass of purely subjective experiences. There can be no "objectivity" at all. Stated differently, sense-empiricists assume that humans exist on the inside of their bodies. If this were true, we would have no grounds for assuming that there is anything but our own subjective sensations and ideas. Objects supposedly exist in a completely subject-independent "outside" world. However, we could have no access to such a world since we would be inside our bodies with nothing but an assortment of our own sensations and ideas. It would be just as valid for me to assume that little green men are what really cause my sensory impulses rather than objects assumed to exist in an unverifiable "external world." We may conclude, therefore, that this radical split between inside and outside is a fabrication and in need of revision.

The Legacy of Rationalism

The first name that is generally associated with rationalism in philosophy is that of René Descartes (1596–1650). What distinguished Descartes' thought from the thought of his predecessors was his bifurcation of all of reality into two fundamentally different, incompatible kinds of "things" or "substances": thinking things and things with extension in physical space (note the subtle implication here that thought does not extend out from itself to the things that are thought about). As Solomon (1989) put it:

> Descartes said that there were two different kinds of substances: mind or mental substances, and body or physical substances. Accordingly, he is usually called a dualist . . . . [Dualism is] . . . the distinction between mind and body as separate substances, or a very different kinds of states and events with radically different properties. (pp. 419, 491)

Descartes' thinking substance and extended substance could each be interpreted as more or less complete and self-sustaining (van Kaam, 1966). In other words, Descartes provided a clearer philosophical framework for the thinkers and scientists that would follow to see the body in a more purely physical way and the soul in a more ghostly, disembodied way. Once we have conceptualized the body and soul in this manner, the problem then becomes how two such radically different substances could interact and influence each other.

A split between body and soul occurs because one has decisively prioritized constituent parts over the whole. The prior unity of the human person's total existence has been passed over. The unitas multiplex is lost. It must be noted, however, that Descartes cannot be held solely responsible for this way of thinking about human beings. Descartes rejected the idea of dualism in theory, and he struggled greatly with the problem of human embodiment to try to overcome it (e.g., see Descartes, 1993, p. 99). It was John Locke's philosophy that established the strict subject–object dichotomy in Western philosophy. Moreover, the first glimmerings of rationalism can be traced back to ancient times, as was noted earlier. Plato held that a human being was a soul and that the body was related to the soul as a cloak is related to its wearer. Descartes rejected this metaphor, but there was a fundamental difference between Descartes and Plato. With Descartes, ideas no longer appeared to be something through which we can understand extramental reality. Ideas themselves, rather than things, became the objects of human understanding. As Solomon (1989) put it:

> Plato . . . would have claimed to know reality itself . . . . But Descartes ultimately claims that we know only the ideas. There is always a gap between the mind and the world that the ancients never allowed and never entertained. (p. 90)

The only thing in existence that Descartes found he could not doubt was his own thought, his own reflection. Descartes did not trust sense experience. Consequently, he went on to maintain that his identity was that of a thing that thinks, that he was a "thinking thing" in some very complicated way attached to a mechanical body (Solomon, 1989, p. 419). "I think, therefore, I am," he claimed. He had split thought off from concrete existence and identified existence with thought itself (Paul II, 1994). This formally established the theory of "a free and rational consciousness set against a mechanical, physical world" (Solomon, 1988, p. 175). Hence, "clear and distinct ideas" were deemed most important in Descartes' philosophy, and the priority afforded to them provided an epistemological foundation for idealist philosophers like Immanuel Kant to propose that human knowledge is governed by a set of logical principles that exist prior to experience and which structure our experience itself (Packer, 1992).

Intellectualistic psychology has many of its roots in this tradition of thought. It shows up in Piaget's genetic epistemology and child-as-scientist approaches to development, the theory-theory view of concept formation, and information processing theory in memory research. It shows up in computational approaches to cognition that utilize computer metaphors or otherwise place an overriding emphasis on the development of logical thought processes in the governance of human behavior. These psychologies emphasize the theorizing activity of "the rational mind," abstract thought processes that operate according to mathematical logic, abstract categories and concepts, theoretical rules, laws, principles, schemata, grammar-acquisition devices, referential structures, and so on. As Packer (1992) put it:

> . . . Cognition is necessarily involved behind and before action in the creation and the determination of truth. Action itself is essentially rational: Meanings are constructed by the logical evaluation of means and ends, based on information about the truth or falsehood of statements and about the world. Action is determined, in the same way that a conclusion is determined from a set of premises, or a sentence from a set of grammatical and semantic rules. (p. 276)

In short, the proper object of study for these psychologists is the workings of a mind that operates at a distance, if not a disconnect, from the real-life dynamics of bodily, affective, and social living.

For intellectualistic psychologists, humans are seen in somewhat of a different way in comparison to sense-empirical psychologists. These thinkers provide a new way of explaining away human existence. Intellectualistic psychologists highlight the role of formal reasoning in human existence instead of undermining it the way sense-empiricists do. However, thought is then emphasized to the point where it is then considered to be the primary cause of our knowledge and behavior. Take, for example, this description of cognitive psychology by Lahey (1989): "

> As you read the word *cognitive* . . . you may try to make sense out of it . . . by recalling that *cogito* means "I think." The focus of cognitive psychology reflects a belief that our behavior and emotions are caused in large part by our cognitions. (p. 20)

The emphasis on causality that one finds among intellectualistic psychologists demonstrates that there is a fundamental harmony between sense-empiricist and intellectualistic approaches to psychology. Both traditions are objectivistic in their general orientation, and much of intellectualistic psychology remains materialist in its philosophical foundations. As two cognitive authors once put it, "The current view of most cognitive psychologists is that the *mind* and *mental process* are ways of describing brain activity" (Ellis & Hunt, 1989, p. 4).

Thinking Otherwise: Toward An Existential–Phenomenological Alternative for Psychology

Sense-empirical and intellectualistic forms of psychology have provided us with a wealth of knowledge about human behavior and shall continue to do so. However, as we have seen, both traditions share an overarching and limiting starting point. They both spilt psychology's object of study, the human unitas multiplex, in two. Both traditions, in their own ways, objectify mind and body and lose touch with their distinctively human characteristics in the process. Each tradition then offers a particular framework for explaining away human experience, knowledge, and behavior in line with its theoretical underpinning. The sense-empiricists seek to do this in terms of physical laws. Intellectualistic psychologists add the abstract principles of the calculative mind to their explanations. Even the more modern combinations and mutations of these two traditions (e.g., "cognitive behaviorism") typically fail to move beyond dualistic thinking and purely explanatory modes of interpretation (see DeRobertis, 2021b). It has been the task of existential–phenomenological psychologists to provide an alternative to these traditions.

By drawing on existential and phenomenological philosophy, existential–phenomenological psychologists have attempted to advance an approach to psychology that does not begin with radical duality, but instead prioritizes the integrative nature of human existence. When it comes to the scientific study of human beings and the phenomena of psychological life, existential–phenomenological psychology places a premium on the complex, multifaceted whole of the person and of psychological phenomena over their parts. In this sense, it can be said to be a *holistic* perspective. It revives the unitas multiplex orientation of hylomorphism, but it also advances into new conceptual territory. Phenomenology was never a mere reversion to pre-Cartesian philosophies, and neither is existential–phenomenological psychology (though the value of hylomorphic insights for the development of both phenomenological philosophy and psychology have long been recognized; e.g., see Sheets-Johnstone, 2022; Spencer 2012; Strasser, 1957b). Existential–phenomenological psychology advocates a twofold conceptual reorientation of the psychologist.

On the one hand, existential–phenomenological psychology espouses a global, metapsychology reorientation based on a revised image of human beings. This is its general perspectival reorientation. Existential–phenomenological psychology perpetually seeks the reunification of mind and body, subject and object, person and world, which began with Franz Brentano's reintroduction of the Thomistic concept of *intentionality* into philosophy and psychology (later adopted and fashioned for phenomenological purposes by Edmund Husserl, the father of phenomenology). As phenomenology developed, the notion of intentionality became enveloped within the broader framework of what is best described as *being-and-becoming-in-the-world* (more commonly expressed in the shortened form, being-in-the-world, Heidegger, 1962; May et al., 1958; Strasser, 1977).

On the other hand, existential–phenomenological psychology reorients the research psychologist in a manner that is reflective of this perspectival holism. This is its research reorientation. Rather than attempting to explain psychological phenomena by an appeal to hypothesized materialistic or intellectualistic causes, existential–phenomenological psychological research prioritizes the systematic and rigorous description of participants' living-experiences. *Living-experience* is more commonly referred to as "lived-experience" in the extant literature, but the gerund form is superior in my view. The term "lived" is more reifying, while "living" better expresses animation (see Sheets-Johnstone, 2022.) Living-experience bespeaks intentionally oriented be-*ing* and becom-*ing* in-the-world. Crucially, the description of living-experience is not a mere preparation for explanation, but is considered substantive in its own right, providing psychologists with a means for accessing the proper conceptual understanding of their subject matter.

Perspectival Reorientation: Reprioritizing the Unitas Multiplex

From the time of its inception, and under the influence of naturalism, psychology progressively developed an abstract conceptualization of human subjectivity as residing deep within the recesses of the brain. To accept this characterization as one's self-understanding is to adopt a third-person perspective that disavows the data of one's immediate experience. But careful attention to the field of human experience tells us that one's awareness is first and foremost caught up in the world. To interpret this involvement in terms of internal biological structures is an act of unusual reflection, a retreat from our typical engagement with other people, things, events, and the situation at large. The internal world of viscera is not the primary dwelling of human psychological life. It can announce itself, for sure, and does so quite loudly when something has gone wrong. On a leisurely stroll, a sudden pain in my abdomen can quickly redirect my awareness away from the swaying trees, the gentle breeze, and my wife's hand in mine. But the point is that while on that walk my experience is best characterized by world engagement. This is not at all to deny the importance of the body. Rather, on this non-dualistic, experience-close view, the body is no longer the objectivized mechanical encasement of my subjectivity. The body is the moving, feeling, orienting, world-engaged body. In existential–phenomenological psychology, the artificial partitioning of subjectivity and objectivity is temporarily set aside (i.e., it is "bracketed"). Existential phenomenologists then attune themselves to the interpenetration of subjectivity and objectivity, which is spoken of in terms of intentionality.

Intentionality and the Graded Nexus of Human World-Involvement

Few concepts have been noted as frequently in connection to the revolutionary nature of the phenomenological movement as intentionality, as it afforded phenomenology a foothold for overcoming dualism. Intentionality refers to the stretching forth or reaching out of the mind toward its "objects" (to be taken in a general sense, and not to imply an exclusive focus on physical things). Intentional consciousness is sometimes metaphorically characterized as a ray or an arrow:

> In Husserlian phenomenology (Husserl, 1962) *intentionality,* metaphorized as the "intentional arrow of consciousness," characterizes our human meaning making activity. We are directed toward objects of meaning in the world. Husserl introduced the fruitful metaphor of the *horizon,* to describe the pathways of meaning coming from other domains of our world of consciousness, present yet invisible, or not yet visible, which contribute to the constitution of the meaning of the object attended to. (von Eckartsberg, 1989, p. 147)

On this view, even when we retreat to the worlds of fiction, fantasy, daydreams, pure ideas, abstract theorizing, and so forth, world-relatedness always remains as the inspiration and the background of mental activity. The existential–phenomenological psychologist refuses to accept the dogma that human beings live "inside their heads." Even when one is in the deepest state of meditation or dissociative withdrawal, one is never literally "behind one's eyes," so to speak. Experts in meditative practice will attest to the fact that to clear one's mind and disconnect from worldly entanglements requires years of practice and can only be achieved in temporary spurts.

For existential–phenomenological psychology, human intentionality is not restricted to the activity of reflective consciousness, much less detached contemplation. In addition to cognitively sharpened acts of intentionality, there are those that function within the flow of prereflective existence, operating within varying horizons of possible experience. Hence, Husserl (1969) spoke of *functioning intentionality*, while Merleau-Ponty (1962) used the term *operative intentionality*. These terms refer to the fact that consciousness is already meaningfully directed toward determinate objects in its ongoing functioning or operation before acts reflection intercedes.[2] Transferring these notions from their philosophical context to psychology, van Kaam (1966) referred to the total field of "intentional–functional behavior" as the focus of existential–phenomenological psychological investigation (p. 53).

One step further, the intentional activity of the living subject perpetually emerges from a field of pre-predicative experiential engagement,[3] wherein meaning is co-constituted in an essentially receptive manner, sometimes referred to with the paradoxical term "passive synthesis" (Husserl, 2001). The paradoxical nature of the term derives from the fact that "acts" of synthesis (i.e., participating in the co-constitution of perceptual meaning and form) are never wholly passive as in sense-empiricism (Husserl never advanced "a clear-cut divide between activity and passivity;" Biceaga, 2010, p. xviii).[4] Strasser (1977) has used the term pre-intentional to refer to this stratum of experiential world-relatedness (we will return to this in Chapter 5). Suffice to say, intentionality is ever-worlded, ever-horizonal, ever-

---

[2] Once again, to speak of objects in this way is not to imply an exclusive focus on physical things.

[3] Pre-predicative experiential engagement refers to experience that has yet to be transformed by acts of judgment and fitted with predicates (Husserl, 1973).

[4] Every human being plays a role in determining what is perceived and how things are perceived in a given environment. Signal detection theory bears this out, as does research on "top-down" processing, for example. Even though perception characteristically feels effortless, subjective participatory involvement is required.

emergent, and graded with respect to its degrees of activity and reflexivity (we will return to this in Chapter 8).

Being-and-Becoming-in-the-World

Instead of understanding person and world as separate entities that must then be reunited, the existential–phenomenological psychologist understands human existence in terms of the unified structure *being-in-the-world,* with others, and alongside things. According to this conception, we very much *are* the experiential worlds of referential significance (i.e., multilayered meaning) we co-constitute. This being-our-worlds is sometimes expressed with the terms *Dasein*, being-there, there-being, being-the-there, and world-openness (see Boss, 1963). Person and world are mutually implicative, together forming what van Kaam (1966) called a "subjective–objective-situational Gestalt" (p. 195). In effect, existential–phenomenological psychology proposes that the most direct way to access and study human psychology is through the detour of living experiential worlds. As van den Berg (1972) put it:

> We get an impression of a person's character . . . when we inquire about [their] world. Not the world as it appears to be "on second thought" . . . . A "second thought" disturbs the verity of this reality. It has been this "second thought" that has considerably hampered the development of psychology.

As described here, the notion of world is far from a mere accumulation of matter suspended in dead space. "World" denotes the network of meanings that are intelligible in light of the person's relatively organized relationships and projects. Being-in-the-world highlights the person–world dynamic that is active from moment to moment, wherein the person is always already physically, affectively, and imaginatively involved in their relationships and projects prior to reflective awareness. Similarly, world space is not a mere container, inherently devoid of meaning, but the space of potential investment and action (Husserl, 1970; Langeveld, 1983; Lewin, 1935).

To be sure, a view of human psychological life that thinks in terms of world-relational interpenetration deviates significantly from traditional, natural scientific psychology. As we saw earlier, the psychological life of the person is split off from the world and "internalized" in both sense-empirical and intellectualist psychologies. The former turns subjectivity into impotent, epiphenomenal residue, while the latter only advances to the extent of embracing the "cold," calculating homunculus of rationalism. From the perspective of existential–phenomenological psychology, the abstract caricatures of psychological life that sense-empirical and intellectualist psychologies generate essentially preclude the question of human *being* as such.[5] In contrast, the intentional orientation of existential–phenomenological psychology, as expressed in the notion of being-in-the-world, brings the question of what it means to *be* a human being to the foreground of its approach (we will return to this issue in greater detail in Chapter 6). Human beings do not merely live "at" and "off of" the world; they live experientially in, with, and through the world. Vegetative life forms are only open systems to the degree that their growth involves environmental interactions that cross a permeable membrane. All animals develop through manifold interactions with the world, as a matter of course. However, human development is far less predetermined than what is found in the rest of the animal kingdom. Humans live in a world of emergent meanings that are the product of cooperative creative-discovery (DeRobertis, 2017). Existential, phenomenological, and humanistic authors have used the term *transcendence* to refer to this peculiarity (DeRobertis, 2021b). As Giorgi (1992) described it:

> Every human situation has a certain gap or leakage which prevents the situation from being closed deterministically, and the gap is human subjectivity which has the power to transform situations through meaning bestowal or interpretation . . . . [Transcendence is] the ability of a person, on his or her own initiative, to overturn any given received structure . . . the capacity of going beyond created structures in order to create others . . . . Humans are not trapped within the context of a specific fixity. One could say that it is the relationship to possibilities that matter, and the power to bring possibilities into being. (pp. 434–435)

The power of transcendence makes human beings extraordinarily "luminous" (Boss, 1963, p. 38) creatures, exhibiting the power to co-

[5] It may be instructive here to think of Abraham Maslow, whose "being psychology" was designed to get psychologists to think beyond non-human animal adaptation, survival, and the gratification of those needs required to adjust to prevailing environmental conditions. The growth-oriented motives of the self-actualizing person (sometimes spoken of explicitly as B- or Being-values) were proposed as a conceptual means for tapping into the human psychological processes involved in *being*.

constitute meaning and shed new light on what lies before them ad infinitum.

The open-ended nature of meaning's co-constitution through ongoing relationships and projects thus exposes a second meaning of the term transcendence in existential–phenomenological psychology: *temporal existence.* As Rollo May (1958a) put it:

> Existence is always in [the] process of self-transcending . . . at every moment becoming . . . . This capacity is already stated in the term "exist," that is, "to stand out from." Existing involves a continual emerging, in the sense of emergent evolution, a transcending of one's past and present in terms of the future. Thus *transcendere*—literally "to climb over or beyond"—describes what every human being is engaged in doing every moment when . . . not ill or temporarily blocked by despair or anxiety. (p. 71)

In other words, human *being* is always human *becoming*. For existential–phenomenological psychology, human psychological life is approached as a participatory process of being-and-becoming-in-the-world. The perspective is inherently developmental. Being human means to live amid both constancy and change, sameness and difference. To be human means that our very being is an enduring issue, a question that is never settled once and for all. It must be worked out in time (Heidegger, 1962; Straus, 1966). As transcendent, being-and-becoming-in-the-world simultaneously implicates one's history, present concerns, and personal outlook as an emergent teleology.

If it is not obvious, transcendence, as the term is used here, implicates the freedom inherent in human being. However, to avoid superficial stereotypes, it is critical to note that existential–phenomenological psychology does not consider freedom to be absolute or arbitrary. Being-and-becoming are structurally housed within finite conditions. Human world-openness always operates within varying degrees of limitation (see Knowles, 1986). It also operates within a motivational network that frames decision making (e.g., see DeRobertis 2008). Every choice simultaneously opens pathways to potential futures while (at least temporarily) closing others. Further, every human disclosure of meaning is what Heidegger (1977) described as an unconcealing that paradoxically conceals other meanings. Suffice it to say, the holism of the existential–phenomenological perspective viewpoint conscientiously recognizes the subtle indeterminacies of psychological life, which exposes existential–phenomenological psychology's connection to the broader current of humanistic psychology (Aanstoos, 2003). Humanistic psychology is an umbrella term for an entire constellation of holistic perspectives in psychology that nonetheless resist the seemingly perennial temptation to intellectually totalize human beings (see Frankl, 1969; Levinas, 1969), to encapsulate them within a system of abstract concepts that would do violence to the complex relational dynamisms that make up the fabric of human living (see DeRobertis, 2015a, 2017). Existential–phenomenological holism is mindful of ambiguity (see James, 1961; Merleau-Ponty, 1962) and paradox in human existence (see DeRobertis, 2021b; DeRobertis & Bland, 2018; Hannush, 2007).

Research Reorientation: The Description of Living-Experience

In developing phenomenology, Edmund Husserl sought to overcome the philosophical schism between empiricism and rationalism by an unparalleled effort to defend the dignity of subjectivity against the ravages of objectivism. In a style reminiscent of Immanuel Kant's philosophy, Husserl deemed subjectivity as playing a participatory role in the co-constitution of reality. Following Husserl, existential–phenomenological psychology rejects the idea that subjectivity is epiphenomenal. Instead, subjectivity is held to play a synthesizing, meaning-bestowing role in the co-constitution of the world. Unlike Kantianism, however, intellectualism is relinquished in favor of a different view of subjectivity, one that reconnects the subject with the body and the whole of the sociocultural–historical and natural world on the basis of living-experience. Here, the influence of Wilhelm Dilthey becomes evident, and the resultant reorientation toward the realm of living-experience has profound methodological consequences.

For Dilthey (1988), living-experience is experience that has not yet become an object of formal reflection, a mere curiosity for the bare intellect. Living-experience is always relational and "in-process." It is experience as it occurs live, in the flesh, in the form of so many world-engaged relationships and projects. It takes place in time as an unfolding meaningful event in the world. But one cannot access and explicate it (at least not clearly or thoroughly) through sense-empirical or intellectualistic explanatory approaches to data collection and analysis. As we will see in Chapter 2, Dilthey proposed the development of an "understanding" psychology as an alternative to a strictly explanatory psychology. Understanding psychology, he held, had to be descriptive and interpretive (i.e., hermeneutic; see Dilthey, 1977). Husserl was sympathetic, but he did not wish to adopt the interpretive thrust of Dilthey's thought, as he suspected it of advancing a form of historical determinism, the form of psychologism called historicism. Rather than following Dilthey into hermeneutics, Husserl drew on Franz Brentano (e.g., see his *Descriptive Psychology*, Brentano, 1995) and maintained that the best way to understand living-experience was disciplined, careful, nonreductive description (for which he spearheaded the development of phenomenology as a method).

When one describes living-experience, the body appears as more than a mere mechanism, and the mind appears as more than a mere calculator. The body offers itself as an owned, human body with a meaningful structural organization that is fundamentally world-relating rather than encapsulated within the epidermis. Similarly, the depth and breadth of the psychic dimension of human psychological life is exposed. Cognition offers itself as inherently bodily, affective, conative, and social, and its world-forming powers are no longer restricted to those of the calculative intellect (a trend that has been slowly catching on in cognitive science with the emergence of 4E cognition, which is *embodied*, *embedded*, *enactive*, and *extended*). In other words, the entire landscape of psychological life looks fundamentally different in comparison to the worldview that has come to dominate psychology conceived as an explanatory, naturalistic science. This is radically unfamiliar territory for the uninitiated.

Preview: What is it Like to Describe Living-Experience?

The core methodological features of phenomenological psychological description will be laid out in Chapter 2. An introduction to living-experience will be provided in Chapter 5. Meanwhile, to make things a bit more concrete for the reader, William James's (1890) analysis of getting out of bed will provide a brief illustration of what it is like to describe living-experience. Of course, James would never have referred to his work as existential–phenomenological, but his account is representative of the basic orientation, and it is very straightforward, parsimonious, and relatable. As James Edie (1987) once observed, "There can now be no doubt whatever that Husserl developed a number of his ideas . . . by reading James. James had a sense of phenomenological method long before the letter" (p. vii–viii).

To appreciate the originality of James's analysis, we must first consider how the act of getting out of bed would be analyzed from sense-empirical and rationalistic perspectives. Since the phenomenon has not been deemed worthy of investigation by representatives of either tradition, we will have to consider the situation from the way each perspective has traditionally approached its object of study. Sense-empirical psychology would inevitably seek explanations for the act of getting out of bed that implicate factors such as the glandular and neurological changes involved in one's circadian rhythms for arousal, the way that these rhythms have been conditioned to respond to light and dark, the reticular activating system, centers of executive functioning in the frontal lobes of the cortex, activation of the somatosensory and motor cortices and their associated afferent and efferent pathways, and the cerebellum for balance and coordination. A rationalist approach would turn from a strict reliance on mechanistic physiological generalizations to explanations that recruit cognitive appraisal mechanisms into the process of getting out of bed: the mechanisms involved in "information processing," logical deliberation, and subsequent decision making. Now, consider James's (1890) account:

> We know what it is to get out of bed on a freezing morning in a room without a fire, and how the very vital principle within us protests against the ordeal. Probably most persons have lain on certain mornings for an hour at a time unable to brace themselves to the resolve. We think how late we shall be, how the duties of the day will suffer; we say, "I *must* get up, this is ignominious," etc.; but still the warm couch feels too delicious, the cold outside too cruel, and resolution faints away and postpones itself again and again just as it seemed on the verge of bursting the resistance and passing over into the decisive act. Now how do we *ever* get up under such circumstances? If I may generalize from my own experience, we more often than not get up without any struggle or decision at all. We suddenly find that we *have* got up. A fortunate lapse of consciousness occurs; we forget both the warmth and the cold; we fall into some revery connected with the day's life, in the course of which the idea flashes across us, "Hollo! I must lie here no longer"—an idea which at that lucky instant awakens no contradictory or paralyzing suggestions, and consequently produces immediately its appropriate motor effects. It was our acute

> consciousness of both the warmth and the cold during the period of struggle, which paralyzed our activity then and kept our idea of rising in the condition of *wish* and not of *will*. The moment these inhibitory ideas ceased, the original idea exerted its effects. (p. 524)

Approached in this way, the phenomenon of getting out of bed is seen as relating to the whole person meaningfully involved in their total situation. James notes that we find ourselves already out ahead of ourselves in the world when we rise up out of bed. The behavior has a meaningful, organized experiential structure. James tracks the subject's intentional directedness (though he did not use that terminology). He observes that when consciousness turns from the objects of immediate perception to those of the impending day, movement follows without struggle or deliberation. The account describes the mutual involvement or interpenetration of the phenomenon's cognitive (e.g., ideas), bodily (e.g., experiences of warmth and cold, the paralysis or activation of motor activity), affective (e.g., suffering, the feelings of deliciousness and anticipated cruelty), conative (e.g., willingness), and social dimensions (e.g., the fear of being late and the sense that the reasons for that lateness would cause public shame or humiliation). Notice that accurately describing the world engagement of the whole person yields generalizable results that make intuitive sense when considering the findings in the light of an individual person's real-time, real-life experience. This is not to say that sense-empirical and rationalistic accounts are disavowed. Rather, the issue is that what James provides offers a vital conduit between the world of the experiencing person's psychology and the psychologist's consciousness, which can operate at varying degrees of closeness or distance from the object of study. James (1890) in no way renounced the importance of things like environmental cues, neurological underpinnings, or the potential for deliberation. He grants these, leaving open the possibility that there could be typological variations on the phenomenon that lead one further into the specialized discourses of sense-empirical and rationalistic viewpoints. James was cognizant of the human potential to act in an "automated" fashion or on the basis of logical deliberation, but these do not form the basic paradigm for understanding human psychological life. For James, the simple act of getting out of bed, when described accurately, illustrates the ambiguous nature of the human will as such: namely, that human willing is not mere *wish*. Yet it would be an oversimplification to explain it away based on the physical forces involved in the exertion of effort and/or the intellectual processes that provide a logic or "rationale" for that effort.

Importantly, James begins his description with the observation that we are all already familiar with a world of living-experience. Yet, we do not stop to examine it closely, on its own terms. Instead, we pass over it, move on with our lives, and then circle back around after the fact, groping for explanations, potentially armed with scientific explanations that we have come across in our daily lives (which have become saturated with natural science interpretations of everything under the sun). Rather than beginning with a predetermined allegiance to physical or intellectual mechanisms, James simply describes the organized, unfolding whole of the phenomenon so that it may be understood from the living point of view. He does not attempt to pin it to conceptual abstractions imposed on the phenomenon in advance, which would circumvent the psychological life of the person. (Again, historically, these abstractions have typically led back to some form of naturalism.) His description of the functional *how* of the meaningfully structured experience leads to insights concerning the intentional *what* of the experience: Getting out of bed is a particular kind of willing. James then transitions away from the specific nature of getting out of bed and concentrates on the nature of the will itself (which was not covered above).

Many years later, phenomenologists picked up where James left off, further explicating the experiential structure of getting out of bed on a similarly holistic, descriptive, and intuitive basis. According to Straus (1966) and Ey (1978), the living-experience of getting out of bed does not present itself as an "internal" psychological phenomenon. Rather, it is founded upon a person's opening to a world of possibilities. To move toward the fulfillment of these possibilities requires the establishment of a sense of self–world orientation wherein mere awakeness increasingly and progressively gives way to intentional conscious relatedness. Becoming oriented involves the imaginative integration of affective impressions and the organization of a living space that potentiates action (Ey, 1978). The ease with which one can imagine oneself capable of moving competently and acting purposefully is proportional to the ease and/or resolve with which one can rise up against gravity and make strides toward the actualization of perceived possibilities (Straus, 1966; see also Knowles, 1986). To get up out of bed is to establish oneself as a willing participant in the temporal unfolding of living relationships and projects. These constitute the fabric of one's world, wherein other people and things are encountered, and the meanings associated with them are disclosed. Optimally, to get up out of bed, to "rise," is to hear and respond to the call of an inviting world. At a minimum, it is to commit to facing the world despite its challenges, holding one's ground in the face of opposition. In any case, it involves the taking of stances with respect to possibilities that transcend the one's present situation.

At this point, one might be inclined to ask, "How can so much be contained in an occurrence as common and otherwise unremarkable as getting out of bed?" The fact is (and this is a patently phenomenological insight) that we take it for granted, just as William James implied. The inherent structure goes under the proverbial radar, as it is part of the ongoing flow of prereflective existence. Given this response, one might then wonder, "Is this just blank check theorizing disguised as research?" Consider consulting with someone suffering from major depression, for whom the experience of getting out of bed in the morning is *not* taken for granted, to see if they find the description presented above to be fabricated. In depression-induced "dysania," the structure of getting out of bed as described here is put in peril, if not short-circuited. Alternatively, consider how worry doesn't just short-circuit but reverses aspects of the structure to produce completely opposite results. In stark contrast to the resignation of depressive dysania, one who worries maintains a false sense of control over relationships and/or projects perceived to be actually or potentially endangered. The world thus loses its cyclical pattern of retreat and invitation. Instead, it looms and stares. Locked in the power struggle of worry, a restful nights' sleep is elusive, and the challenge is that of going to bed rather than getting out of it. Of course, to see how results like these are derived from formalized, systematized phenomenological psychological research requires a more detailed introduction to the methodology. It is to this task that we will turn next.

The Tasks Ahead

In the current chapter, we began with broad historical, philosophical, and perspectival considerations as the context within which to introduce the descriptive, phenomenological–methodological reorientation of psychological research. We will now reverse this manner of coverage. Phenomenological research findings provide the justifying bases for existential–phenomenological psychology's general perspective assertions. They are what allow existential–phenomenological psychology to develop and grow. Accordingly, we will proceed by examining the phenomenological method as conceived for psychological purposes and then, in the second section of the text, transition back to a broadened discussion of issues representing the existential–phenomenological perspective in psychology.

Key Terms, Concepts, and Themes

- Sense-empirical psychology
- Atomism
- Mechanistic theory
- Naturalism
- Natural scientific/natural science psychology
- Rationalistic/intellectualistic psychology
- Third-force/humanistic psychology
- Hylomorphic philosophy
- Soul/ensoulment
- Rational–social–political animal (i.e., the human animal)
- Dimensional ontology
- Unitas multiplex
- Positivism
- Materialistic monism
- Epiphenomenalism
- Physicalism
- Psychologism
- Neurologism
- Sociologism
- Anthropologism
- Historicism
- The theory of sensation
- Dualism
- Being-in-the-world
- Becoming
- Living-experience
- Intentionality
- Functioning/operative intentionality
- Intentional–functional behavior
- Pre-predicative experiential engagement
- Passive synthesis
- "World" as experienced or experiential world

- World space
- Transcendence
- Temporal existence
- 4E cognition

Part I:

Methodology

Chapter 2

Phenomenological Psychological Research: A Conceptual–Methodological Outline and Introduction

To review, existential–phenomenological psychologists have sought an approach to psychology that is not utterly dependent on explaining (away) human behavior but also allows for descriptive understanding. Once one is no longer restricted to looking at human experience, knowledge, and behavior in impersonal, cause-and-effect terms, one can investigate the structurally meaningful events (of living-experience) that we participate in by describing them on their own terms, as *given*, without the imposition of scientific abstractions in advance of study. Phenomenology is the method of this approach.

Phenomenology falls within the wider tradition of qualitative research in the social sciences. It typically begins with individual, case-specific data and then transitions to a trans-individual level of analysis to yield generalizable findings. Stated differently, it begins idiographic and ends nomothetic. Its character as a method is illustrated in the thematic overview provided in this chapter, outlined as follows:

I. Returning to "The Things Themselves" (as Given in Experience)
   A. The Epoché: Bracketing
   B. Confronting the Irreal: Non-Sensuous Givens
   C. Returning to the Participants Themselves: Empathic Attunement
II. The Methodical, Rigorous Description of Living-Experience
   A. Attending to the Complex, Multifaceted Whole
   B. Attending to the "What" of the Phenomenon
   C. Attending to the "How" of the Phenomenon
      1. Temporality

III. Intuition and Elucidation of Essential Meanings
   A. Studying Variations for Invariant Meanings
   B. Explicating a General Structural Description

To be clear, this chapter provides a broad conceptual introduction to phenomenological methodology as applied to psychology. It is designed to convey a conceptual understanding of the major aspects and phases of phenomenological research in psychology. There can be a degree of diversity in how these are "manualized," actualized, and carried out by the development and implementation of specific procedures (see Giorgi, 2018; Wertz 2023). There is even more diversity in how they are custom tailored for use in diverse disciplines (e.g., see Finlay, 2009). The current chapter is not a detailed procedural introduction. Many authors have outlined specific phenomenological procedures for research purposes in psychology (and many more in related fields). For detailed procedural applications related to what appears in this chapter, the reader is referred to Churchill (2022), Giorgi (1987, 2009), Churchill and Wertz (2015), Wertz (2015), and Fischer and Wertz (1979). To concretize this introduction, the chapter will conclude with an example of phenomenological research, an actual study that was completed and published in the *Journal of Phenomenological Psychology* (DeRobertis & Bland, 2020a).

Returning to "The Things Themselves" (as Given in Experience)

In contrast to what has traditionally been taught in conventional methods classes, phenomenological research is not founded upon hypothesis testing. Instead, priority is given to unprejudiced openness and seeing afresh. Originally described by Edmund Husserl (2001) as a process of returning to "the things themselves" (p. 168), phenomenology places a premium on attaining the most original, faithful description of the data possible. Phenomenology is a rigorous, disciplined attempt to avoid prefiguring phenomena so that they are optimally situated to reveal themselves. Thus, hypotheses cannot be allowed to dictate data collection and analysis. As van den Berg (1972) once noted, "the phenomenologist never needs hypotheses. Hypotheses emerge where the description of reality has been discontinued too soon" (p. 124).

Taking inspiration from the philosophies of both Aristotle and Descartes, Husserl revived and rehabilitated the notion of intuitive self-evidence as an alternative to sense-empirical induction and rationalist deduction. To state the matter rather crudely, Husserl sought a more direct, immediate access to reality than what bean counting or abstract argumentation could account for. This aspiration was expressed vividly in what he considered phenomenology's principle of all principles:

> *Each intuition affording [something] in an originary way is a legitimizing source of knowledge... whatever presents itself to us in "Intuition" in an originary way* (so to speak, in its actuality in person) *is to be accepted simply as what it affords itself as,* but *only within the limitation in which it affords itself there.* (Husserl 2014, p. 43, emphasis in original)

In accordance with the phenomenological principle of all principles, the reflective, intuitive processes involved in phenomenological description prohibit taking away from the fullness of phenomena (as in reductionism) or adding things that are not there either because one is compensating for holes in reductionistic explanations or because one is engaging in creative interpretations of the data. Along similar lines, compare the following directive offered by William James (1996) almost a decade before Husserl: "To be radical, an empiricism must neither admit into its constructions any element that is not directly experienced, nor exclude from them any element that is directly experienced" (p. 42). Returning to "the things themselves" means describing things precisely and only as they are given.[1]

This value of unprejudiced description should not be mistaken for conventional psychology's value of "pure objectivity," since that notion is founded upon a subject–object dichotomy which assumes that the "real" world is untainted by the presence of human subjectivity and the life of consciousness. Phenomenology rejects this as an indefensible presupposition and a form of scientific idealism: an all-encompassing objectivism. A world can only be a world for those who participate in its co-constitution (see Boss, 1963, p. 51). To say this is not to imply that phenomenology celebrates subjectivistic relativism. The need for objectivity is not merely rejected. Rather, without pitting objectivity against subjectivity, phenomenology advocates for a more sophisticated approach to unbiased observation. From a

[1] Recall the phenomenological reduction noted in the Preface. One is "reducing" one's field of vision to precisely what presents itself through experience rather than allowing presuppositions to prefigure one's investigation.

phenomenological perspective, hypothesis testing can constrict the scientist's openness to new understandings by stifling original contact with the object of study. As the research in any given area moves forward, the new is filtered through the lens of the old. In other words, what is overlooked in conventional methods education is the propensity for hypotheses to hide phenomena. A habitual reliance on hypotheses tends to create blockages, gaps, or slippages between the researcher's worldview and what is being researched. It puts the researcher and the researched at a prefigured distance from each other. To be sure, even quantitative researchers have sensed this, which has led some (e.g., Rodgers, 2010) to argue for a revolutionary shift away from testing the null to a modeling–building orientation that would allow the research to freely "go fishing" in the data collection process (p. 10).

This critique notwithstanding, it should also be noted that phenomenologists do not ignore conventional research or disavow research findings from hypothesis-driven studies. Quite the contrary, phenomenologists often directly confront traditional research, mining it for raw materials that can be reinterpreted in the light of fresh, descriptive phenomenological insight (e.g., see Giorgi, 1967; Merleau-Ponty, 1962, 1963). The phenomenological critique of hypothesis testing is not an all-out objection to the use of hypotheses in scientific research. Rather, it is a criticism of the assumption that data can only be interpreted via the scientist's representation of reality. As an alternative, phenomenology proposes that the researcher engage in a systematic, descriptive explication of how the data present themselves originally, prior to the introduction of hypotheses.

The global thrust of the existential–phenomenological approach to psychology is the impetus to connect with the original sense of psychological life, what presents itself prior to the imposition of scientific constructs. This impetus was anticipated by William James. As Ashworth (2009) noted:

> William James . . . insisted repeatedly that it was fallacious to assume that the research participant's experience was to be understood in terms of the readily-available categories of the researcher. The psychologist's fallacy (of which all researchers concerned with experience may fall foul, not only psychologists) involves a confusion of the standpoints of the researcher and the researched. The "subjective world" of the

> research participant must be understood in its own terms. (p. 195)

Accordingly, there is no attempt in existential-phenomenological psychology to reify its research foci. At the same time, however, existential-phenomenological psychology does not seek methodological alternatives that revolve around formal logic and deductive reasoning.

The *Epoché*: Bracketing

Introduced by Edmund Husserl, the *epoché* is a methodologically specified way to circumvent the psychologist's fallacy. Phenomenological researchers wish to work from what is immediately given rather than from what is intellectually handed down, assumed, or projected into the data. They strive to be fully present throughout the processes of data collection and analysis so as not to have one's field of vision restricted by preexisting conceptualizations. But this sustained, ongoing effort is no simple matter for phenomenology. To transition from hypothetical representations to descriptive presentations of data requires a reorientation of the researcher with respect to the natural attitude of everyday consciousness and the naturalistic assumptions of conventional psychology (i.e., psychology envisioned as a natural science). The perspective of the natural attitude gives us the world as ordinarily and tacitly understood (Husserl, 1970). There are many aspects to it, but there is one aspect in particular that would stand in the way of phenomenological research if it were left unquestioned. It is a certain kind of naivete: that the world is simply there, preformed, and having nothing to do with our involvement in that world (i.e., our participatory co-constitution of it). Husserl calls it "the naïve and natural straightforward attitude" (p. 143), naive because it is full of unexamined presuppositions. In the natural attitude, the world has already been thematized in accordance with received opinion. The naturalistic attitude of conventional psychology is an offshoot of the natural attitude that evolved over the course of Western cultural history and became sedimented in scientific discourse. It harbors idealizations of the natural attitude, interpreting all the world on the basis of thing-ness, of sheer materiality, quantifiability, and causality. Together, the natural attitude and the naturalistic attitude form a double envelopment of presumptiveness that truncates the learning process.

Faced with the natural and naturalistic attitudes, phenomenological psychological researchers adopt the contrasting attitude of the epoché. As Fuller (1990) described it:

> Employing the phenomenological method means taking a step back from our usual everyday involvement in things, from our normal fascination with things and projects—with beings in their sheer obviousness—and in particular from what has become the commonsense commitment to a "scientific" view of the universe . . . our everyday tendency to treat things as absolute and in-themselves, ready-made, "out there," and the same for everybody . . . . (p. 27)

Adapted for psychological purposes, the epoché is a "bracketing" or provisionally setting aside what one knows (or thinks one knows) about the object of study. It facilitates a phenomenological attitude of disciplined openness to meanings, especially those meanings that may deviate from what the research would otherwise expect to find. In the attitude of the epoché, presuppositions are not doubted or deleted, but are rather provisionally held in check, suspended. The metaphor of temporarily placing presuppositions "in brackets" is revelatory of a fundamental value of the phenomenological researcher: to not rush to judgment. First, describe what presents itself without imposing preexisting beliefs that would oversimplify or obfuscate what is given, see the phenomenon afresh, then arrive at one's conclusions. If data analysis brings preexisting beliefs to mind, if it arouses natural attitude assumptions (ranging from presumptive personal impressions to folk psychological accounts) or scientific accounts, they are neither de facto accepted nor rejected. They are not assumed to be on target because the data analysis aroused them; nor are they assumed to be biased (and thus rejected) because they already existed. The point is, rather than assuming, keep judgments in check for the time being. Once the description is completed and one is satisfied with its rigor and faithfulness to the data, things like natural attitude assumptions and scientific accounts, such as what one would have discussed in the literature review portion of the study, can be checked against one's findings. Through it all, one maintains a posture of always being able to ask questions like, "Is this really true here?" "How can I check that?" "Is there sufficient data here to warrant that conclusion, or might it be different?"

The attitude of the epoché frees the researcher from the naivete of the everyday natural attitude and the formalized objectivism of the naturalistic (natural scientific) attitude. This temporary suspension facilitates a heightened attention to the meaning-bestowing, co-constitutive activity of consciousness. The resultant heightening of attention is bidirectional and dynamic. On the one hand, the researcher does not take the participant's meaning-giving participation for granted. On the other hand, the epoché attunes the researcher to their investigatory perspective as they strive to make sense of the data without prejudice (i.e., it affords radical investigatory self-transparency). In both instances, the phenomenological attitude allows the researcher to understand the natural attitude and the naturalistic attitude better than they understand themselves (see Giorgi, 2009). Giorgi (2018) recently provided the following account of this orientation to the research process:

> The attitude employed is . . . like the attitude Merleau-Ponty (1962, p. 28) described as one of "circumscribed ignorance," an attitude that has an "empty" but already determinate intention," which is what attention is. It has to be appreciated that the method being employed is a "discovery-oriented" method and not a "hypothesis-verifying" one. With a discovery-oriented method, especially one involving morphological phenomena, new insights in the very criteria being used are possible. (Morphological phenomena are descriptively based phenomena with irregular dimensions that cannot be fully determined by formal implications.) The lack of an initial explicit statement of criteria . . . allows the researcher to tap into prepredicative levels of functioning (Husserl, 1973) or indeterminate zones of experiencing (Merleau-Ponty, 1962) whence new aspects of the objects of experiencing can be encountered. The method is not an intellectualistic one, but an existential or embodied one. After all, not everything is already known, and space must be left for the new to announce itself; maximum openness is necessary for that to happen. This is especially important for prelogical or pararational phenomena, categories within which most psychological phenomena reside. (pp. 102–103)

Thus, the purpose of the epoché is twofold. "Negatively," it serves to liberate the researcher from making premature judgments and operating under the auspices of unexamined presuppositions. "Positively," the epoché serves to instantiate a radical reawakening of the researcher to the participatory life of consciousness. As Morley (2010) described it:

> The full power of the *epoché* is too often taken for granted by qualitative researchers and even sometimes by those of us professing to be phenomenologists. We too often assume it is a simple matter to suspend judgments, hold back our prejudices, or become aware of our assumptions. But what Husserl meant by the *epoché* is much more radical than we often recognize. To hold back our existential commitment to the very existence of the world, i.e. the reality positing power at the very core of consciousness itself, is a profoundly challenging and painfully difficult undertaking. It would be incorrect to treat the *epoché* as a simple mental technique or "professional" procedure that could be easily taught in an institutionalized manner as one would instruct a simple craft or practical skill. For the *epoché* is an action that involves one's total existential position toward the world and is thus profoundly personal. In other words, the *epoché* is not a merely intellectual operation. It is often likened to a type of a conversion experience that can be a shock to one's previously held convictions. Furthermore, achieving the intellectual flexibility that permits one to stand back at a distance from the natural attitude involves an extended preparation and intellectual familiarization with phenomenological literature. (p. 225)

A major consequence of this transitional form of experiencing is the opening of the researcher to the domain of the irreal.

Confronting the Irreal: Non-Sensuous Givens

Conventional psychological research exalts what can be presented to the senses in the process of knowledge acquisition (i.e., it is strongly allied to sense-empiricism). Traditional, natural scientifically oriented psychological research is so oriented toward *the real* that it has no language to deal with what Husserl (2014) referred to as *the irreal*, which is neither real nor unreal. Stated differently, natural science psychology is explicitly oriented toward the visible, but it has no language to deal with the invisible (Merleau-Ponty, 1968). In contrast, phenomenology does not restrict "data" to what can be presented to the senses. As Giorgi (2014) observed, phenomenological psychological research orients the researcher to non-sensuous givens that would be impossible to study with conventional methods. As he put it:

> If we want to uphold the philosophical perspective that humans, while partially natural, also have dimensions that are nonnatural, where do we turn? I want to turn to the most obvious, and yet the most difficult phenomenon for nonsupporters of our approach to embrace: the presence of irreal phenomena or irreal dimensions of phenomena. Until psychology tackles this issue, it will not make significant headway in understanding human psychological phenomena. (p. 236)

Broadly speaking, the data of phenomenological psychology are in each case an amalgam of the real and the irreal (not to be mistaken for the un-real or fantasized). But such phenomena as consciousness, meaning, belief, organizational processes, reason, memory, attention, anticipation, judgment, conscience, and imagination (to name a few) are not reduced to their material substrates. Phenomenological psychological research does not prefigure its topics of investigation on a sense-empirical basis (that impetus would be bracketed). This does not mean that phenomenology is anti-empirical. If empiricism means making observations and working from experience, then phenomenology is quite empirical in its own way (see DeRobertis, 2022). Husserl referred to phenomenology as simultaneously a universal empiricism and a universal rationalism (Husserl, 1971). The empirical nature of phenomenological psychology may be seen as "impure" when viewed from the perspective of conventional (sense) empirical psychology. But, from the perspective of phenomenology, it is sense-empiricism that is tainted and biased because of its myopic appeal to the "raw data" of sensory impulses as the source of knowledge. Phenomenologists are not alone in noting this myopia. This line of thinking has roots that extend all the way back to William James's (1996) radical empiricism, where the sense data of traditional empiricism are reconceptualized as always shot through with conjunctive relations that cannot be reduced to sensible realities. James spoke of these relations as those aspects of experience that join and unify sense data, expressed in words such as, "with, near, next, like, from, towards, against, because, for, through, my," and so on (p. 45). In more recent history, Jean Piaget, one of the most cited and influential psychologists of all time, contributed a similar criticism, noting:

> The empiricist tradition . . . regards knowledge as a kind of copy of reality and intelligence as deriving from perception alone . . . as if there were nothing more in mental life than sensations and reason—forgetting action! (Piaget & Inhelder, 1969, pp. 28–29)

Here, in a roundabout way, Piaget is calling attention to an unfounded grand assumption that is pervasive throughout conventional research training and much of psychology at large: that every human being responds to two separate worlds, an external, objective world, and a paradoxical internal world of neural tissue and worldless subjectivity. Once this assumption is bracketed, the phenomenological researcher is afforded opportunities for empathic, intuitive participatory engagement with research participants, witnessing and "entering" their worlds, as it were.

Returning to the Participants Themselves: Empathic Attunement

Since phenomenological psychology does not pit objectivity against subjectivity, it adopts a radically different attitude toward human participants in the data collection process. In phenomenological psychological research, data are most often gathered from written protocols and transcribed interviews where participants are given instructions to describe their experience in as much detail as possible. As part of its return to "the things themselves" (i.e., the phenomena under study as experienced rather than reified) phenomenological research returns the participants themselves (i.e., the source of the data) with a value on letting the other person freely and openly participate in the research process without the imposition of scientific prejudices. Thus, Halling (e.g., 2005; Halling et al., 1994) has conceptualized the phenomenological research process as an unfolding relationship, an ongoing dialogue between participants and researchers that explicitly rejects the historical ambivalence toward the subjective in psychology. Phenomenological psychology does not seek data gathering techniques designed to restrain the subjectivity of the participant, filtering their responses to bring them in line with the researcher's hypotheses.

In contrast, conventional methodology prioritizes a detached, third-person perspective, pursuing a kind of objectivity that requires guarding one's data collection against contamination by the participants subjectivity. Data is collected from subjects by channeling their responses, conceptually through hypotheses, and concretely through tests and measurements. Relative to phenomenology, there is a stronger emphasis on keeping the firsthand experience of the participant at a distance for the researcher to do good science. Phenomenological psychology is quite different in that it secures a legitimate scientific place for the first-person perspective of the participant and the second-person perspective of the researcher in dialogue with the participant. Even "third-person" readings of participant data are not done as a detached outsider. They are deliberately, reflectively, and empathically attuned to the experiential world of the participant. The phenomenological researcher wants to answer their research questions in a way that is organic and remains faithful to the experiential world of the participant as encountered by the researcher.

The important, though often neglected role of second-person perspectivity in phenomenological psychological research has recently been discussed at length by Scott Churchill (e.g., 2012). Second-person perspectivity is contrasted with both impersonal third-person perspectivity and first-person perspectivity that is projected onto the other. That is, second-person perspectivity does not refer to experiences of the other as coopted and envisioned by the self "at a distance," as it were. A description rendered from the second-person perspective is an empathically situated description that deliberately and continually seeks resonation with the other's total living (embodied, affective, perceptive) viewpoint to whatever extent that is possible. As Churchill described it:

> "Second person perspectivity" is a special mode of access to the other that occurs within the first person plural: in experiencing the other within the we, we are open to the other as a "thou", another "myself" - and, in this same moment, I become an intimate "Other" to the one with whom I find myself in an "exchange." (p. 2)

The history of this orientation has strong historical ties to the work of Wilhelm Dilthey. Dilthey is seminal for phenomenological psychology, as he was perhaps the first thinker to point out that the methods of the natural sciences (e.g., physics, chemistry, biology, etc.) were insufficient for the establishment of a science of human beings (i.e., psychology). As van den Berg (1972) put it:

> Like the physicist, the psychologist tried to dissect the object of his studies; he tried to isolate the elementary factors of mental life to reconstruct actual mental life with these elementary factors. While it was obvious, even then, that . . . an all-embracing psychology, could not be achieved this way, Dilthey was the first to point this out . . . . In his opinion, the essential characteristic of the psychic aspect of human life is that it is . . . not a collection of elements. The psychologist . . . must try to find a method that originates from the subject itself. (pp. 126–127)

As an alternative, Dilthey proposed a psychological science that would develop original methods for dealing with human phenomena, those that would seek to understand human psychological life based on a living, feeling relation to the other. As Strasser (1985) described it:

> According to Dilthey, the [human] "sciences of the mind" share the methods of all empirical sciences: observation, description, classification, even quantification; they are, however, distinguished from them by the method of "Verstehen," i.e., the comprehension of mental acts like thoughts, strivings, feeling, emotions, etc. In consequence, for Dilthey the sciences of the mind were not inferior to the natural sciences; in a certain sense they were even superior, because they were able to give an account of the phenomena of life. Since we are living beings, we need not reconstruct those phenomena in the abstract manner in which natural sciences reconstruct the phenomena of nature. We experience them immediately, we know them "from within." "Life understands life" was one of Dilthey's favorite sayings. (p. 4)

Through the influence of Dilthey, the social sciences and the tradition of phenomenology became acquainted with the notion of *Verstehen*. Verstehen denotes the "understanding" that results from a strategic use of the human capacity to see and feel with the other for investigatory purposes. The "method" of Verstehen is to use the imagination in a concentrated effort to experience as the other does. Dilthey preferred the term *Mitfühlen* for "feeling with" the other, which is sometimes translated as empathy or sympathy (Gallagher, 2019). Thus, as Bourgeois, (1976) once noted, throughout the social sciences Verstehen has come to carry with it "the idea that a social scientist must empathize with . . . subjects in order to understand [their] actions as social actions" (p. 27).

Drawing on Dilthey and the philosopher Theodor Lipps (who spoke of empathy as *Einfühlung*), Edmund Husserl came to see empathy as a central problematic in the formation of the phenomenological method. Husserl also used the terms *sich Einfühlung* (i.e., to feel one's way into) and Mitgefül (i.e., fellow feeling; see Moran & Cohen, 2012), and he considered empathy to be the royal road to genuine interhuman encounter. Accordingly, it has become a critical aspect of phenomenological psychological research. As Meacham (2013) put it:

> In *Ideas II*, Husserl talks about a kind of sensitizing of our empathic capacities such that we can come to better understand the motivational structures of another (here he means human person) as both generally similar to our own and distinct in the sense of individuated from a more general style of being motivated (or sense-forming) in a typical manner: typical to the form of our bodies, our cultural background, and at a more general level species-typicality. (p. 15)

Drummond (2020) has more recently observed that empathy in Husserl's works is not a primarily affective experience, but one that allows an individual to both maintain the intersubjective distance needed to see the other in their foreignness and transition into experiences of sympathy and compassion. The latter are the affective yield of empathy, constituting the more concretized connective tissue between the experiential worlds of the self and the other. Thus, for Husserl, Einfühlung is a more cognitive–constitutive dimension of intentionality. It refers to the attunement through which other people are experienced as conscious embodied subjectivities. Einfühlung founds the possibility of Mitgefühl as co-feeling.

The Methodical, Rigorous Description of Living-Experience

When it emerged in the middle of the 20th century, humanistic psychology needed a method that could save human subjectivity from its objectivist exile (see Maslow, 1946, 1966, 1969; Rogers, 1953), and existential phenomenology was a perfect fit (see DeRobertis, 2021c). Existential phenomenology offered a rigorous form of methodical qualitative description. As noted in Chapter 1, this descriptive orientation has strong historical ties to Franz Brentano. In his 1874 book, *Psychology from an Empirical Standpoint*, Brentano (2015) argued for a descriptive psychology to counterbalance what he considered psychology's two dominant viewpoints: a physiologically based genetic–explanatory psychology and introspectionism. The former emphasized an externalist viewpoint; the latter emphasized an internalist viewpoint (thus reflecting an inherent dualism in the field). In contrast, Brentano held that psychology ought to study the intentionality or "aboutness" of diverse conscious acts (thus, calling attention to the neglected "in-between" realm of world-relationality). Consciousness is always a certain kind of "direction toward an object" (Brentano, 2015, p. 92). Intentional acts can be studied with "objectivity," but only if the psychologist is not bound to objectivism. Intentional acts will never be adequately understood when studied wholly "from without," as it were. For Brentano, the third-person, externalist viewpoint needs to be supplemented by an appreciation of "inner perception," which needs to be investigated with descriptive rigor. Introspectionist psychology's alternative of studying the "inner contents of the mind" lacked this rigor because it was founded on the faulty (similarly objectivistic) assumption that one could, in an instant, stop the temporal flow of consciousness and catch a static snapshot of one's own mind (Mulligan and Smith, 1985).

Attending to the Complex, Multifaceted Whole

Brentano (along with the philosopher Gottlob Frege) was also influential in turning Edmund Husserl toward the *meaning* of the subject's intentional acts (Bell, 1990). In existential–phenomenological psychological research, meanings are considered non-discrete moments of unfolding experiential events. Meanings are not analytically reduced to reified standalone elements because phenomenologists are primarily interested studying the living-experience of the real rather than the static abstractions of "objective" natural scientific consciousness (Husserl, 1970; Knowles, 1986, p. 115). As was noted in Chapter 1, natural scientific psychology takes the ambiguous phenomena of life and systematically reduces everything down to an artificialized "clear conception of dependencies" (Dilthey, 1988, p. 85). The object of study is broken into pieces or parts and studied as a collection of hypothesized causes and effects. Experience is objectivized as the holistic, living flow of human experience is entirely displaced and covered over by *representations* of experience. Phenomenology plots a very different course in its study of structural meaning. Meanings are seen as constituents of a living Gestalt, which includes the total structural meaning of the phenomenon under study (discussed below as the phenomenon's "what") and its manner of unfolding (discussed below as the phenomenon's "how"). The unfolding structural whole of a meaningful human experience is the alpha and omega of the existential–phenomenological psychological investigatory process.

As was also noted in Chapter 1, this non-objectivizing approach to phenomena reflects a broader, holistic view of persons. Subjectivity and objectivity are not artificially partitioned in advance of study, so the researcher does not attempt to isolate internal and external causes and effects. The focus is on the living, meaning-bestowing activity of persons as it unfolds in their respective situations. The process is not linear, as in a cogitating subject projecting meanings at the world, which would suggest an intellectualist or idealist perspective. Intentionality is both world directed and world embedded. It is ordinarily prereflective, with varying potentials for reflective insight depending on the situation (recall the discussion of functioning or operative intentionality from Chapter 1). Thus, Frankl (1967) once noted, "Phenomenology, as I understand it, speaks the language of . . . prereflective self-understanding rather than interpreting a given phenomenon after preconceived patterns" (p. 2). Along similar lines, van den Berg (1972) characterized phenomenology as a method that allows the researcher to reconnect with *"prereflective existence"* (p. 130). In prereflective existence, the cognitive, bodily, affective, conative, and social dimensions of living-experience do not appear as so many atoms of psychological life (we will look at this more closely in Chapter 5).

Attending to the "What" of the Phenomenon

Phenomenologists seek to clarify the nature of the phenomenon under investigation (as revealed by its meaning), what makes it the specific kind of phenomenon that it is. If, for example, I am interested in studying compulsion as a phenomenologist, I will first want to know what it means for the experiencing person engaged in such a behavior and what it is like for them rather than how compulsion figures into a prefigured psychological framework of explanation. This allows the psychologist to truly access the deepest possible understanding of what *being* compulsive is all about. Phenomenologists, while seeing the value in explanation, do not see it as self-sufficient; nor are they content to remain at the level of explanation when studying a topic of interest. Explanation alone is no guarantee that the researcher will be able to achieve a genuine understanding of what the phenomenon under study is primordially, as a meaningful aspect of human psychological life. Take the example of swimming. One may give many fabulous explanations of how swimming becomes a possibility via biology, physiology, chemistry, physics, behaviorism, and so on. But, in the end, these kinds of analysis do not yield the clearest understanding possible of what it really means to swim for the swimming person. Thus, as J. H. van den Berg put it (1972):

> Phenomenology is a method, it can be called an attitude . . . . The phenomenologist . . . distrusts theoretical and objective observations, observations at a closer inspection, the kind of observations made by the physicist . . . standard opinions, and quickly formed opinions like projection, conversion, transference, and mythicizing. To write a discourse on swimming, he [*sic*] will . . . swim and repeat . . . until he [*sic*] knows and can express what swimming is. (p. 77)

Rather than grounding research in an explanatory "why" question or asking what causes a phenomenon to occur, phenomenology begins with a different kind of "what" question: "What is the meaning of the phenomenon?" The question sounds simple, but it is not, because the general or "overall" meaning comprises many constituent meanings that are structurally configured so that the phenomenon takes on its specific qualitative form in the life of human subjects. Sometimes significant aspects of this structural configuration jump right out at the researcher, but phenomena can also be quite opaque, requiring a lot of follow-up inquiry, deep reflection, and empathic attunement (see Churchill, 2018).

Regrettably, psychology has always looked upon methods that allow researchers to quantify data and apply inferential statistics as a kind of Holy Grail. Thus, researchers trained in conventional methods often overlook phenomenology, passing it off as just another of many descriptive, qualitative techniques. From the traditional viewpoint, description only offers surface-level snapshots of phenomena, which can have high heuristic value (i.e., the potential to stimulate or encourage further thinking) but do not explain why the data appear as they do. From the viewpoint of phenomenological psychology, this is uncertain, as it depends on the nature of the descriptive method in question. Phenomenology offers a unique form of methodical description, with the power to explicate and clarify the fundamental structure of what the psychologist is studying. Structural clarity of understanding is no trivial matter. As May (1958b) once observed:

> This is a point . . . phenomenologists make consistently, namely, that to know fully *what* we are doing, to feel it, to experience it all through our being, is much more important than to know *why*. If we fully know the *what*, the *why* will come along by itself. One sees this demonstrated very frequently in psychotherapy: the patient may have only a vague and intellectual idea of the "cause" of this or that pattern [of] behavior, but as he [*sic*] explores and experiences more and more the different aspects and phases of this pattern, the cause may suddenly become real . . . not as an abstracted formulation but as one real, integral aspect of the total understanding of what he [*sic*] is doing. This approach also has an important cultural significance: is not the *why* asked so much in our culture precisely as a way of detaching ourselves, a way of avoiding the more disturbing an anxiety-creating alternative of sticking to the end with the *what*? That is to say, the excessive preoccupation with causality and function that characterizes modern Western society may well serve, much more widely than realized, the need to abstract ourselves from the reality of given experience. Asking why is generally in the service of a need to get power *over* the phenomenon, in line with Bacon's dictum, "knowledge is power" and, specifically, knowledge of nature is power over nature. Asking the question of *what*, on the other hand, is a way of *participating* in the phenomenon. (p. 83n)

Attending to the "How" of the Phenomenon

As phenomenologists describe a phenomenon, they simultaneously seek to describe the structured, temporally unfolding meanings embedded in immediate experience. They attend to the phenomenon's "how" (i.e., the specific way that it emerges from within its context, takes shape, and unfolds). Human psychological life is always situated, manifesting within an inexhaustible web of meaningful relations to others and things (i.e., relationships and projects). While some aspects of a phenomenon are salient, other aspects remain latent or even hidden in the worldly backdrop of experience. Thus, to be truly empirical and faithful to experience, the phenomenologist must acknowledge that things present and hide themselves at the same time. Disclosing what is latent or hidden in our experience is also important in phenomenological research. Since things are primordially tied to other things, people, and situations, phenomenologists seek to elucidate the meanings of things as they appear against the total horizon of a person's being-and-becoming-in-the-world-with-others, alongside-things. As Fuller (1990) put it:

> To describe the full structure of an event of meaning—all that a meaning is, the complete phenomenon—involves displaying the manner in which the meaning takes place, the qualitative "how" of its occurrence. How something happens in its lifeworld setting is essential to what it is. A meaning never exists in isolation but always in a lifeworld context of other meanings and always for someone who has some interest in the matter... Not content with what for the most part does show itself, meanings as we are straightforwardly involved with them in our daily rounds, phenomenology attempts to render explicit any meaning's largely hidden event character, its being. (p. 29)

Phenomena are understood as related to a human body and therefore having a place from which actions originate; as belonging to a social structure, a culture, and a language; as belonging to a history; and as oriented toward the horizon of future possibilities.

Temporality

To speak of history and future possibilities as contextual factors highlights the fact that time is a critical aspect of phenomenological psychological research. As noted above, the "how" question implicates the inherent temporality of human experience with its attention to emergence and unfolding. This question, which is more genetic in character, can spiral out from participant data to questions concerning the wider sociocultural and historical horizons of the phenomenon (Husserl, 1970). Of course, the researcher may or may not pursue these lines of inquiry, and there are different ways of going about it. We will return to this issue in Chapter 3. For now, the more important point here is that phenomenological description will eventually bring one to the precipice of such questions.

Time has always been a central theme of phenomenology. Its founder, Edmund Husserl, dedicated an entire text to the study of time consciousness (Husserl, 1964) and time figures prominently throughout his unpublished manuscripts. Time, in this context, is not objectivized time, however. It is not the linear procession represented by clocks and calendars that we are taught in elementary school. Those are abstracted derivatives of time as it is originally lived and experienced as both a natural phenomenon (e.g., sunrise and sunset, the change of the seasons) and a personal phenomenon (e.g., minutes can seem like hours when you are bored). As Donohoe (2004) noted, Husserl characterized the original sense of time as a *streaming living present*. It is the time of living-experience. The streaming living present is where human beings find themselves always already taking up a personal and collective past in anticipation of a future (whether immediate or remote). To reflect on the present moment is to disrupt a preexisting, forward-moving flow and catch a glimpse of what is already slipping into the past. Moments cannot be fixed as discrete points, snatched up, and manipulated like clay in the hands of a potter. Similarly, Heidegger (1962) once wrote that human lived-time is not a succession. The future cannot be reduced to what is later and the past cannot be reduced to what is earlier. The future, says Heidegger rather poetically, is present in an enduring process of already having been moving in a given life direction (thus highlighting the fact that the future is always already woven into the present as it continually slips into the past).

Intuition and Elucidation of Essential Meanings

As noted above, conventional research values quantification. Quantitative data and statistical analyses are not universal in conventional research (see Shadish, 1995), but the value of quantification is steadfast. In the field of psychology, lines of research are held in higher esteem where statistical data are readily available. Thus, Marchel and Owens (2007) concluded from their study of American Psychological Association (APA) journals that if you want to publish something that is not quantitative, "do not begin with the Tier 1 journals" (p. 320). The scientific reasoning process that undergirds the impetus to quantify and calculate is probabilistic inductive generalization. Conventional research is committed to the idea that the researcher systematically observes varied empirical manifestations of a phenomenon and then derives from these observations a heightened ability to say what is most likely (i.e., probably) the case in terms of explaining it.

In contrast to the emphases on quantification and probabilistic inductive generalization, phenomenological psychology emphasizes experiential quality and intuitive insight to make its claims of generalizability. Rather than relying on inductive inferences that "leap" back and forth between a quantity of factual "hard data" and the researcher's hypothesized interpretations, phenomenology seeks intuitive, self-evident understandings of phenomena gleaned directly from its descriptive analyses. Here, intuition is not relegated to the status of a mere feeling, hunch, or guess (see Osbeck & Held, 2014). Rather, for phenomenological psychology, intuitive self-evidence refers to insight into essential structural meanings. It is *essential intuition* or *Wesensschau* in German. Essential structural meanings are what give the phenomenon under study its qualitative distinctiveness. They give phenomena their specific psychological identity so that the scientific community clearly knows, with reflective understanding, what it is studying. Without this clarity, there will always be an epistemological slippage between data and interpretation, which can unnecessarily incite and/or prolong scientific debate.

The Search for Invariant Meanings

The phenomenological method relies on intuitive self-evidence to explicate essential meanings by searching for invariants that run across participant descriptions. Findings are derived from a reduction process that does not lapse into a reductionism. Of course, essential intuition does not just happen of necessity in the process of a descriptive analysis. One can describe and describe without focusing one's attention on essential meanings. The key is to be able to differentiate between meanings that are incidental to the phenomenon and those that constitute the *sine qua non* of the phenomenon (i.e., without them, the phenomenon would not be what it is). Here again, the influence of Aristotle is palpable as it was he who introduced the distinction between the essential and accidental properties of things. To accomplish this differentiating task, the phenomenological researcher identifies and reflects upon the meaningful themes that run across actual (empirical) variations of the phenomenon. Diverse cases are examined with attention to meanings rather than objectivized "facts." At each turn of the descriptive process, the researcher wants to know about the relevance or significance of this or that aspect of the expressions being analyzed. When phenomenologists engage in description, they are not interested in simply taking an inventory of facts; nor are they compiling a chronology of meanings. They aim to reveal what is most essential to the meaning of the experience as lived.

Individual cases are examined first. But empirical variations are not enough. To rely on empirical variations alone would restrict the results to the status of an empty generalization based on nothing more than frequency of occurrence within a given sample (i.e., a probabilistic inductive generalization, perhaps backed by a p-value where statistics have been employed). The generalization is said to be "empty" because there is no scientific role assigned to the process of achieving intuitive insights into the nature of the phenomenon under study. To achieve such insights, phenomenologists also use *imaginative free variation.* They imaginatively vary the constituents and meaningful relationships given with the experience of the phenomenon to intuitively discern which are most vital to the experience of the phenomenon in question. The researcher varies the meaningful constituents under scrutiny in imagination asking, "If this were different, would the experience be fundamentally different, or would it be basically the same with respect to the specific phenomenon being studied?" The same procedure is then repeated across all the participant data. The phenomenological researcher studies diverse empirical and imagined variations of the phenomenon with the aim of explicating general structural meanings, thus taking analysis from the level of the individual case to a trans-individual level that yields generalizable psychological findings. Here, phenomenological psychologists speak of an eidetic reduction, where the object of study first encountered in specific observed instances with all their concrete embeddedness is "reduced" to its essential psychological meanings and thereby conceptually clarified. Having said this, it is important to bear in mind that the descriptive effort is not intended to rise to the level of philosophical description, which deals with higher level generalizations. As Giorgi (2009) put it:

> We want to claim that imaginative variation is employed so that an eidos is obtained, but we also want to claim that the eidos is a type rather than a universal category. Its scope is much more limited, yet it is also not an empirical generalization. An empirical generalization refers to a category arrived at based upon the number of cases on hand, but an eidos is a generalization that sets the boundaries for possible instances of occurrences because possibilities are considered. However, unlike in philosophy, in psychology the boundaries are set by a type of the phenomenon and not its universal characteristics. The idea of a generalized type is further reinforced by the awareness that, since we are dealing with experiential contents, the essence is a morphological one. For Husserl . . . morphological essences are in principle inexact. (pp. 196–197)

Explicating a General Structural Description

Conceptual clarity is brought to fruition by the articulation of an essential meaning profile. Invariant meanings must be transformed into robust thematic expressions of the phenomenon under study. That is, they must be synthesized to become invariant, general-level themes. When these now thematized expressions are woven together in a way that exposes the fabric of their organized unfolding, one has arrived at a general structural description of the phenomenon.

This is a skill set all its own as the researcher is tasked with choosing the most appropriate expressive terms to explicate the essence of the phenomenon under study. In terms of propriety, the researcher must bear in mind that they are doing research that is focused on faithfully describing psychological meaning. The expressions that they choose ought to pointedly and accurately represent the domain of psychological discourse while (under the epoché) resisting the temptation to resort to the use of abstract terminology from psychology or some other science, which would undermine the method. The researcher must find those words that will bring the phenomenon to life for the reader, so there is an element of creative writing involved. But the writing of the results is not a mere exercise in creativity. Quite the contrary, one is reporting scientific results. Thus, to reiterate an above noted point, the researcher must avoid oversimplifying (thus neglecting essential structural constituents) or obfuscating (i.e., embellishing).

An Illustration: A Phenomenological Investigation of Cross-Cultural Learning

Now that a thematic, conceptual introduction to phenomenological methodology has been provided, an example of its application is in order. This will show how the kinds of ideas presented here can be translated into a series of concrete steps for doing psychological research. The results that follow were taken from a study of cross-cultural learning (DeRobertis & Bland, 2020a) that utilized what has become known as the Giorgi method.

Recruitment and Participants

IRB approval for research with human participants was obtained for this study in October of 2018. Participants were solicited via announcements made around my college campus. I met with volunteers as they came forward to determine if their experiences matched the focus of the study. In total, eleven volunteers were screened until a baseline of 3 participants (see Giorgi, 2009) were identified. These included: (a) a 54-year-old Chinese female who moved to the United States when she was approximately 30 years old, (b) a 36-year-old White American female, and (c) a 32-year-old White American male. No compensation was provided for participation.

Procedure

Having provided written consent, the participants were duly informed that the proposed research involved voluntarily disclosing personal experiences of having encountered another culture, initially feeling threatened, and then overcoming this feeling in a cross-cultural learning experience. Each participant responded to the following query:

> Please describe an instance where you were exposed to another culture's lifestyle and/or viewpoints and initially felt threatened, but then learned something that broadened your personal horizons. Please include in your response how the experience began and played out. Proceed as if you are speaking to someone who knows nothing at all about such experience but who wants to know what it is like to go through it.

Participant interviews were transcribed for protocol analysis. In accordance with the phenomenological epoché, tentative pre-understandings (both informal and those gained from the literature review) were not doubted or deleted, but provisionally held in abeyance.

The analysis calls for a synoptic reading of the data to obtain a holistic sense of each response. This entails deriving both a coherent grasp of each participant's global intentional orientation and a sense of the ways the meanings embedded within each description are structurally related to one another. Once completed, "units" of psychological significance are identified in each protocol. Meaning "units" are deemed non-discrete moments within the temporal unfolding of the phenomenon. To identify them, the researcher notes when and where noteworthy shifts in meaning occur within the participant's experiential stream (Giorgi, 2009, p. 130).

The researcher identifies meaning units with the aim of understanding the significance of this or that aspect of the whole to the person experiencing the phenomenon. Persons, places, things, and processes of all kinds are not brute facts, objects, or discrete quantifiable entities. They are interrogated in terms of their interdependent, interwoven constituent meanings with the intent of explicating the qualitative *what* and *how* of the phenomenon. Here it must be remembered that the researcher's reflective analytical delineation process is but a temporary conceptual convenience for penetrating the fabric of participant accounts in order to progress toward the achievement of deepening insights. Given the flux and flow of living-experience, this step in the research process admits of a degree of fluidity and flexibility from researcher to researcher (see Giorgi, 2009). Diversity in the way that researchers delineate meaning units does not pose a problem for the research because all one is doing is earmarking places within a total temporal flow to gain a foothold from which to articulate the structure of the phenomenon holistically.

The participants' expressions that originally appear in the meaning units are then transformed so that they clearly convey the psychological meanings inherent to the phenomenal whole of each participant's protocol. Here, the researcher transforms the first-person everyday ("natural attitude") expressions of the participants into third-person thematic expressions that are amenable to the higher level conceptual understandings of psychology while maintaining the phenomenological attitude (i.e., without resorting to the imposition of preconceptions). During this step of the analysis, meaning units are made into themes. The first-person language of each participant is changed to third-person language to prepare for the explication of psychologically generalizable findings. If the researcher is from a different discipline, their description would strive to articulate different kinds of meanings. In the current context, we are talking about psychological research. As Giorgi (2009) put it, one is making a psychological interpretation by means of a descriptive method.

During this step, meaning units are also transformed with the aim of distinguishing incidental psychological meanings from essential psychological meanings (sometimes called psychological *eidetics*) at the level of each individual participant description. The phenomenological researcher "wants to know more precisely how to articulate what makes the object [of study] a specific example or instance of the type of phenomenon it is" (i.e., "what is essential about it"; Giorgi, 2009, p. 88). To transform the meaning units into themes, the researcher uses imaginative free variation. One asks whether the moment in question could be different and, if so, whether it would fundamentally alter the nature of the phenomenon as experienced by the participant. This facilitates the transition away from the sheer embeddedness of the meanings in the data toward an articulation of greater generality. If a determination cannot be made from within the context of the available data, the researcher will have to return to the participant to collect more information.

Individual themes are then studied across participant data to delineate and explicate the meanings that were significant to the phenomenon in general as revealed by the participant sample. By using the method of imaginative variation, the phenomenon is "reduced to its essence" and explicated (Giorgi, 2009, p. 90). General themes are integrated into a general structural description of the psychological significance of the phenomenon.

Results: Transitioning from the Experience of Personal Threat to Cross-Cultural Learning—a General Structural Description

For the phenomenon of transitioning from the experience of personal threat to cross-cultural learning to occur, the learner begins in a state of essential unfamiliarity with the real lives of others belonging to the culture that one finds threatening. That is, the learner has had either (a) no (or very little) contact with this culture or (b) if there was sustained contact, substantive relating was lacking.

From the learner's initial viewpoint, the behavior of others belonging to this culture is held to radically deviate from the norm to which one is accustomed. This radicality is founded upon a judgment concerning the core of one's social value system, a belief that members of the other culture fail to meet a certain standard of how one ought to conduct oneself in relation to other people. Consequently, the others' behavior is deemed impenetrable, incomprehensible, and personally unacceptable from the learner's preexisting worldview. The others' behavior is also looked upon as somehow dangerous based on negative stereotyped associations (e.g., such people are likely to be radical, mentally ill, diseased, etc.). These associations can be formed via mere hearsay, or the learner can generalize beyond known facts.

Thus, the threatening character of the others' behavior rests upon a twofold foundation, appearing as a substandard social foreignness that also harbors the potential to place the learner's well-being in jeopardy. The feeling of threat can be rooted in an exceptionally high degree of moral preoccupation with the others' lifestyle, which is deemed objectionable on this basis (e.g., as decadent, evil, sinful, etc.). In this instance, there may be an additional concern over being socially rejected for tolerating the other culture's ways. However, the phenomenon can unfold without a pronounced, fervent moralism. In either case, the learner will have formed an implicit assumption of the others as people of a relatively impoverished humanity. This is an emotionally driven process of creating an oversimplified conceptual bifurcation that portrays oneself and the others as different "kinds" of people.

For change to unfold, currently held assumptions regarding the others' culture must be shown to be untenable from other people who provide different information that challenges one's beliefs and implicit expectations. To put the process in motion requires a laying of the foundations for dialogue, an openness manifested concretely as freedom of expression, listening, and a modicum of respect at a minimum. The learner is then confronted with a perspective on the others' culture that proposes a new possibility: that their lives are more complex than what the learner had imagined. Once this possibility is seriously entertained, the learner begins a gradual process of opening to a new experience of the others that requires the development of a revised, more multifaceted, and refined sort of intellectual understanding. However, this revision cannot be brought to fruition by purely intellectual means, as the new understanding must also become concrete and relatable, with grounding in an intuitively grasped, bodily manner of knowing. Thus, it is possible for the change process to begin based on new input from any number or variety of others, be they proximal or remote. However, having already presumed the others to be radically different in an emotionally driven manner, a fully revised understanding can only be achieved via personalized experiences with the threatening others themselves.

Firsthand experience makes it possible for the learner to get to know specific others whom they perceive as threatening face to face, in the flesh, in person—and to find that in reality they are not as different as was assumed. The learner discovers a wealth of contextualizing data within the flow of live interaction that makes specific situated others comprehensible, which would not have been possible from mere discussions about the others in the third person. Most importantly, the learner witnesses spontaneous and genuine emotional expression and particularly vulnerable interpersonal emotion, which indicates to the learner that these others have rich affective lives that make them "like any other human being." The most significant contributor to the decisive unfolding of a gradual change in the learner's thinking and general orientation toward the others is instantiated upon seeing their range of emotionality in response to universal human needs, desires, and struggles. In full sway, the change process involves the learner co-existing courageously with the now less threatening others amid a free-flow of information that is incongruent with what was initially expected. Threat progressively diminishes and courage progressively builds as the learner comes to increasingly see these others in the abundance of their humanity, which thereby outmodes any compartmentalized, intellectualized understanding that conceptualizes them and their life situations anonymously and in the abstract. Within the learner's field of experience, the radically different, incomprehensible others that threaten are in the process of being transformed into familiar others who struggle and suffer "like we all do." These increasingly familiar others are coming to be seen as representing a widening field of positive human values and social goodness. The learner is becoming capable of seeing these others as individuals with legitimate human viewpoints that the learner can accept and validate from their own point of view.

Once this form of learning occurs, it engenders an intellectual humility in the learner in which one is no longer quick to maintain assumptions and make prejudgments concerning the others' culture. The learner becomes better able to shift from an avoidance orientation to a relative openness orientation through deepening intrapersonal and interpersonal dialogue. This is, however, a process and it takes varying amounts of time to unfold. Even after the learning has occurred, the others are still relatively new to the learner and in ways still unknown. The learner will struggle to keep assumptions and stereotypes in check and work to resist the temptation to pass judgment as an ongoing task. The learning impresses upon the learner the need to repeatedly leave the comfort of a self-protective posture, allowing one to be temporarily vulnerable. Effort is required to remain empathic and relational. The emergence of a new orientation toward the others does not mean that apprehensions instantaneously vanish. The learner continues to feel unease to differing degrees. Apprehensions progressively diminish without necessarily going away altogether, although they may with the passage of time

Final Remarks

Having seen results from a formal phenomenological study, the reader will notice that in describing the phenomena above no recourse was made to hypotheses or scientific constructs. "Objective factors" were never pit against "subjective factors," and there was no attempt to explain away the phenomena under study. Emphasis was given to the living structural meaning of the experience as it unfolded within the total context of human being-in-the-world. Some of the things you saw you might have already known about the phenomenon from your own experience. Other things you might have suspected or sensed but did not know explicitly. While still other things might have even surprised you.

It is important to note that when one is doing this kind of research, researchers sometimes come up against unresolvable discrepancies in the explication of general themes. This may mean that more data need to be collected or that errors have been made. If the data appears robust and adequate and no errors are apparent, the researcher must consider the possibility that they have procured data on a similar but ultimately different phenomenon. In Chapter 4, for example, we will see that embarrassment, shame, and guilt have long been considered overlapping experiences, but with subtle differentiating contours. Participants do their best to provide the data that the researcher is asking for, but they are not perfect, nor are they social scientists. Obtaining and differentiating data is the researcher's responsibility. This can be a hiccup and/or a productive learning experience in the research process.

Another possibility is that one has collected data that are suggestive of a typological (sometimes called morphological) variation. Here, one is confronted with the fact that seemingly diverse phenomena can share higher level core similarities. As we will also see in Chapter 4, there can be varied manifestations of the same basic kind of experience. If one suspects that there is a typology emerging from the data, this will then need to be identified, described, and properly delineated, potentially with the addition of new participants to fulfill sample size requirements. In the cultural learning research noted above, the possibility of a typological variant emerged when one of the participants emphasized a culturally embedded moralistic dimension to her experience of threat. She noted that in her culture gay people were considered, among other things, disease spreaders. But the rest of her description was fully commensurate with the data from the other participants, so a mere caveat was added to the general structure. This is one of the more difficult aspects of this kind of research. If the data that she provided forced me to articulate the general structural description at such a high level of abstraction that the general structure did not represent the psychological essence of the phenomenon as revealed by the rest of the participant data, a typological variation would have presented itself (for illustrations, see DeRobertis, 2016b, 2017).

To conclude, it is also important to note that the kind of results provided by phenomenological research are *not* offered in opposition to the kind of information provided by strictly explanatory approaches to psychological phenomena (e.g., see DeRobertis, 2015a; Mruk, 1985). Rather, phenomenological results fill an important gap between conventional psychology's distanced, hypothesis-oriented manner of theorizing and its quantitatively driven, causal-explanatory research. Phenomenological research allows one direct access to phenomena, unhampered by the limitations imposed by the purely explanatory impulse.

Key Terms, Concepts, and Themes

- "The things themselves"
- Phenomenology's principle of all principles
- Intuition
- The epoché/bracketing
- The natural attitude
- The naturalistic attitude
- The irreal/non-sensuous givens
- Empathy/empathic attunement
- Second-person perspectivity
- *Verstehen*
- Meaning-bestowing world relating (co-constitution)
- Prereflective understanding
- The "what" of an unfolding phenomenon
- The "how" of a phenomenon's unfolding event structure
- Horizon
- Temporality
- Essential meanings
- Essential intuition/Wesensschau
- Invariant meanings
- Imaginative free variation
- Morphological essences
- General structural description

Chapter 3

Phenomenological Psychological Research in Perspective: Controversies and Horizons

When I have shared phenomenological research with colleagues whose training is limited to conventional methodology, their critical remarks have revolved around two themes. First, they will comment on the smallness of the sample size and assert that this is problematic because it diminishes one's ability to generalize. Second, they will interpret the results as having been wholly derived from evidence that is merely anecdotal and assert that this makes the research findings suspect because there were inadequate protections against participant bias. After all, participants are not trained scientists, so they make mistakes in drawing conclusions about their experiences. Of course, these observations (mine) are themselves anecdotal, but they are worth mentioning because they bring up issues concerning the quantity and quality of phenomenological research evidence, both of which should be discussed in further detail.

On the Quantity of Evidence

The concern over sample size reflects conventional psychology's commitment to probabilistic inductive generalization. Larger quantities of data make for higher probability in that kind of generalization process. But, as we have seen, phenomenological psychology's primary concern is not saying what is "probably" the case when it comes to this or that object of study. Instead, it wants to know what makes the phenomenon the kind of phenomenon that it is. Thus, the sheer number of empirical variations per study is not as important for carrying out phenomenological research. Still, it is important to bear in mind that this difference is only one of relative importance. As noted in Chapter 2, phenomenological research in psychology typically uses a baseline of three participants, so sample size is a consideration (Giorgi,

2009). There are other ways that the number of participants matters as well. Recall from Chapter 2 that phenomenological psychological essences are characteristically morphological, sometimes manifesting in numerous typological variations. Additional empirical variations allow the phenomenological researcher to encounter and explicate these typologies. Moreover, in phenomenological psychological research, it is assumed that any given general structural description may need to be revised and refined in the light of new data. Thus, one of the goals of phenomenological research is to be able to repeat its findings with new participants. For reasons such as these, phenomenological psychological research has sometimes been referred to as empirical phenomenology (bearing in mind that this usage of the term *empirical* is broader than what one finds in sense-empiricism). This can be confusing for students, as if they are getting mixed signals about the empirical status of phenomenological research. This is especially the case when it comes to the issue of replication, which is a bit more complicated, so more needs to be said about it.

As part of its objectivism, conventional psychology is focused on the sum of facts pertaining to a topic of investigation. Even "subjective" variables are interpreted as factual contingencies seen in terms of cause and effect. The ideal aim is to explain away the phenomenon based on the evidence of empirical replication carried out by the control and manipulation of these factual contingencies. In contrast, phenomenological psychology does not objectify the subject and, instead, turns its attention to intended meanings. Meanings are not deemed mundane facts. They are not epiphenomenal or merely derivative. Meanings are held to be substantive and non-discrete, requiring a method that faces them head on, reflectively, rather than reducing them to so many facts of nature. Should a researcher catalogue all the facts contingent upon their participants' environments, count and even code all their words and phrases, there is still no guarantee that they have entered the realm of intentional meaning, much less structural (organized, integrated) intentional meaning or essential intentional meaning. Thus, it simply makes no sense for phenomenological research to get involved in a "sheer numbers" game, so to speak. Counting, calculating, and accruing volume are more suited to a psychology of facts than meanings. The repetition of findings in phenomenological research pertains to the refinement of its general structures, not the sheer accumulation of higher quantities of data.

On the Quality of Evidence

The anecdotal evidence critique is a typical follow-up to the issues raised above, and this critique leads to questions concerning the quality of the data as well. The criticism is that one's analysis is tainted by the subjectivity of the participants, detracting from scientific objectivity. This would be difficult to refute were it not for the fact that the phenomenological researcher is not consulting with participants for an explanation of the phenomenon under study. The criticism assumes that the aim of all social science research is to extrapolate cause-and-effect relationships from data and, further, that phenomenological research must be about taking the participants' folk psychological accounts or "lay theories" (Keltner & Buswell, 1997, p. 252) to be authoritative. What the critique misses is the possibility of a non-propaedeutic role for methodical descriptive rigor in psychology.

It is wise to do justice to this critique, however, and to take it as seriously as possible. Participant accounts are reliant on recall and, as such, harbor the potential to be distorted and disorganized. Thus, Giorgi (2009) has noted that phenomenological psychology's reliance on retrospective accounts is a potential vulnerability. But there is no reason to assume that the possibility of distortion in recall is uniform across all participants and experiences. There is literature to suggest that negative events and information are more prone to distortion than positive events and information (see Schachter et al., 2011). Yet, even this cannot be taken as gospel. For example, Pezdek and Roe (1994) observed that a child's memory tends to be resistant to distortions brought on by force of suggestion when recalling emotionally distressing instances of abuse.

In any case, no research is without vulnerabilities of various kinds, including those related to its samples. The landscape of mainstream psychological research is full of self-reported data. The fact that instruments from questionnaires to fMRIs are used to control and/or "filter" participant data in anticipation of the researcher's interpretation of findings does not make natural scientific research in psychology immune to problems of distorted recall. One could even make the argument that instrumentation adds extra layers of controversy to the problem of interpreting participant data (e.g., Aue et al., 2009; Murphy, 2016).

To be sure, the deeper underlying assumption of this critique is that subjectivity is a potential contaminant that must be contained. However, as we have seen, this is an assumption of naturalistic objectivism. From a phenomenological psychological perspective, "objectivity" can be increased (rather than decreased) by a respectful, attentive, sensitive, and reflectively discerning intersubjective encounter. The accusation of anecdotal bias would have more merit if the role of the phenomenological researcher is to be a passive observer, absorbing participant data in the most superficial manner, going on faith, merely inferring what's going on "in the participant's head." But such is not the case. In phenomenological research, the researcher is bound to what is given, but not as a passive receiver of data as in sense-empiricism. Phenomenological psychological research is explicitly oriented toward the overcoming of prejudices by the attitude of the epoché. This is compounded by the demand for empathic attunement and methodical descriptive rigor (Churchill, 2022). The interpersonal skill set that belongs to good counselors, parents, teachers, and friends must be developed under the auspices of the epoché so that the phenomenological researcher can detect and follow-up on leads without "leading" the participant. The researcher is not an inert word collector, powerless in the face of what is not so obvious or latent. One listens with one's mind and body to what is said, how it is said (in terms of both intonation and body language), what cannot or will not be said, and so forth. As Churchill (2018) observed, people can mean more than what they articulate in words. A person with good interpersonal skills is regularly attuned to this without having to reflect on it. But, as Churchill noted, training in phenomenological research involves becoming explicitly attuned to this stratum of dialogue so that open-ended queries can be used to productively broaden and deepen the data. The qualitative "how" of participant accounts is shot through with clues concerning contextual factors related to their manifold relationships and projects (e.g., personal and interpersonal history, real and perceived strengths and vulnerabilities, points of pride and regret, self-justifications and self-satisfactions, latent interests and motives, and so forth).

On Interpretation

As noted, phenomenological research most often analyzes data in the form of written protocols and transcribed interviews. But many forms of expression can be phenomenologically analyzed, such as play, body language, art, cultural artifacts, historical documents, and even participant responses from quantitative studies (Fink, 2016; Giorgi, 1967, 1968; Merleau-Ponty, 2020; van den Berg, 1961; Wagemans et al., 2006). These data sources suggest a more pronounced role for interpretation in phenomenological research. Moreover, to suggest, as I have above, that the phenomenological researcher listens to how things are said or not said will most certainly incite a discussion over the need for interpretation (sometimes called *hermeneutics*) in phenomenological research.

Irrespective of the data source, phenomenological analyses demand that researchers strive to painstakingly describe the experiential quality and meaningful structure of human comportment from what is available without imposing their own prejudices into the data. Nonetheless, the researcher may be confronted with obscurities in the data. Crystal clear evidence is sometimes wanting, so the researcher must face what was previously referred to as a phenomenon's "hidden event character" (Fuller, 1990, p. 29). Recall that phenomena are nested within a body, social structure, culture, language, and history; they are oriented toward the horizon of future possibilities, and the meanings that come forth as figures in a phenomenological analysis do so against the background of these contextualizing factors. Sometimes these aspects of an experience announce themselves quite forcefully as participants open up, but their extended meanings and implications may be unclear. At other times, it will occur to the researcher that certain contextualizing factors are setting the stage for certain meanings to form, but there is little in the data that has been collected to explore them. What are the researcher's options? According to Wertz (1983), one may pursue these leads and articulate those contextualizing factors in the participants' lives that are relevant to the phenomenon under study. He referred to this as the interrogation of opacity and noted that one may remain more descriptive in doing so. Alternatively, one may transition to a more interpretive posture.

If remaining descriptive, one may make do with what one has in the data, present one's findings, and handle any remaining opacities as limitations of the research that need to be handled by future studies. Another option is to collect more data, to ask participants, "Can you tell me more about that?" One can press on with open-ended questioning until relevant data emerge. How the researcher is to proceed once they have reached the limits of current understanding is a place of some controversy within phenomenological psychology. As suggested above, there is a continuum of views on this issue ranging from various descriptive to interpretative postures. On one end of the continuum stand those perspectives that remain pointedly descriptive and represent a genetic phenomenology "in the transcendental register"

(James, 2007, p. 22). Recently, Davidson (2021) has made a plea for this sort of option. He begins by noting issues raised here:

> Now that we have a reasonable handle on the structure and meaning of [an] experience, where do we go from here? What is the next step in our psychology? Is it enough to understand the internal logic, the lived necessity, of . . . actions, or is more to be demanded of a scientific psychology than simply this? What do we do once we have arrived at the structure of our subject's experience? How are we to make further sense of it, and is it imperative that we do so? Are we, as psychologists, content with this level of analysis? Can we stop here? (p. 276)

Davidson recommends that the researcher uses interdisciplinary data as clues, but remains oriented toward the implicit constitut*ing*, meaning-making activities of the individuals under study. The researcher focuses on the way participants passively and actively, implicitly and explicitly, take up meaning-laden positions with respect to their circumstances. Emphasis is placed on the originality of the constituting subject's meaning-making activities or participatory contributions as transcendentally framing all the interpretations and psychosocial dynamics inherent in their world relations. In his words:

> Psychology, like all other positive sciences, is to be subordinated to the transcendental perspective in which it is situated. Each discipline is taken to be only one beam of light shone on what is to be considered an essentially transperspectival subject matter. It is the transcendental life of the Person that always remains primary; the presence of the Person as non-psychological of which psychology only provides one glimpse among many. (p. 309)

This transcendental perspective advocates for a more pronounced role for philosophical reflection in the research process. The alternative, mid-position strategy is to remain focused on the ways in which meaning-making is existentially immersed, as a constituting that is dynamically and paradoxically constitut*ed*, working reflectively and critically (rather than naively) within the natural attitude of situated, everyday life. This is sometimes referred to as a *diacritical* posture (e.g., Englander & Morley, 2021). Rather than having to press on toward the "heights" of a universal, transcendental perspective (more proper to philosophy), the researcher's work involves the progressive delineation of culturally embedded typological variations. On this view, one can remain essentially descriptive (e.g., Giorgi, 1970, 2009), working in a slow and steady manner by the collection of new participant data. Or one can transition to the other end of the methodological continuum and adopt explicitly interpretive or "hermeneutic" procedures (e.g., Packer & Addison, 1989; van Manen, 1990, 2014; see also, Giorgi, 2018). As we will see below, this can include the consideration of theoretical frameworks in the light of participant data.

The interpretive dimension of phenomenological research has not been made an explicit theme until now for two reasons. First, I am of the conviction that description is the gateway for understanding phenomenology, especially as regards the process of deriving findings that stand a chance of being taken seriously by the scientific community in psychology. To the uninitiated, anything that smacks of "it's all interpretation" will inevitably lead to accusations of post-modern anti-scientism in psychology. (How ironic, if not hypocritical, in a discipline that is so committed to interpreting findings based on hypotheses!) At any rate, the introduction of interpretive themes greatly complexifies the discussion of phenomenology and leads to issues concerning diverse applications that move beyond phenomenological psychology. It even leads one beyond the scope of phenomenology itself. This holds true in philosophy as well. The more that thinkers like Martin Heidegger, Maurice Merleau-Ponty, Emmanuel Levinas, and Paul Ricoeur turned toward interpretive themes, the more they spiraled outward away from a focus on phenomenology to engage broader ontological, epistemological, and metaphysical concerns (Ihde, 1971; Solomon, 1988; Strasser, 1986). Second, the issue of interpretation has become bitterly contentious in social science research and is still being debated. Part of the debate concerns the phenomenological status of methods calling themselves "interpretive," and questions have emerged over the rigor of such approaches (e.g., see Churchill, 2018; Giorgi 2006; van Manen, 2018). "Interpretive" may, for some, appear as a blank check to operate in a freeform qualitative manner under the banner of phenomenology while producing results that are neither phenomenological nor capable of withstanding conventional methodological criticism. Suffice it to say that it seemed inappropriate to expose the reader to such issues in the middle of a basic introduction to phenomenological psychological methodology.

To provide some background, phenomenology's descriptive and interpretative dimensions have repeatedly reemerged as controversial since the days of Husserl himself. Most notably, Martin Heidegger took up the theme of interpretation as part of a fundamental disagreement with Husserl concerning the nature and role of phenomenology in philosophy (e.g., see MacDonald, 2006; Sheehan, 1997). The theme of interpretation, already prominent in the groundbreaking work of Wilhelm Dilthey, was revived by Heidegger as a way of turning phenomenology away from the ideals of Husserl's transcendental aspirations. For Heidegger, primacy was to remain on the ego, "I," or self as situated in a particular time and place, disavowing any striving toward the ideal of achieving a universal philosophical perspective, which is more commonly associated with Husserl's transcendental reduction and transcendental ego.

This reprioritization generated a decisive shift in emphasis toward the finitude of the individual subject and the limited, perspectival nature of their existential knowing and understanding. The attitude of the epoché becomes a less prominent theme as more relative importance is placed on owning and taking up one's world-embedded access point to the data in any given inquiry. The specific world-situated interests and motivations of the person seeking answers to their existence take center stage, as does the language systems used to carry on one's investigations (Nicholson, 1984). The ideal of achieving understandings that rise above the limitations of one's bodily, sociocultural, and historical conditions is deprioritized. In its stead, there emerges a view that human knowledge-gathering efforts of all kinds always hide phenomena even as they illuminate them. A given set of interests, facilitated by a specific vocabulary, can open one to new understandings, but they will hide others in the process. This means that the interpretive turn reorients phenomenology toward the challenge of confronting the obscurity and strangeness of all that we encounter in the world. Experiential "absences" (as contrasted with experiential "presences") come to the foreground of the research process.

Herein lies the stepping-off place for Max van Manen's program of hermeneutic phenomenological research in the area of pedagogy. As he described it, the hermeneutic phenomenological method not only utilizes the epoché, phenomenological intuition, and phenomenological reduction, it also involves an engagement with language and aesthetics to excavate the hidden dimensions of phenomena and bring about deep, resonant phenomenological understandings (van Manen, 1990, 2014).

A similar view was advanced by Moustakas (1994), who advocated for the use of self-dialogues, stories, poems, artworks, journals, diaries, and other personal documents to depict experience. Overall, this leaning in phenomenological research can be traced back to the divergence between Husserl and Heidegger and the tension that it created between subjectivity conceived as transcendental and subjectivity conceived as existentially situated (with a particular emphasis on linguistic relativity). This returns us to the existential–phenomenological paradox noted in the Preface. As described by Natanson (1970), phenomenology depicts the typical (better, the typological) and strives toward the elucidation of essence and the structure of consciousness. Existentialism wants to highlight the unique in its concreteness, expressing the reality of the individual (in other words, as situated). Some researchers place more relative emphasis on one or the other side of the paradox. So, although both Giorgi and van Manen have referred to their phenomenological orientations to research as existential, the way they translate this into a research orientation is somewhat different. For van Manen (1990), the challenge of phenomenological research is to articulate findings in a way that captures both the "unique and universal" (p. 39). For Giorgi, it is neither of these when phenomenology is usually applied to psychology. Findings are typologically oriented, general structural descriptions of morphological (inexact) phenomena that are rooted in the description of situated individual accounts. It is also important to bear in mind that the Giorgi method does not preclude the study of individual cases to arrive at the essence of a singular experience or higher level analyses that tap into the human condition as such. Indeed, an individual-level focus is a required inclusion in areas of research like personality, developmental psychology, assessment, and many other clinical and applied areas, especially when dealing with rare conditions.

To cite a brief example of how this divergence has trickled down into the practices of individual researchers, a recently completed dissertation on learning (Maser, 2023) cited results I derived by using the Giorgi method. The author recognized "alignment" between my results on learning and his own, using a self-made amalgam of several methods, including van Manen's (p. 179). He nonetheless cast my general structural descriptions as committing an objectifying essentialism, stating that my general structures sound too psychological and thus do not "resonate" enough with the reader (p. 179). Maser proposed a van Manen-inspired alternative, reframing his descriptive results by repeated "hermeneutic" detours that presented the idiosyncratic manifestations of learning in the lives of individual participants. This was done with the intention of increasing the readers' sensitivities to the learning process and was justified on the basis of what the author considered van Manen's (2014) insistence that results should be mediated by empirical material drawn from life, such as anecdotes, stories, fragments, aphorisms, metaphors, memories, riddles, and sayings (Maser, 2023, p. 128).

Giorgi and van Manen come from different disciplines, which helps to account for their difference in emphasis. With van Manen focusing specifically on pedagogy, research participants are more likely to be children. The younger the child, the more one will be faced with slippages between the language and worldview of the researcher and the participant. Interviews and protocol analyses could not be carried out as they are with adults in phenomenological psychology. New observational strategies may be required. The younger the participants, the more one feels the need for interpretive moments in the research. Thus, Moran (2004) once noted of Husserl, "In his middle years, Husserl likes to speak of 'interpretation' . . . with regard to grasping the mind of a child, animals, and so on in a developmental or genetic manner" (p. 300).

Coming from different disciplines, Giorgi and van Manen speak to different audiences and thus pursue slightly different aims, but there is much overlap in their insights and adaptations, and Giorgi (2018) has recently made it clear that he sees interpretation as important. At the same time, Giorgi objects to hermeneutic universalism. Not unlike conventional psychology, hermeneutic universalism looks upon description as too simplistic and surface level (e.g., see McCall, 1983, pp. 63–64). But rather than opting for a return to the methods of the natural sciences, hermeneutic universalism maintains that hermeneutics is the only method of research for the human sciences (see Giorgi, 2018, pp. 46–47). For his part, van Manen (2014) has recognized the complementarity of the two approaches (i.e., Giorgi's and van Manen's), citing his post-Husserlian focus on language as the distinguishing characteristic of hermeneutic phenomenological research in pedagogy. With its interpretive focus, hermeneutic phenomenological research stresses the need to confront the dynamics of concealment and unconcealment (obscurity and clarity, absence and presence) by attending to manifold forms of human expression, even to the extent of dealing with interpretations of interpretations, as in the arts. (To analyze this difference in perspective further would demand an entire detour through the literature on the linguistic relativity hypothesis, which is too far afield for the current discussion.) One must further become skilled in the art of creative writing to present findings. Giorgi (2018) has similarly noted the need to be a skilled creative writer in presenting phenomenological findings, but he would be far more cautious about emphasizing "creativity" in the process of deriving findings from the data. Giorgi is emphatic about the phenomenological principle of all principles (see Chapter 2), according to which the researcher is bound to the limitations of what is afforded in the data. In other words, the phenomenological researcher should not take creative license when presenting findings.

The unfortunate way that this has played out historically is that phenomenologically oriented social scientists have often come under the pressure of a false dilemma: One must decide to become a descriptive or an interpretive phenomenological researcher. Introductions to phenomenological psychology have blurred or completely covered over the distinctive characteristics of description and interpretation, merely resting on the assertion that description is just another name for interpretation (e.g., Keen, 1975; Spinelli, 1989). In the process, phenomenological approaches that focus on the primacy of description are sometimes miscast as relics of a "Husserlian idealism." This is a regrettable fact of the history of phenomenological research in the social sciences, as researchers have too often come to take sides in a debate that tends to have more to do with labels than practice (Churchill, 2016).

To illustrate, Giorgi (2009, 2018) has been the most ardent advocate of the descriptive approach, applying Husserl in modified form to do psychology. Yet, as we have seen, his modification of Husserl does not necessitate any press toward a transcendental reduction. For Giorgi (2018), the process of doing psychology is pointedly existential and embodied. On the one hand, one is engaged in making *psychological interpretations* with a descriptive method (see Giorgi, 2009, p. 181). Here, Giorgi refers to interpreting in the sense of making meaning from within a situation and a vantage point. On the other hand, interpretation as a creative *going beyond* what is known and currently knowable (a second meaning of the term) becomes necessary when what is available in the data has reached a point of obscurity (Giorgi, 2018). Where the possibility for descriptive clarity has reached its limits, interpretation can intervene to offer creative contributions to a phenomenological exploration, taking its lead from clues appearing in what the participants have provided.

Methodical description, to describe with disciplined openness, is the necessary centerpiece of phenomenological psychological research, which is de facto existential in nature. Interpretivists never tire of citing Heidegger (1962, p. 61), who asserted that descriptions are simultaneously interpretations. But it is important to bear in mind that before doing so Heidegger insisted that the term *descriptive* phenomenology is a tautology, a redundancy (p. 59). Unprejudiced description marks the inception of phenomenology. The circumscribed ignorance of methodical descriptive rigor is the power and freedom within situated perspectivity to access the given and take responsibility for one's limited access to the phenomenon under study. Methodical descriptive rigor allows a community of researchers to refer to the data and mutually affirm that something is clearly observable and evident. Interpretation straddles this effort as the situated access point of a phenomenological description on the front end and as a creative, responsible confrontation with obscurity on the back end. The former pertains to the inevitability of perspectivity in psychological research; the latter pertains to method in terms of research activities or procedures.

On Theory

What we have seen thus far is that by assuming the attitude of the epoché phenomenological research temporarily disengages preexisting conceptualizations of phenomena. This includes theories that one would have come across in the literature review process. In this specific sense, phenomenological research can be said to be "atheoretical" in character. However, one must not mistake this to mean that theory plays no role whatsoever in phenomenological research. There are at least five points of contact between theory and phenomenological psychology.

First, the entire enterprise of phenomenological psychology rests on a philosophical and theoretical (global perspectival) reorientation of the psychologist. At the most basic levels, phenomenological psychology offers a new theoretical approach to psychology, one might say an alternative metapsychology or paradigm, founded on the philosophical insights of Husserl and those who have carried on the phenomenological tradition. With phenomenology, psychology is reconceptualized as a human scientific rather than natural scientific discipline (Giorgi, 1970). Even the adaptation and development of the methodology for psychological application is founded upon philosophical and theoretical principles which, as we just saw, are not as a matter of course immune to ongoing debate. What is revolutionary about phenomenological psychology is that it draws from a philosophical source that is not limited to "pure" argumentation, but also anchors its dialogue in descriptions (van den Berg, 1972). As Strasser observed, phenomenological description provides a groundbreaking alternative to both the deduction-driven approach of traditional philosophy and the induction-driven approach of psychology (Strasser, 1977). But, as we just saw, it would be quite naive to think that phenomenological philosophy and psychology are comprised of nothing but descriptions.

The second point of contact between theory and phenomenological psychology is founded on the notion that there are different kinds of theorizing. When phenomenological psychologists express caution, concerns, or misgivings about theories, they are typically referring to formal theories (see Giorgi, 1979), especially those that have been developed under the auspices of unreflective objectivism. As Strasser (1977) observed:

> The metaphysic which lies hidden in the various psychological and psychopathological "systems" is for the most part already present in the categories and concepts which are selected for describing the normal or pathological movements of the heart. Thus one who is not trained philosophically is unaware that, by taking over certain supposedly technical and descriptive concepts and methods, he [*sic*] has already adopted a determinate path which may lead . . . into a hedonistic, naturalistic, idealistic or mechanistic anthropology. (p. xiv)

The more formalistic a theory, the more it is mediated by implicit and/or explicit hypotheses. Such theories are more likely to rely on the (sense) empiricist theory of induction, which obscures the Wesensschau and invites the development of obfuscating conceptual contrivances. This makes it less likely that the theory will evidence compelling connective tissue to the world of living-experience. To use Husserl's (1970) terminology, the theory will appear increasingly groundless, resulting in the compensatory inclination to generate abstractions that substitute for unbiased descriptions.

To illustrate, in the next chapter we will see an example of how formalized theorizing operates in conventional research. The theories deal with the phenomenon of embarrassment based on hypothesized causes and effects. We will see that the theorists have persistently sought a general structural description, but their progress has been held back because they lack the (human) scientific methodological resources to provide anything other than revised conceptual definitions and theoretical descriptions informed by new hypothetical explanations. But, as we will also see, the theorists and theories are diverse, with some being more formalized and objectivistic than others (or at least more formalized and objectivistic in certain respects than others).

So, to reiterate, the more formalistic and objectivistic a theory, the more the phenomenological researcher must proceed with caution. But there is also such a thing as non-formalistic, descriptive theoretical activity, and this is to be welcomed with open arms. On this view, psychological theorizing is "simply thinking made systematic and rigorous" (Giorgi, 1979, p. 75). As Giorgi put it:

> From a phenomenological perspective, the essential activity of theorizing is conceptualization, and Husserl distinguished two forms of conceptualization, formalization and generalization. Formalization . . . divests itself of intuitive content, is basically an empty content that can be applied extensively. Generalization, however, refers to the achievement of rich or filled concepts because the material or intuitive content is deliberately taken into account. The process of generalization can also lead to essences or structures. (p. 74)

In this light, phenomenological psychological research always aims to be a kind of grounded theoretical research operating within any given area of investigation. Thus, van den Berg (1972), who spoke against the habitual reliance on hypotheses, was nonetheless quite clear in noting:

> An accurate description of an incident necessarily involves a judgement concerning the incident, *according to a theory of the incident. Only then, if needed, is a theory on the incident permitted.* The first theory is the one of the incident and of the actor in it. (p. 64, emphasis in original)

For van den Berg, the basic principle of all phenomenology is that the investigator remain true to an event of meaning as it happens on a firsthand, living basis. That is what guides the first theory, the primordial theory "of" the event rather than the theory "on" the event. Similarly, Gurwitsch (1974) asserted that the "purpose and sense" of the sciences are "to provide a theoretical account of the life-world," the world of living-experience that precedes scientific abstraction and idealization (p. 139).

This aspect of phenomenological psychology is too often overlooked, even by phenomenological psychologists themselves. This is most likely due to the enthusiasm with which phenomenologists embraced post-Husserlian currents of phenomenology, especially Heidegger, who spoke adamantly against theory (see Sheehan, 1997). In contrast, Husserl (1970) praised theory in his *The Vienna Lecture*. For Husserl, to take the Greek notion of *theoria* seriously is to embrace the notion that philosophy and science have infinite tasks laid out in front of them. This then becomes the basis for a phenomenological critique of those dogmatic aspects of the natural attitude and of naturalism that preclude open exploration and discovery. There is a difference, in other words, between theories that authentically represent the ideal of theoria, its openness to infinite tasks, and those that do not. The one-sided rationalism of the Enlightenment was a flawed attempt to actualize theoria, in his view, as was the objectivistic, "mathematical natural science" that followed (p. 295). Thus, Husserl's effort to revolutionize philosophy and science on phenomenological grounds featured a privileged place for theory rescued from the groundlessness of its natural scientific exile. Taken on its own, formal (hypothesis-based) theorizing incites sometimes spurious debate, which can remain active on a prolonged basis with enough crafty reconceptualization and data dredging. Following Husserl, the infinite tasks of science ought to be fine-tuned for optimal (efficient, effective) disclosure by a phenomenological rehabilitation of theorizing activity.

The third point of contact between theory and phenomenological psychology pertains to the fact that the epoché is not doubt or deletion. It is temporary disengagement so that the researcher can see the phenomenon afresh, to encounter what one is studying with the originality that results from disciplined, methodic description. Theories are encountered in the literature review process, temporarily disengaged, and then reengaged at the conclusion of one's study (see Churchill, 2018). Thus, when it comes to addressing theory in an investigation, phenomenological psychological research is not unlike conventional research at the front and back ends of study. The primary point of divergence lies in the process of collecting data and analyzing findings. In conventional research, pre-understandings (which come from many sources, including theories), remain active throughout the research process by way of hypotheses. For phenomenological psychological research, the hypothetical must give way to original contact with the data.

This leads directly into the fourth and fifth points of contact between theory and phenomenological psychology. The fourth point of contact concerns the critical examination of theories as an important task in human science research. Far from being glibly discounted, even highly formalized, highly objectivistic theories are scrutinized for intuitive insights into living-experience in a phenomenological investigation. Phenomenological insights tend to be peppered throughout formal theories, though admittedly to different extents, even though the theorists may be unaware of them as such (e.g., see DeRobertis, 2021a, 2021b). As we will see in the next chapter, this is part of what accounts for how there can be implicit phenomenology embedded within conventional research. From a phenomenological point of view, a formal theory that is more in touch with living-experience is inherently disposed to have more enduring relevance, as those who would seek to apply the theory will always have tangible, relatable touchstones to work from. This would be especially so with a theory that is more in touch with the essential structures of living-experience and their different typological variations. Since phenomenological insights (i.e., essential structural insights) are oriented toward necessity rather than probability, higher level descriptions offer exceptional external validity (see Churchill, 2022), while lower level (more context embedded) descriptions allow for greater discernment when it comes to understanding the phenomenon's diverse worldly variations. Critical assessment in the light of phenomenological findings can lead to important clarifications and/or correctives to formal theories. In the United States, critical reengagement with reviewed theories has been part of phenomenological dissertation research since the development of phenomenological psychological methodology at Duquesne University toward the end of the 1960s. As we will see, the Vallelonga (1986) research on embarrassment mentioned at the conclusion of the next chapter is one such example.

The fifth and final point of contact between theory and phenomenological psychology pertains most directly to the infinite tasks of phenomenology. Critical assessment of formal theories need not end with clarifications and correctives. Placed in a dialectical relation to informal theory, formal theorizing can be another avenue for phenomenological researchers to productively confront obscurity and unclarity. As Jager (1988) noted, the guiding metaphor of theorizing has for millennia been "one of a formative journey of exploration leading to an intimate contact with and knowledge of little-known regions and distant peoples" (p. 12). This can be done in a manner that prioritizes maintaining close contact with living-experience and descriptive evidence, or in a manner that spirals away from the phenomenal field toward more distant indeterminant horizons. Everything depends on how hermeneutic in orientation one wishes to be (see DeRobertis, 2015a). In either case, this engagement with formal theory can inspire new avenues of phenomenological research, even if that research is not carried out through hypothesis testing.

Suffice it to say, the phenomenologist does not use theory in the traditional way (i.e., deducing a hypothesis, operationally defining its variables, conducting an experiment, quantitively analyzing the outcome, and inferring support or lack of support for the hypothesis). The phenomenologist utilizes theories, hypotheses, prior explanations, and so on heuristically—that is, as a possible way of understanding what a phenomenon is and if it can be borne out by a careful examination of what shows itself in the phenomenon itself (i.e., as directly or "originally" experienced, without taking a detour through a conceptually prefigured examination of evidence). This is what Wertz (1986) found in psychoanalytic research performed by Freud and others throughout its history. Specifically, he found that the phenomenological method was performed in very much the usual way by psychoanalysts, but they added an operation not typically found in phenomenology. They also utilized a theoretically informed or sensitized examination of experience to engender new insights into the way phenomena show themselves. To illustrate, a doctoral student, Paulson Veliyannoor (2011), an Indian priest, developed a formal method with Wertz for his dissertation, a study of the meanings of the Eucharist among persons of the Catholic faith. He analyzed interview data describing experiences of the Eucharist first using Giorgi's phenomenological procedures, without any theory, and then analyzed the same data through the heuristic lens of object relational psychoanalytic theory (Melanie Klein, Wilfred Bion, James Grotstein, and Thomas Ogden). After completing an explication of ten situated (ideographic) structures and one general (nomothetic) structure of the experience using Giorgi's method, Veliyannoor identified four central dynamics postulated by psychoanalysis implicit within the experience (that did not emerge in the phenomenological analysis). He then explicated a fifth experiential dynamic that emerged in a psychoanalytically extended phenomenological analysis. This project demonstrated how, using strictly delineated procedures, psychoanalytic theory can be used heuristically within a thoroughgoing phenomenological methodological framework.

Final Remarks: Revisiting the Epoché

Having reiterated the importance of the epoché several times in this chapter, a few more words need to be said about its specific role in phenomenological psychology in contrast to phenomenological philosophy. The epoché played an important role in the transcendental philosophical project of Edmund Husserl, and it plays an equally important role in the project of offering a phenomenological alternative to conventional psychological research. The following quote illustrates its foundational significance to Husserl (1970):

> When we become conscious of [unquestioned and available] "presuppositions" and accord these their own universal and theoretical interest, there opens up to us, to our growing astonishment, an infinity of ever new phenomena belonging to a new dimensions, coming to light only through consistent penetration into the meaning and validity implications of what was thus taken for granted—an infinity, because continued penetration shows that every phenomenon attained through this unfolding of meaning, given at first in the life-world as obviously existing, itself contains meaning and validity implications whose exposition leads again to new phenomena .... (p. 112)

Phenomenological psychologists seek to tap into the power of the epoché for breaking through the myopic naturalism of conventional psychology. Only then can the "infinity of ever new phenomena" come to light. However, phenomenological psychology leaves the task of realizing a "universal" theoretical interest to philosophy.

Adopting the epoché for psychological purposes, one should not make the mistake of thinking that phenomenological research involves articulating all of one's preconceptions or seeking a view from nowhere—a God's eye view, as it were. Rather, bracketing represents a radical willingness to take responsibility for one's own manner of making sense of data through self-transparency and, above all, to not take anything for granted in reaching conclusions. The attitude for examining the data is "innocent until proven guilty," so to speak (see Giorgi, 2009). What presents itself to the phenomenological psychologist does not go unquestioned. Above all, phenomenologists refuse to make judgments based on received knowledge. The basic posture is that of intellectual humility, always returning to the data for answers. Those who get caught up in Husserl's introduction of the epoché for transcendental philosophical purposes sometimes pass it over as inessential to phenomenological psychological research (e.g., Zahavi, 2021). But this teleo-centric view trivializes the more fundamental, far-reaching contribution of phenomenology to psychology. In fact, there are those who have recently argued just the opposite: that phenomenological psychology has not taken the epoché seriously enough (e.g., Davidson, 2021; James, 2007).

Of course, one might argue that a psychologist who is explicitly informed by phenomenological philosophy might apply its many insights directly to an object of study without the epoché. But is that really being a phenomenological psychologist? I suggest not, or perhaps only by proxy at best (this will come up again at the close of Chapter 5). The attitude of the epoché makes all the difference when employing this strategy. As Wertz (1983) observed, if guiding concepts are taken from a preexisting theoretical context (even a phenomenological one), there is a danger of "imposing notions alien to psychology proper or the particular matters under analysis" (p. 45). Is not the point of a truly phenomenological psychology to describe what is given with disciplined openness rather than operating under the auspices of received knowledge? Applying philosophical phenomenological results without the epoché would put philosophers squarely in the proverbial driver's seat, diminish the autonomy and specialized role of the phenomenological psychologist, and confirm the suspicions of our natural scientific colleagues that phenomenological psychology is an attempt overturn psychology's purported liberation from metaphysics (May, 1958b).

Psychology has enshrined naturalism since its origins. Naturalism is sedimented in psychological scientific consciousness, arguably more than any other social science. To pass over the epoché is to place phenomenological psychology's ability to dig below the world of natural scientific representationalism on methodologically shaky ground, or at least fundamentally weaken its claim to this largely uncharted territory in psychology. Naturalistic objectivism is far too entrenched in the history of psychology for an alternative to emerge and stand its ground without the epoché as adopted for psychological purposes. Recall that Piaget waged a war that was purportedly against empiricism and became one of the most influential psychologists of all time, yet he remained bound to the tradition of psychology envisioned as a natural science. As Rennie (1995) has observed, the rhetoric of natural science has persistently overwhelmed, overtaken, and absorbed the rhetoric of human science. For more recent examples of this trend, the reader is referred to Giorgi's (2018) analyses of grounded theory research and neurophenomenology. Meanwhile, in the next chapter, we will see a concrete example of how the epoché plays an important methodological role in distinguishing phenomenological research from conventional research.

Key Terms, Concepts, and Themes

- Empirical phenomenology
- Interpretation
- Hermeneutic universalism
- Horizon
- Transcendental perspective
- Diacritical posture
- Experiential presence and absence (clarity and obscurity)
- Linguistic relativity
- Formalistic/objectivistic theory
- Non-formalistic/descriptive theory
- Epoché

Chapter 4

Unclarified Phenomenology in Conventional Psychology: Lessons from the Study of Embarrassment

Psychological research does not always reflect what is taught in college courses and handed down through textbooks (see Shadish, 1995; Strasser, 1963, 1985). The principles of what Costa and Shimp (2011) have dubbed *textbook science* are derived from varied source that may or may not be theoretically harmonious, such as positivism, logical positivism, and the hypothetico-deductive model of science (see Clegg, 2016; Park, et al., 2020). If one were to look at the history of a given line of research in psychology, one would find both similarities and differences in comparison to what has become canon in methods education. More importantly for the purposes of the current discussion, one would also find similarities and differences in comparison to phenomenological methodology. This chapter will show that conventional research sometimes shares affinities with phenomenological research, including the striving to achieve certain similar aims.

The inspiration for the chapter comes from the phenomenological philosophy of Maurice Merleau-Ponty. Drawing on Edmund Husserl's (e.g., 2009, 2014) analyses of the relationship between phenomenology and science, Merleau-Ponty (1964) once suggested that phenomenological insights regularly emerge on an implicit basis in psychology. However, these insights are unclarified and incomplete because conventional psychology only approximates phenomenological understanding. This is due to its reliance on empirical induction. Psychology habitually makes empty generalizations based on probabilities, such as the estimated strength of a correlational or the likelihood of a causational relationship. As Merleau-Ponty put it:

> Husserl says . . . that "everyone is constantly seeing ideas or essences and that everyone uses them in the operations of thought, in spite of the widespread opposition put forth in the name of points of view in the theory of knowledge." The empiricist theory of induction is one of these points of view (in the pejorative sense of this phrase), a vague opinion without rigor, which prevents us from seeing ourselves when we practice the *Wesenschau*, especially in making inductions. (p. 72)

In other words, conventional psychology unwittingly and confusedly pursues knowledge of essences, but this knowledge remains vague because it lacks an explicit, articulated means to arrive at intuitive insights into the essential structures of phenomena.

The current chapter extends this line of thinking. It proposes to examine conventional psychological research on an established topic and then show how it is embedded with unconscious phenomenological leanings. This will also provide the opportunity to then see why it is that these leanings are prevented from achieving their unclarified aims. In what follows, I present a selection of peer-reviewed scholarly works on the psychology of embarrassment to track its evolution since the emergence of Goffman's (1956a, 1956b) groundbreaking research.[1] The literature review is a bit lengthy, so I ask for the reader's patience. Thorough coverage is necessary to avoid the charge of having made a straw man out of either the embarrassment research or conventional research. This presentation will provide a concrete example of how a problem in psychology is handled, without implying that psychological inquiry always unfolds this exact way. Still, the methods and style inherent in the psychology of embarrassment are commonplace. This presentation will be followed by a critical analysis of its implicit phenomenological aims and the ways in which they have been prevented from being fulfilled. This, in turn, will deepen the

[1] Any given line of research in psychology would show more or less similarities to phenomenological research depending on the methods used. Wertz and colleagues (2011), for example, have shown that the underlying principles of phenomenological research are palpable when psychologists employ qualitative methods. But Wertz has also argued that phenomenological principles are nowise restricted to qualitative methods (we will return to this in Chapter 9). For this chapter, I did not deliberately choose a line of research that relied heavily on qualitative research. Instead, I simply elected to pick a research topic that has been researched in a very commonplace manner over a long period of time in psychology.

readers' appreciation for the unique role that phenomenological analysis plays in the world of psychological research.

Conventional Psychological Research on Embarrassment, A Dramaturgical Brush with Everyday Life: Erving Goffman Creates a Theory

Erving Goffman introduced the study of embarrassment to the social sciences by developing a theoretical framework constructed from the research that was presented in his doctoral dissertation (Goffman, 1953). In this study, Goffman used a variant of naturalistic observation called participant observation. He studied the real-time communicative interactions of people in a rural community in Great Britain located near the small island settlement of Baltasound, which he referred to as "Dixon." Goffman involved himself in the lives of the people of Dixon to get a ground floor look at their behavior in its natural setting. He interviewed people informally so that they would not suspect that a study was being done. He observed and recorded his observations inconspicuously in field notes whenever the opportunity presented itself and analyzed the data in private.

Goffman called the theory of embarrassment that he built from these observations a "dramaturgical" perspective (Goffman, 1956b, p. 8). This theoretical perspective focused on the way in which people present themselves to others in social situations. To begin to appreciate this perspective, it helps to think of the Shakspearian phrase "All the world's a stage, and all the men and women merely players." As Goffman described it, human beings are engaged in performances, playing parts or roles in their interactions with other human beings. The parts and performances are a cooperative creation in the sense that they are defined and shaped by the expectations and efforts of everyone involved. On this view, the entire fabric of social existence is co-created by people mutually defining situations, which is carried out by enacting the "appropriate" parts to be played in accordance with provisional, preestablished cultural norms. Within varying limits, the participants can alter the parts as they go. Everything depends on the nature of the given situation. Scripts can be very implicit, loose, and casual, or very explicit, rigid, and formal (think of the "part" you play at a party versus the "part" you place at a ceremony like a graduation, a wedding, or a funeral).

Since people are born and raised in cultures that define the parts that they play in advance of their personal involvement to varying extents, there will always be differing degrees of wholeheartedness in the performances that people undertake (Goffman, 1956b). More important is that human social interaction is permeated by a need to appear competent in one's role, so that the successful projection of one's ideal self would mean that one is playing one's part "well" and is thus more likely to allow one to "fit in" without raising eyebrows. To use Goffman's (1956a) words, "face," persona, or ideal self is merely a kind of individual "application of legitimate organizational principles" (p. 271). The idea that people can play parts more or less "well" for a given situation injects a value dimension and thus a moral aspect into each social interaction. But this moral aspect must not be mistaken to mean that all people in all situations are expected to act virtuously. The exact opposite could be the case. Some social roles might require acting like a "badass," for example. To play a part "well" or "good" implies the ability to orchestrate a presentation of self that is "at once coherently unified and appropriate for the occasion" (Goffman, 1956a, p 268). The part must be matched to the social norms of the particular situation.

From a "dramaturgical" perspective, embarrassment is rooted in a botched performance. The self that is being projected suffers a kind of breakdown that allows other, incompatible self-presentations to appear. In the best circumstance, the other people involved might simply overlook the misstep, either by pretending not to see it or by writing it off as trivial. Or they may even collude in spontaneously altering the standards of the situation to disqualify the behavior as a gaffe. People regularly engage in preventive practices and corrective practices to deal with discrediting performances. When they fail, the results are anomie and a "flustering syndrome" (Goffman 1956a, p. 246). The flustering syndrome refers to a state of temporary disorganization such that poise and comfort are lost. It can be set into motion by different kinds of life events, like being showered with congratulations and compliments, having a heated argument, or (Goffman's focus) a failed performance. In Goffman's (1956a) view, the flustering syndrome can be divided along the lines of subjective and objective signs. The signs that he deemed "subjective" included constriction of the diaphragm, a feeling of wobbliness, consciousness of strained and unnatural gestures, a dazed sensation, dryness of the mouth, and tenseness of the muscles. Now and then he would speak of a heightened potential for feelings of shame and guilt, and the relationship between the three emotions of embarrassment, shame, and guilt would go on to become a central concern for later embarrassment researchers (e.g., Keltner & Buswell, 1997). The signs that Goffman (1956a) deemed "objective" included blushing, fumbling, stuttering, an unusually low- or high-pitched voice, quavering speech or breaking of the voice, sweating, blanching, blinking, tremor of the hand, hesitating or vacillating movement, absentmindedness, malapropisms, a lowering of the eyes, bowing of the head, putting of hands behind the back, nervous fingering of the clothing or twisting of the fingers together, and stammering (sometimes incoherent) speech.

Broadly speaking, the flustering syndrome is a paradoxical phenomenon. It is a loss of naturalness in performance that is nonetheless quite natural. Goffman (1956a) recognized that it would be tempting for Western researchers to interpret the flustered disorganization of embarrassment from a stereotypically individualistic viewpoint as a person being "irrational" and "maladjusted" (pp. 270–271). But to stop one's analysis here would be to stop prematurely and render an incomplete account of what happens in the everyday life of human beings. Goffman saw that it would be far stranger and far more socially problematic if people were incapable of embarrassment. Embarrassment is uncomfortable, but without it a person would be more vulnerable to social rejection.

Embarrassability and the Problematic of Subjectivity: Enter Self-Esteem

Just a few years after the publication of Goffman's theory, Modigliani (1968) revisited Goffman's psychology of embarrassment and put a slightly different spin on it. What struck Modigliani about embarrassment was the fact that the phenomenon can be elicited by such a "surprising range of apparently dissimilar situations" (Modigliani, 1968, p. 313). As he put it:

> Consider, for example, the case of being embarrassed by sheer volume of attention as when one is being introduced to an unfamiliar audience, or is the focal point of "Happy Birthday to You." Because it is not possible for one to project a situational-public-identity through some active flow of conduct, it is not possible to control others' inferences about oneself. The result is a sense of vulnerability, of foolishness—as if negative attributes were "leaking out" through nonconscious, deficient aspects of behavior and appearance. (p. 316)

Goffman focused his attention (though not exclusively, as we have seen) on the actual discrediting of an ideal self by way of things like gaffes, missteps, and errors. But for Modigliani the imagined example above suggests that embarrassment is rooted in the loss of control and sense of exposure that would make one vulnerable to the potential discovery of inadequacy by others. Embarrassment results specifically from the perception of a loss of personal empowerment and feelings of competence when it comes to how one is seen by other people. In Modigliani's view, this generates embarrassment by threatening the person's *perceived self-esteem*—in other words, without necessarily having to lower self-esteem in any "objective" sense. After all, singing to someone at their birthday celebration is meant to honor them, not belittle them. From this perspective, perceived (potential or actual) threats to self-esteem lie at the core of the experience of embarrassment. Thus, to attain a better understanding of how the same experience (embarrassment) can be elicited across diverse situations, one must look closer at the experiencing subject and their implicit and/or explicit self-interpretations in relation to others in any given social situation. Modigliani studied how a person's participation in a social situation, the way they enter it and cognitively navigate their way through it, can make them more susceptible to becoming embarrassed, which he referred to as embarrassability. In Modigliani's view, to understand embarrassment, one needs to move past Goffman's more general situational focus and attend more closely to the subjective, interpretive factors at play in any given social situation. Modigliani thus asserted, *"embarrassment is the psychological state associated with a loss in situational-self-esteem that is caused by loss in situational-subjective-public-esteem"* (pp. 315–316; emphasis in original).

Revisiting Goffman's Theory, Part I:
How Researcher Presuppositions Hide Phenomena

Research supporting the esteem interpretation of embarrassment continued alongside dramaturgical research into the 1970s (e.g., Apsler, 1975). Things got more complicated in the 1980s, which was a period of intensified theoretical reflection on Goffman's groundbreaking work. Schudson (1984), for example, observed Goffman's theory as proposing what looked on the surface to be a kind of counterpoint to Freudian theory. Whereas Freud highlighted human beings' selfish animal desires, Goffman emphasized a natural human need to remain within the bounds of socially acceptable behavior. Schudson applauded Goffman's originality and insight, but he also questioned the way in which Goffman collected data. To be more specific, he accused Goffman of having committed confirmatory bias:

> So far as one can tell from Goffman's dissertation, he had no intimate contact with . . . family life. There is no indication that he made any friends; there is no special "informant" that anthropologists have often discussed with such feeling. Indeed, Goffman is intentionally anti-anthropological. He claims that he was not doing a study "of a community" but a study "in a community." [But] he inadvertently wound up examining primarily the social interactions that most resembled interaction in the most detached and impersonal settings of modern life. Rejecting time and place, undoing tradition and history, eschewing intimacy and friendship, Goffman created the setting for pure "social man" . . . and then claimed to have discovered him. (Schudson, 1984, p. 640)

According to Schudson, Goffman presented his findings as if he had studied the structure of a traditional society. But he instead focused on social interactions that were more indicative of a market society (i.e., of people doing business) and social exchanges between people of different social classes. In both instances, a higher degree of formality is demanded, and people in these situations are more notably cautious about how they present themselves. In this light, there is reason to doubt that Goffman's theory of embarrassment is grounded in observations that would allow for a faithful, unprejudiced rendering of the phenomenon as it manifests in day-to-day living. He employed a qualitative, experience-close style of research, but it was nonetheless susceptible to the projection of scientific preconceptions onto the data.

If Goffman was not open to the ways in which embarrassment ordinarily emerges in the world of daily life, it follows that his account of the phenomenon would be too formal and too artificial. On the one hand, embarrassment is always deemed the outcome of a kind of act, a show, a performance (albeit a botched one), rather than a spontaneous human interaction. On the other hand, the dramaturgical theory always seems to characterize the embarrassed performer as perpetually at the mercy of the audience. To be fair to Goffman, he duly recognized that people co-participate in defining situations, that they can redefine them, and that they can play their roles with different levels of wholeheartedness. Yet, he downplayed or ignored the significance of these factors as he built his theory of embarrassment. The phenomenon of embarrassment lacks the personal quality of ownership when viewed from the dramaturgical perspective. In embarrassment there is little more than the loss of a face or persona to the other. Recall that for

Goffman (1956a) the self that is offered to others in any given situation is merely an "application of organizational principles" (p. 271). Embarrassment is never one's own. Embarrassment that is backed by genuine conscience is nowhere to be found. Goffman, as it turns out, does not provide a genuine alternative to Freud. He merely turns Freud on his head by focusing on the fear of punishment associated with the psychoanalytic superego.

Thus, for Schudson, the dramaturgical theory is grounded in a mistaken view of human nature. It takes the metaphor of acting too far. Goffman's theory fails to account for what goes on "off-stage" even though Goffman had recognized this aspect of human life in his dissertation (Schudson, 1984, p. 641). The idea of a person being embarrassed "to oneself" or "by oneself" is precluded by the dramaturgical theory. But, as we will see, this is not a foregone conclusion for other embarrassment researchers. Goffman quietly passes over the total, developing, autobiographical self that transcends the limited parameters of given situational circumstances. He only analyzes the situational self that is relegated to immediate demands. The dramaturgical theory illuminates the phenomenon of embarrassment in terms of the contingencies of the present, but it is silent regarding the past and the future in which the experience is nested. As Schudson phrased it, "The fact that people are historical beings makes it possible . . . for them to be indifferent to the fear of embarrassment [or] recognize the possibility of embarrassment and to invite it rather than avoid it" (p. 644).

If this critique finds Goffman's viewpoint to be too limiting on the autobiographical self, it is no less limiting on the social dimension of embarrassment. The dramaturgical viewpoint speaks of social participation, cooperation, and encounter, but this is deceptive. Other people must merely be made to believe a performance. The disapproving gestures of the other in the experience of embarrassment are a means for the embarrassed person to learn how to put on a better show. How does the learning experience rendered by embarrassment treat the other as an end rather than a means? There is something missing in Goffman's theory when it comes to the social nature of human beings:

> To maintain continuity of interaction people learn to follow rules and to observe them with tact. For some reason (on what the reason is, social scientists have been silent), the maintenance of the definition of the situation and adherence to

> both role and rule is enormously important to people. (Schudson, 1984, p. 636)

Here, Schudson had discovered that the psychology of embarrassment was burdened with a proverbial elephant in the room. Everyone could see that the phenomenon of embarrassment was connected to profound sociality, but no one had dared enter that territory.

Revisiting Goffman's Theory, Part II: Defending Dramaturgic Turf (the Essence of Embarrassment as Revealed by its "Necessary" Features)

In stark contrast to Schudson's theoretical assessment, Silver and colleagues (1987) sought to defend the psychology of embarrassment as dramaturgic turf, especially against the developing esteem accounts of embarrassment that we saw above. In refutation of Modigliani's (1968) birthday party example, Silver and his colleagues maintained that the guest of honor's awkward state is simply that of "anticipatory embarrassment" (p. 49). True to the dramaturgical viewpoint, they held that embarrassment as such is always a flustering caused by the perception of a fumbled or botched performance. In their 1987 work, the researchers offered an expanded articulation of the dramaturgical approach to embarrassment, in which they hoped to identify and clarify its primary structural features. They began with a list of features that appeared to be "special to embarrassment" as a psychological phenomenon (Silver et al., 1987, p. 49). They then proceeded to "test" their theory with logical analysis, appealing to the evidence available from the research of their day wherever possible. Their goal was to discern which features of embarrassment were "necessary" for the phenomenon to occur rather than merely "contingent" (p. 50). Among their conclusions, three stand out as relevant to the current discussion.

First, the unpleasant nature of embarrassment is necessarily caused by a potential or actual performance disruption (which creates anticipatory embarrassment and embarrassment proper). Loss of esteem is only a frequently occurring contingency. Second, embarrassment can be disarmed by things like tact and wit if (and only if) there is a working consensus among everyone present, which does not always happen. Embarrassment thus necessarily occurs where working consensus (which is merely contingent) falls through. Third, embarrassment is necessarily social. Embarrassment requires that a shattered consensus has led to an inability to act a part or social role.

Silver and colleagues (1987) thus argued against the "solitary" nature of solitary embarrassment as follows:

> *Solitary embarrassment.* Sometimes we feel embarrassed even though we are not in a focal interaction. Consider: Don't we occasionally feel embarrassed when we slip in public even though we don't see anyone looking at us? People sometimes report that they nonetheless feel that they are the centre of attention—"the buildings have eyes." We follow Goffman in arguing that even this sort of incident has properties of a social interaction . . . we constantly remain alive to the possibilities of interaction when we are in public. Our embarrassment at slipping is a reaction to a vague anticipation that others *might* see us. Perform this gedanken [thought] experiment: Are we more likely to be embarrassed when we slip while in public even though no one is obviously around or while we are alone at home? (p. 53)

Summarizing their viewpoint, Silver and colleagues insist that people are first and foremost "avoiders of embarrassment," as Schudson (1984) put it (p. 646). Silver and colleagues (1987) conclude as follows: "Embarrassment is the flustering caused by the perception that a flubbed (botched, fumbled) performance, [by] a working consensus of identities, cannot, or in any event will not, be repaired in time" (p. 58).

Revisiting Goffman's Theory, Part III: The Problematic of Subjectivity Reemerges

To be sure, the 1980s was a theoretically turbulent time for the psychology of embarrassment, and 1988 brought with it another pendulum swing, once again veering away from the highly externalized view of the dramaturgical account. More in line with Schudson's (1984) critique of Goffman, Babcock (1988) advanced a view of embarrassment that proposed an increased importance for the embarrassed person's personal standards and self-evaluations. For Babcock, embarrassment results from a perceived rift between one's self-ideals and actual behaviors. The evaluations of other people matter, but less so than what the dramaturgical or even esteem accounts had suggested. In Babcock's theoretical assessment, both the dramaturgical and esteem accounts of embarrassment unjustifiably downplayed the subjective, personal nature of the phenomenon and underestimated the extent to which embarrassment reflects a concern with personal identity. Recall that for Goffman embarrassment ensues when the face, persona, or ideal self that a person projects into a situation is discredited because it failed to meet the standards of performance inherent in a social situation. In contrast, Babcock (1988) advocated for a more personalized view of embarrassment. Embarrassment ensues when an individual finds themself acting in a way that is inconsistent with their personally owned/endorsed persona or conception of self. Embarrassment is not mere concern over what others will think but a concern with upholding personal standards. It is a more personal "mechanism of self-control" than a reaction to a fear of negative evaluation by others (p. 459).

A Persistent Search for the Structural Invariants of Embarrassment

In the 1990s, there was a continued striving to account for the basic structural components of embarrassment. Notably, Keltner and Buswell (1997) made significant inroads in terms of compiling these components from diverse research contributions and offering some clues as to how they might factor into the formation of a coherent experience. Their work represents a persistent, implicit search for a general structural account of embarrassment, one that had been present since Goffman's original formulations. What we have seen thus far, however, is that a fully articulated general structural account has been elusive. Instead, with each new contribution, new data, ideas, and insights have been suggested as ways of improving upon the structure embedded in Goffman's work (i.e., embarrassment fractures and discredits a projected persona, breaks down social structure, creates flustering, and ultimately provides a means through which people can become better adjusted to their social surroundings). At best, modified conceptual definitions such as those proposed by Modigliani (1968) and Silver and colleagues (1987) have been proposed in lieu of a revised general structural articulation.

Keltner and Buswell's (1997) work marks a significant step forward, somewhat ironically, because they take a step backward and return to the most fundamental of research questions: Does embarrassment as a psychological phenomenon have a "distinct form" (p. 250)? Keltner and Buswell noted that there had been no consensus in psychology regarding how to conceptualize embarrassment. In response, they stressed the need to first consider whether embarrassment is a distinct emotion, as opposed to some other form of arousal (e.g., a mood), or merely a variant of another emotion (e.g., shame or guilt). To ascertain whether embarrassment had a form of its own, Keltner and Buswell (1997) performed a comprehensive review of the empirical and theoretical evidence relative to their time in history. This included their own studies of the behavioral displays specific to embarrassment, which asked respondents to judge emotions in still photographs (e.g., Keltner, 1995; Keltner & Buswell, 1996). Their review covered a wide array of research including naturalistic observations, case studies, survey research, correlations, and experimental "laboratory studies" (Keltner & Buswell, 1997, p. 254).

Considering the available evidence, Keltner and Buswell determined that embarrassment has the quick, adaptive quality that distinguishes an emotion from a mood (see Ekman, 1992). Moreover, embarrassment possesses enough distinctive features to make it different from other emotions. As they put it, "The evidence indicates that the antecedents, experience, and display of embarrassment, and to a limited extent its autonomic physiology, are distinct from shame, guilt, and amusement and share the dynamic, temporal characteristics of emotion" (p. 250). What kind of evidence did they offer in support of these conclusions? Drawing on the work of Miller (1992), they characterized embarrassment as having the following distinctive antecedents: physical ineptness, cognitive shortcomings, loss of control, failures of privacy regulation, loss of script, knowledge of situational transgression of social norms, the co-transgressions of others, others publicizing the transgression, others teasing, and the vicarious embarrassment of witnesses. They characterized embarrassment as having the following distinctive appraisal mechanisms: the involvement of others' evaluations, lack of control, the perception of a temporary cause, low effort, and uncertainty. They characterized embarrassment as having the following distinctive experiential dimensions: funniness, awkwardness, foolishness, nervousness, worry, surprise, self-consciousness, mildness, brevity, abruptness, withdrawal, and the perception of others' laughter. Drawing on Keltner's (1995) own work on behavioral displays, embarrassment was characterized as having the following distinct behavioral unfolding:

1. Gaze downward
2. Smile control/expression containment
3. Smile

4. Non-Duchenne smile (which is restricted to the muscle movements that pull the corners of the lips upward)
5. Gaze shifting, and gaze aversion or turning one's head away from others.

Finally, Keltner and Buswell (1997) noted moderate, inconsistent evidence that the physiology of embarrassment is most closely related to "the blush response and heart rate deceleration" (p. 257).

If these are the distinguishing characteristics of embarrassment, then how does it differ from shame and guilt, the emotions with which it appears to have "considerable overlap" (Keltner & Buswell, 1997, p. 252)? This question had lingered ever since Goffman's work. Drawing on research that utilized questionnaire self-reports and participants descriptions, including those that consisted of responses to imagined scenarios (Mosher & White, 1981), Keltner and Buswell drew the following distinctions. Embarrassment is a briefer, milder, more light-hearted experience in comparison to shame and guilt. It displays milder surprise and emotional negativity in comparison to shame. Blushing is more typical of embarrassment, and it is more correlated with the perception of others' laughter, which may be connected to efforts to remediate the transgression. Shame, in comparison, results from a failure to live up to one's own or other people's expectations relating to one's core self, ego ideal, or overall character. It is defined by the feeling of being a bad, immoral person and the feeling of isolation from others. It involves a long-lasting anger and disgust at oneself, the sense of others' anger and disgust, and the inclination to apologize. Keltner and Buswell (1997) referred to shame as the experience of a "devastating sense of personal incompetence" (p. 254). Finally, guilt results from a violation of moral rules that govern social interactions (e.g., lying, cheating, stealing). Guilt displays less self-consciousness and feelings of inferiority when compared with shame and embarrassment. Moreover, guilt is linked to other people's pain, likely the outcome of the individual's moral transgression. Keltner and Buswell (1997) concluded that their review of extant research allowed them to "converge on what one might consider a prototypical process of embarrassment" (p. 256). They articulated this prototype as follows:

> Embarrassment typically begins when an individual acts in a way that violates rules of a conventional nature, thus momentarily threatening the individual's social identity within the interaction. The individual responds with submissive and

> affiliative behavior. This behavior, in turn, evokes reconciliation-related behavior in others that restores the social interaction and, more broadly, the individual's social identity. (p. 265)

(Notice that, for all this hard work, the prototype offers nothing new in terms of clarifying one's understanding of the phenomenon of embarrassment.)

Revisiting Goffman's Theory, Part IV: A Persistent Search for a General Structural Account of Embarrassment

In the new millennium, Miller (2001) attempted to provide the general structural account that had yet to crystallize in the psychology of embarrassment. Although he did not explicitly refer to his narrative as a prototype or general structure, it clearly qualifies as such:

> Embarrassment is the acute state of awkward and flustered abashment and chagrin that follows events that produce a threat of unwanted evaluations from real or imagined audiences. It almost always occurs in public. If people do experience embarrassment when they are alone, it is inevitably because they are vividly imagining what others would think if they were present (Tangney, Miller, Flicker, & Barlow, 1996). The mere knowledge that others are aware of some misstep or misbehavior—no matter how they respond—is enough to trigger embarrassed emotion. Importantly, embarrassment is a discrete emotion: It occurs automatically and involuntarily, lasting moments instead of hours, and it is accompanied by a coherent, obvious sequence of nonverbal behavior that clearly distinguishes it from related states such as amusement or shame (Keltner, 1995). It is also accompanied by unique physiological changes, such as (in many cases) blushing, the visible reddening of the face and neck that signals one's chagrin. Altogether, then, a person's embarrassment is ordinarily plain to anyone who is watching; observers can tell when someone among them is embarrassed (Marcus & Miller, 1999). The converging data suggest that, at its core, embarrassment springs from people's concerns about others' evaluations of them and that it results when undesired evaluations are imminent. (Miller, 2001, p. 31)

Miller's narrative is an attempt to fulfill the persistent, implicit need for a general structural description of embarrassment. Miller was another of Goffman's apologists, but he also felt that Goffman's theory had overstepped certain bounds and needed to be put into perspective. As he put it:

> Tying so many specific behaviors to a motive to save face and avoid embarrassment is too narrow a conception. The reason why face, fear of embarrassment, and embarrassment itself are so influential in social life is that they all reflect humans' extensive and enduring concerns with what other people are thinking of them. (p. 32)

Thus, Miller added his voice to Schudson's (1984) in calling attention to the unaddressed social motives that found human interaction and embarrassment as well. Miller arrived at the same precipice as Schudson, questioning the unexplored social nature of human beings as the backdrop against which experiences of embarrassment occur. Unlike Schudson, Miller did not take issue with the characterization of human beings as embarrassment avoiders, but he clearly sensed the dire need for embarrassment researchers to contextualize the phenomenon by exposing what underlies embarrassment avoidance: "a fundamental, universal, prepotent social motive, the 'need to belong'" (Miller, 2001, p. 32). Moreover, Miller astutely observed that the widespread and persistent avoidance of such a fundamental issue is likely the result of scientific prejudices, the repeated projection of researcher presuppositions onto the data:

> [The need to belong] is a motive that experimenters rarely study. I suspect that we scientists are sometimes like the participants in actor/observer studies, who attribute importance to the influences we happen to notice at the time (Storms, 1973), and different theorists may form different attributions for the same event. (Miller, 2001, p. 32)

With Still Unclarified Social Underpinnings, Embarrassment is Upgraded to "Prosocial"

In the 2010s, the significance of human sociality remained steadfast as an important aspect of embarrassment research. To illustrate, Feinberg and colleagues (2012) took up the idea, first proposed by Goffman, that those involved in an embarrassing incident will take measures to repair the damaged social situation. They performed five studies, which showed that "individuals who display higher levels of embarrassment tend to be more prosocial and that observers attribute more prosocial intention and express greater trust toward individuals who express greater embarrassment" (Feinberg et al., 2012, p. 89). These results notwithstanding, the social foundations of embarrassment remained unaddressed, along with the question of whether the "prosocial" effects of embarrassment are better accounted for by a dramaturgical theory, an esteem theory, or some other theory.

The Delineation of Public and Private Typologies of Embarrassment: Viva Imagination!

Approaching the 2020s, old themes resurfaced in new efforts to achieve an increased degree of refinement in the psychology of embarrassment. Krishna and colleagues (2015, 2018) confronted the relative publicness versus privateness of embarrassment, thoughtfully considered the evidence for each view, and proposed a way of conceptualizing embarrassment that offered a higher level of generality and integrative understanding than what had been previously developed. They generated a new conceptual model of embarrassment based on a revised "integrated definition" of the phenomenon (Krishna et al., 2018, p. 3). They began by proposing the following imagined scenario:

> Visualize yourself as an 8-year-old waking up in the middle of the night. You are on your way to the bathroom. You glance in the direction of your parents' bedroom, only to see them having sex – the door has been left open! They do not notice you and you quickly run back to your room. You know what they were doing, but you have never seen it before. You feel uncomfortable and hide under the covers. No one sees your transgression and you do not imagine them doing so. Importantly, you do not necessarily imagine anyone judging you—the negative feelings come from you judging yourself. (p. 1)

This imagined variation of embarrassment poses an interesting prospect. Krishna and his colleagues pointed out that Modigliani (1968) had suggested a model of private embarrassment based on a reduction in self-esteem, but he never discussed or explored the model. It was based on the private experience of failure as evaluated in the light of personal standards of competency. Krishna and colleagues (2015, 2018) proposed to pursue this model further and give private embarrassment its due. This is embarrassment as a failure to live up to personal standards of conduct rather than a concern over what others will think. The researchers noted that Babcock and Sabini (1990) found this type of personal standard violation to be particularly embarrassing when an individual finds their transgression to be out of character. To further illustrate, Krishna and his colleagues (2018) cited the research of Higuchi and Fukada (2002), who conducted a study in which they presented participants with two imagined embarrassing scenes representing either public or private contexts (e.g., falling on a crowded platform versus failing an examination due to lack of studying). The participants rated the scenes in terms of how much they believed the experience would lead to embarrassment. The authors concluded that public embarrassment is driven by concerns of social evaluation and uncertainty about how to act around others, and that private embarrassment is caused by inconsistencies in one's self-image and lower feelings of self-worth.

Krishna and colleagues (2018) built a conceptual model based on a typological schematic that characterized embarrassment as potentially occurring in public or private, involving either other- or self-appraisals (see Krishna et al., 2015). They tested their schematic in several studies. For example, in one study, they asked participants to imagine experiencing incontinence. The participants then read about the experience of purchasing a drug for their incontinence, one in public at a drug store and one in private online. Prior to reading the purchasing scenarios, the participants were primed for other- versus self-appraisals by writing about and providing examples for either their own general evaluations of themselves or their perceptions of other people's evaluations. The authors found evidence for four typological variations of embarrassment:

- Type 1: Where other people are present, the actor deliberates on their perceptions of others' appraisals of their transgression
- Type 2: Where other people are present, the actor deliberates on their own appraisal of their transgression
- Type 3: Where no other people are present, the actor deliberates on their perceptions of imagined others' appraisals of their transgression
- Type 4: Where no other people are present, the actor deliberates on their own appraisal of their own transgression

Building on this schematic, Krishna and colleagues (2018) offered a broader definition of embarrassment that "recognizes a conceptualization of embarrassment . . . extending beyond requirements of 'social presence' and 'other- appraisal'" (pp. 4–5). In their words, "Embarrassment reflects an aversive emotional state in which one feels chagrin following deliberation on perceived negative appraisal by others or negative appraisal by oneself for transgressions that occur either in public or in private contexts" (p. 4).

Critical Analysis

The above overview of embarrassment research reveals certain methodological similarities and differences when compared to phenomenological research. The outline provided in Chapter 2 can be used to make an overall comparison:

I. Returning to "The Things Themselves" (as Given in Experience)
   A. The Epoché: Bracketing
   B. Confronting the Irreal: Non-Sensuous Givens
   C. Returning to the Participants Themselves: Empathic Attunement
II. The Methodical, Rigorous Description of Living-Experience
   A. Attending to the Complex, Multifaceted Whole
   B. Attending to the "What" of the Phenomenon
   C. Attending to the "How" of the Phenomenon
      1. Temporality
III. Intuition and Elucidation of Essential Meanings
   A. Studying Variations for Invariant Meanings
   B. Explicating a General Structural Description

Over the course of its history, embarrassment researchers have been working on select aspects of the second and third levels of this outline, but within strictures that are typical of conventional psychological research. The conventional research on embarrassment utilized descriptive data and descriptive methods to access experiential and behavioral aspects of the phenomenon. Embarrassment researchers have attended to the phenomenon's multifaceted presentation (i.e., its cognitive, bodily, affective, conative, and social aspects). They have been debating the nature of the phenomenon, what it means to be embarrassed in its essence (versus not feeling embarrassed, feeling guilty, or feeling ashamed), even though they have not used this terminology. They have also studied the temporal structure of the phenomenon. These characteristics relate to level II of the outline above. The conventional research on embarrassment studied both real and imagined variations of the phenomenon in attempts to identify its invariant features. This served the aim of articulating a general structural description (i.e., what embarrassment researchers called a "prototype") of embarrassment. These characteristics relate to level III of the outline.

Resonances of Level II

Methodically Describing the Phenomenon

Since the middle of last century, conventional psychological research on embarrassment has relied on description and descriptive data, and this was not limited to what are called descriptive methods in psychology. Self-report descriptions, which were analyzed in various ways, were foundational in allowing researchers to check their understandings against participant experiences. This dual descriptive emphasis is a point of convergence with phenomenological psychology (albeit a loose convergence of sympathies) because phenomenological analysis is fundamentally descriptive in orientation. To carry out a descriptive analysis, the data are most often gathered from written protocols and transcribed interviews where participants are given explicit instructions to describe their experience in as much detail as possible.

The research on embarrassment diverges from phenomenology in that the history of embarrassment research harbors conflicting research values when it comes to description. Goffman's groundbreaking work grounds the psychology of embarrassment in descriptive work as intrinsically and uncompromisingly valuable, targeting the experience of participants interacting in natural settings. Yet, throughout the history of embarrassment research, there is a certain uneasiness and ambivalence over the use of such data (e.g., see Lizardo & Collett, 2013; Schudson, 1984). There is a traditional (natural science inspired) sentiment threaded throughout the research that description is basically a preparatory or merely propaedeutic research tactic. On this view, description is inherently inferior to those methods that allow the researcher to quantify data and apply inferential statistics. The highest value is assigned to research methods that allow the greatest amount of control over participants and their responses (especially controlled laboratory experiments). This allows the researcher to infer causal relationships.

The underlying assumption of this tactic is that the subjectivity of the participant is a danger to the researcher's quest for objectivity. This has put embarrassment researchers in a bit of a double bind. One the one hand, they need to get at the subject's experience to understand the phenomenon. On the other hand, their conventional training demands that this subjectivity is a potential contaminant. What are typically offered as "descriptions" in psychology are really interpretations of the researcher. We saw this in the psychology of embarrassment, where participant self-reports were regularly filtered through the researchers' predesigned survey questions, imaginatively constructed scenarios, observer rating criteria, and coding procedures. From a phenomenological perspective, the problem with these strategies is that they place such a stranglehold on the subjectivity of the participant that the prejudices of the researcher inevitably come to dominate the scientific discourse. When confronted with the inevitability of their interpretations, the traditional researcher will defer to the data-collection process as a safeguard against bias, claiming to be data driven. But the argument is circular, as the data-collection process repeatedly employs the same tactics, embedded with the same disproportionate emphasis on the observer over the participant.

Attending to the Complex, Multifaceted Whole

From Goffman's original formulations to the present, embarrassment has been looked upon as a complex phenomenon involving clusters or categories of components. Embarrassment is associated with various cognitive processes such as perceptions of social norms, perceptions of other people's judgments, self-perceptions, and judgments concerning one's own behavior in relation to the total situation. Embarrassment is considered identifiable by bodily displays associated with flustering, such as blushing, smiling, gaze aversion, and head turning. Embarrassment is considered an awkward sort of emotion that is similar to and sometimes associated with other affective phenomena, such as shame and guilt. Finally, embarrassment is discussed (in varying degrees depending on the theorist in question) in connection with the conative potentials of the person (meaning related to purposive action), especially the ability to redefine situations as they unfold. These potentials always exist in relation to the social dimension of the person, including the uniquely human prosocial dimension (Feinberg et al., 2012).

Phenomenological psychology also approaches phenomena with an openness to this cognitive, bodily, affective, conative, and social diversity. However, whereas the embarrassment research characteristically approaches this diversity by way of unquestioned naturalistic interpretations, phenomenology begins with what is descriptively given in living-experience. Both traditions place emphasis on understanding the object of study as a multifaceted whole, but the abstract representationalism and concomitant atomism of the former prevents it from achieving genuinely holistic understandings.

As a significant point of convergence, the embarrassment literature casts the phenomenon as rooted in perception and judgment. The perception of social situational norms, other people's judgments, and one's own behavior were deemed critical to the self-judgments that give rise to embarrassment. Similarly, perception and judgment were critically important to Edmund Husserl in the development of phenomenology, especially his work on pre-predicative experience. However, in the embarrassment literature, cognitive processes are interpreted as mundane causal factors among others in the emergence of the phenomenon. Such is not the case for Husserl, for whom cognition is an embedded, interdependent part of dynamically unfolding, living-experience. As Moran and Cohen (2012) put it:

> Strictly speaking, no mental episode is an independent part of the flow [of living-experience], mental episodes are always embedded in one seamless flow of consciousness. Conscious processes have a priori no ultimate elements as such. Furthermore, conscious life is not a chaos of intentional processes but a highly structured, layered and unified complex. (p. 195)

Cognition is involved in the perpetual co-constitution of meaning and, as such, it is bodily, affective, social, and agentic.

Phenomenologically speaking, the blushing, head movements, and muscular changes of the face that are associated with the bodily aspects of embarrassment cannot be reduced to the status of mere physiological side effects. Rather, they are nonverbal (or at least preverbal) expressions of the living body. The fact that they are unwelcome and not altogether under the control of reflective consciousness in no way lessens their lived status or significance. There are many subtle levels of bodily knowing (Gendlin, 2018).

For phenomenology, cognition is not only situated in a body, as noted above, it is also affective or emotionally toned. As Fisette (2022) has shown, Husserl considered emotion to be a form of evaluative predication (i.e., a form of experiencing that invokes judgments and values). As situations unfold, one's emotional state can transform to become more positive or more negative, creating alterations in a person's motivational state, decision making, and resultant actions. On this view of emotions, emotions are intentional states. Their intended "objects" are values. The evaluative dimension is strewn throughout the embarrassment literature, as the phenomenon has been connected to the violation of social norms and personal standards in different ways and to different extents depending on the researcher. To be sure, this aspect of the phenomenon has been quite contentious, as represented by widely contrasting views on the extent to which the emotion of embarrassment is a function of objective social factors or subjective personal factors. This came to the fore very early in the history of embarrassment research (e.g., Modigliani, 1968), reemerged with considerable force in Babcock's work (1988), and returned once again in the work of Krishna and colleagues (2018). From a phenomenological perspective, the embarrassment research is marked by a valid recognition of the valuational essence of the phenomenon. But the nature of that essence is problematic and embroiled in ongoing controversy; this is not merely because the phenomenon is complex, but because there is no theory of intentionality to help ground the research in participant's living-experiences and the identification of its typological variations (i.e., its morphologies). What the research of people like Krishna and colleagues (2018) demonstrates is a valiant, unclarified attempt to take decades of research that has struggled to understand embarrassment as intentionally stretched out between the subjective and objective poles of value (Frankl, 1967).

For phenomenology, emotions are also the intentions of an agent, a volitional decision maker. Emotions are "attitudes that the agent takes toward an object presented in sensory perception" (Fisette, 2022, p. 224). This crosses over more decisively into the conative domain of human psychology. At the center of this domain lies the transcendent aspect of psychological life. In Giorgi's (1992) words, "Every human situation has a certain gap or leakage which prevents the situation from being closed deterministically, and the gap is human subjectivity which has the power to transform situations through meaning bestowal or interpretation" (pp. 434). As we have seen, the transcendent, agentic self has a spotty history within the embarrassment research. It is there, but controversial. The agent who lives out and "owns" the phenomenon was implicit in the background of Goffman's work, coming nearer to the surface in later discussions of the subject's perceptions and judgments, but never explicitly. The agentic aspects of embarrassment emerged as particularly contentious with the works of Schudson (1984) and Miller (2001), both of whom took issue with the tendency to overemphasize "blind" social adjustment, as it were. Schudson (1984) put it best when he observed, "The performer, the clown, the continual avoider of embarrassment—the modal person in Goffman's universe would be, in Erikson's analysis, a human and moral failure" (p. 647). As we have also seen, the possibility of agentic, owned embarrassment continues to drive discussions of private embarrassment (e.g., Krishna et al., 2015, 2018).

To the extent that the totality of the embarrassment research can be seen as representing a dynamic, dialectical tension between the conative and the social, it is commensurate with a phenomenological perspective. The primary point of divergence is the ambivalence over this relationship in the embarrassment literature. All the embarrassment researchers recognize the highly social nature of human beings, even if only implicitly. Yet, there is a constant struggle apparent in the literature to decisively move beyond social determinism and mere mutual (mechanical) causality. Goffman (1956a) spoke of social encounters, but he never articulated the relational self–other mutuality (sometimes dubbed "I–Thou" experience) needed for genuine encounter to occur. He established a trend in the embarrassment literature that places undue restrictions on the image of humanity that underlies the research. There is a tendency to overemphasize the socially defined self, sometimes seen as ambiguously connected to a human need for belonging, at the expense of the relative agency of the subject embedded within the intersubjective world. From a phenomenological perspective, what is required is a delicate balancing act that does not assume in advance that the self is a mere collection of reflected appraisals (i.e., an effect) or default to the hyper-rational ego of Western individualism (i.e., a cause). People are historical beings with the potential, no matter how small or imperfect, to release themselves from the sedimentations of their past in an act of transcendence (Husserl, 1970). There is a mutually implicative relationship between the personal and the interpersonal, the exact nature of which must be allowed to reveal itself in the context of every investigation without the prejudices of the researcher getting in the way.

All in all, what the history of the psychology of embarrassment shows is an aspiring holism that cannot find its footing. The whole of the phenomenon is elusive and remains controversial. Embarrassment is repeatedly subjugated to a form of analysis that seeks to isolate the elements belonging to each of its major aspects (cognitive, bodily, affective, conative, and social), interpreting them in terms of causal explanations. The approach is basically atomistic. Embarrassment is viewed as a cluster of causes and effects that need to be mapped out rather than as a Gestalt. The body, the naturalistically evolved body, is interpreted as manifesting various objective and subjective effects of embarrassment, most notably the blush response. The judgments that underlie embarrassment are seen as the result of social norms and subjective perceptions, but the role and importance granted to each varies greatly depending on one's theoretical approach. The actions and intentions of the embarrassed person are sometimes seen as the effect of context and the pattern of antecedent conditions. At other times, they are seen as causal forces, and this drives considerations of private embarrassment and raises global questions concerning human nature.

Phenomenology appreciates and engages in analytical breakdown, but nests analysis within an approach that makes the whole the alpha and the omega of the analysis. From a phenomenological point of view, if one does not begin and end with an explicit value of the whole phenomenon, analysis creates a disconnect with the full reality of what it proposes to understand. Lacking a deliberate, systematized fidelity to the whole, a community of researchers will always seem to struggle in vain to put the pieces of the phenomenon it is studying back together again with mutual consensus. The door will always be left open for psychologists to inject hypothetical mechanisms into the phenomenon "from without" on a prolonged basis, as we have seen. As the conventional embarrassment research amassed its formidable laundry list of findings, it developed a pressing need for an integrative prototype to compensate for this proliferation. But holistic structural descriptions, which would be the key to attaining such a prototype, were rare. The most holistic description, offered by Miller (2001), was not derived directly from participant data, so it presents more like a robust theoretical narrative distilled from empirical research. Consequently, embarrassment research has had to settle for an ongoing series of newly proposed conceptual definitions and theoretical models. The strategy of phenomenological psychology is to derive holistic descriptions directly from participant data to counterbalance the atomistic tendencies of traditional research.

Attending to the "What" of the Phenomenon

Throughout the history of embarrassment research, conventional researchers have been trying to work out what embarrassment is. Is it or is it not an emotion? If it is an emotion, is it a variant of shame or guilt, or does it have its own distinctive presentation? These researchers have been attempting to gain clarity on what does and does not make for an embarrassing situation to be able to say what does or does not count as a genuine case of embarrassment. This was done in the hopes of arriving at a prototype of the phenomenon and (without using this language) delineating its typological variations, which implicates extended considerations of how the phenomenon can unfold in varying situations. The history of embarrassment research yielded numerous results, asserting that embarrassment is:

- The flustering caused by a perceived consensus that a botched performance cannot or will not be repaired, resulting in the exposure of unwanted self-presentations
- The loss of situational self-esteem caused by a loss of situational, subjectively perceived, public esteem
- The perception that one has suffered a temporary loss of self-control, resulting in behavior that is both inconsistent with one's conception of self and a violation of one's personal standards of conduct
- The experience, following a violation of conventional social rules, that momentarily threatens the individual's social identity
- The acute state of awkward and flustering that follows events producing a threat of unwanted evaluations from real or imagined others
- The chagrin experienced after deliberations on perceived negative appraisals by others or one's own negative self-appraisals for transgressions occurring in public or in private

These conceptualizations display varying degrees of overlap in meaning, while other issues remain contested, such as the relative importance of social and personal esteem and social or private embarrassment. Areas of dispute have persisted for decades at least in part because none of these conceptualizations were derived from a direct, systematic study of the phenomenon as experienced firsthand by the participants themselves. For that matter, the "what" of embarrassment never rose to the level of an explicit focus. It has constantly driven the research but primarily as an implicit given, only occasionally rising to the level of an explicit concern. Phenomenological research, in contrast, makes the description of the meaningful structure of a phenomenon, its essential meaning, not only an explicit focus, but it does so by investigating research participant's living-experiences without imposing theoretical or procedural constraints on subjectivity in advance.

Attending to the "How" as Manifested in the Temporality of the Phenomenon

The conventional psychological research on embarrassment approached the phenomenon as a temporal or time-dependent phenomenon. Embarrassment was seen as comprised of diverse antecedents, real-time experiences, preventative measures, and subsequent repair efforts. Sympathetically, time has always been a central theme of phenomenology. In phenomenological psychological research in particular, phenomena are approached as unfolding events comprised of meaningful moments rather than static elements (Giorgi, 2009).

From a phenomenological perspective, however, the understanding of time in the embarrassment research is nonetheless wanting on two accounts. First, the embarrassment literature tends to characterize the temporal aspects of the phenomenon in terms of clusters of elements standing in linear, ordinal relation (e.g., recall the summative lists offered by Keltner & Buswell, 1997). At no point does one obtain a thick description of the lived temporal flux and flow of embarrassment as experienced firsthand by participants. This is to be expected since there is no methodological procedure for apprehending the phenomenon as a qualitative unfolding.

Second, there is phenomenological divergence with respect to the wider context of time in human psychology. Recall that Schudson (1984) based one of his most damning critiques of Goffman on the notion that the dramaturgical theory fixates on the situational self of the current moment. Schudson was a rare voice of protest in the history of embarrassment research on this point. Schudson's notion of the autobiographical self was the closest cognate to a phenomenological viewpoint with respect to the dimension of time in the embarrassment literature. For phenomenology, the phenomena studied by psychology are embedded in a history and are simultaneously given form by the future outlook of the participants under study. The human capacity to *ex-sist* or stand out in time is a transcendent quality of human existence that implicates agency (Corballis, 2007; Heidegger, 1962; Schudson, 1984). Yet, agency has been a controversial aspect of embarrassment research since its inception. Goffman established a norm wherein the patterns of social interaction were the primary object of study, not agency (Romania, 2019). In contrast, Modigliani's (1968) work inspired a dissenting, discordant current of thought that has more of a tendency to refer back to the embarrassed subject's personal standards (e.g., Apsler, 1975; Babcock, 1988; Krishna et al., 2018; Schudson, 1984). To be sure, the embarrassment research is not exceptional in this regard. While psychology has long viewed the past as a potent causal force determining human behavior, the future orientation of the person is rarely given serious attention. By default, the same can be said of agency (DeRobertis, 2021b). Phenomenological psychology demands an attitude of openness to all dimensions of time and agency, however they may appear, so long as the description is true to the participant's living-experience with respect to the phenomenon under study.

Resonances of Level III

Studying Real and Imagined Variations of the Phenomenon: The Search for Invariants

Psychological research on embarrassment has been studying a combination of real and imagined variations on the phenomenon. The data have included real experiences of embarrassment in various settings as well as imagined scenarios generated by the researchers. The latter of the two widened the researchers' analytic reach beyond available empirical variations. And, as we saw from the studies of Krishna and colleagues (2015, 2018), it continues to rely on findings derived from such data. This is implicit in their work, but in phenomenology the need to reach beyond what is empirically given is an explicit aim of the research. Phenomenology names and formalizes the process: *imaginative free variation*. The use of imagined variations in the embarrassment research is deliberate and pragmatic, but the reasons for its utility are quietly passed over because conventional research is committed to a very traditional, very limited notion of empiricism (DeRobertis, 2022). As a sense-empiricism, it is explicitly oriented toward the real, but it has no language to deal with the irreal. It uses the imagination to get beyond the "hard" reality presented to the senses, but only under the auspices of researchers' hypotheses. Thus, imaginative variation is held in less esteem than empirical variation and bears a tenuous relationship to participant data.

The search for structural invariants has been implicit throughout the history of embarrassment research. The research repeatedly sought to determine what was most consistent across its empirical and imagined variations. More consistency means more probabilistic predictive power from the vantagepoint of traditional research. Without saying it, all the researchers were seeking (and inevitably relying on) what phenomenologists would call essentials that are trans-situational, going beyond contingences of a given time and place. Silver and colleagues (1987) were the closest to explicit in this regard in their attempts to separate what is necessary to embarrassment from what is incidental to its occurrence. What we have seen in the psychology of embarrassment was that empirical and imagined variations were an unspoken means to arrive at invariants that undergird and structure the object of study. Likewise, the derivation of invariant structures from empirical and imagined variations is an explicit methodological aim of phenomenological research. In phenomenology, however, these invariants are referred to as invariant structural themes because the structural components or "constituents" of the phenomenon are meanings rather than brute facts. In contrast, the embarrassment research has vacillated between quantified factual data and qualitative meanings derived from interpretations of data. These interpretations provided the connective tissue for its periodic revisions of the phenomenon's conceptual definition as it pressed on toward the hope of obtaining a sufficiently high level of generalization or prototype. This is directly related to method. The traditional embarrassment research was and remains committed to induction and interpretation. It has no place for intuition among its scientific procedures and, as we saw above, its approach to description is marked by ambivalence. Phenomenology, in contrast, speaks of the intuitive grasp of essential structures as the researcher systematically and reflectively pours over the empirical and imagined variations. The structure emerges in intuitive self-evidence (recall the Wesensschau). In the embarrassment research, intuition is only mentioned to put it down as astute guesswork (e.g., see Keltner & Buswell, 1997).

Pursuing a "Prototype" (or a General Structural Account of the Phenomenon)

As noted, in the psychology of embarrassment, there has been a concomitant, persistent striving to derive a prototype of the phenomenon from the data. Researchers have sought a general structural description that can be used to ground and orient the whole domain of inquiry, including its efforts to delineate different kinds or typologies of embarrassment. But the search for a general structural description in the embarrassment research diverges from phenomenology because of its ambiguous commitment to probabilities alongside its search for the necessary conditions of the phenomenon. This is a stumbling block in the pursuit of a general structural description. A prototype that is framed in the language of probability is fundamentally different from a general structural description that is meant to represent the essence of a phenomenon. The former is an empirical generality, a truth claim based on what has typically been observed to be the case. As such, it cannot directly or decisively address the necessary and sufficient conditions for a psychological phenomenon to be what it is. As we have seen in the embarrassment research, there is an implicit, persistent sense that probability is not good enough. Yet, the embarrassment research taken as a body of literature is far more able to offer an evolving stockpile of findings, conceptual definitions, and models rather than holistic descriptions of living-experience. This is because their methods were simply not designed to move directly toward general structural descriptions. Speaking of what is probably the case as derived from a given sample of participants always seems to leave ample room for a proliferation of hypothetical explanations for the phenomenon. This is exactly what has been going on for the better part of 70 years of research in the psychology of embarrassment.

Conclusions

This chapter began with an observation from Merleau-Ponty (1964) that conventional researchers practice unclarified phenomenology, unable to clearly see and understand their scientific sense-making process as they unconsciously approximate the Wesensschau. The chapter provided a concrete example of how this can play out. As illustrated by the study of embarrassment, when conventional psychology seeks to determine the precise nature of a phenomenon (its "what"), it has no language for explicating essential structural meanings. It possesses no formalized intuitive process for doing do. In its search for the invariant features inherent in what it studies, conventional research vacillates confusedly between quantified facts and qualitative meanings. It then seeks to compensate for discrepancies that emerge with attempts at increasingly precise and/or comprehensive conceptual definitions and prototypes, which are repeatedly revised in the light of new quantitative data and more formal (hypothesis-generating) theoretical arguments.

The above analyses also buttress Merleau-Ponty's insight, contextualizing it with several additional observations:

- While conventional psychological research prefers induction and hypothesis-based interpretation to description, description can play a critical role in the unfolding of its research. However, the rhetoric of psychology envisioned as a natural science contradictorily, if not hypocritically, casts description as merely propaedeutic to its hypothesis testing. The devaluation of description is part of a larger worldview that sees subjectivity as a potential contaminant in the data collection process that needs to be inferred, filtered, and contained by the researcher through the use of instruments. This limits the benefits that can be gained by a descriptive approach to research.
- Conventional psychological research may deem it important to study the multifaceted whole of a phenomenon. But these many facets are de facto interpreted naturalistically. Thus, the whole is approached as a cluster of hypothesized causes and effects that need to be mapped out rather than a true Gestalt. The resulting abstraction and fragmentation of the phenomenon creates conceptual gaps and vagaries that researchers attempt to disambiguate by creating more hypothetical mechanisms.
- When time is deemed an important aspect of an investigation, conventional research prefigures it in accord with a naturalistic worldview as well. Temporality is restricted to clock time, so the lived flux and flow or meaningful unfolding of the phenomena under study cannot emerge and contribute to a holistic understanding of its structuration.
- Even in conventional research, the use of the imagination is important for achieving a broadened, more generalizable understanding of what is being studied. The imagination frees the research from the confines of the "hard" reality presented to the senses, but this is unspoken. Conventional

psychology has no language to deal with the irreal. The liberating function of the imagination only operates under the auspices of researchers' hypotheses. Imaginative variation is held in less esteem than empirical variation and bears a tenuous relationship to participant data.

This last conclusion (which requires more than a bullet point) highlights the fact that the most pronounced differences between conventional research and phenomenology pertain to Level I of the outline provided above. Conventional research has no place for the irreal, it reserves no scientific role for empathic attunement, and it knows nothing of the epoché. Here, traditionally trained researchers will likely object that there is an analogue to the epoché in their striving for objectivity. But this assessment misses the significance of the epoché as a radical starting point for phenomenological research. While phenomenological psychologists share with traditional researchers a likeminded impetus to avoid bias, the epoché involves suspending judgment on the entire set of taken-for-granted beliefs that founds traditional psychology's notion of "objectivity," as counterposed to subjectivity. The epoché puts being true to what presents itself to the researcher above the unreflective acceptance of inherited wisdom. Accordingly, neither the assumption that objectivity and subjectivity exist in two discrete worlds (one publicly accessible, one merely inferred) nor the idea that the latter must be constrained so that the former can shine forth are taken on faith. The epoché puts the subject–object dichotomy temporarily out of play to see what reveals itself with respect to what is under investigation. To perform the epoché is to see the experiential field afresh, including the meaning-making activity of participants and researchers alike. The epoché frees the researcher not only from the subjectivistic forms of bias known to conventional psychology, but also from the objectivism or objectivistic biases of both the everyday natural attitude and its naturalistic/natural scientific derivation (Husserl, 1970).

Interestingly, an analogue to the epoché almost emerged in Goffman's impetus to enter the everyday world of his participants rather than relying on more distanced quantitative methodologies. But, as later analyses would show, Goffman had a scientific agenda that took priority over unprejudiced description. As the subtitle to the Goffman section indicated, his was but a "brush" with everyday life. In his defense, Goffman courageously sought to achieve a widened view of what counts as good empirical science that phenomenologists can related to. He was uncharacteristically open to the qualitative and the social aspects of human reality. And rather than assuming a rationalistic clinical–scientific perspective, he came to see embarrassment as neither pathological nor even irrational, which is akin to an insight that would result from the epoché. But conventional psychology has no language to accommodate the widened view of empirical science that Goffman sought. The embarrassment research in general teetered on the edge of this widened viewpoint, always prevented from crossing over by the sedimented, traditionalized assumptions of a psychology patterned after the natural sciences. There is no epoché and no theory of intentionality or the co-constitution of meaning that allows the researcher to operate outside the influence of the subject–object dichotomy on its methods. If it is not obvious by now, the consequences of the epoché are tremendous. Assuming the attitude of the epoché means to maintain a disciplined openness, to be a perpetual beginner in one's research, this is neither trivial nor easy (see Morley, 2010). But it does make all the difference. Without it, conventional research strives to actualize phenomenological insights but struggles against unnecessary hurdles because it cannot get behind its time-honored objectivistic, naturalistic prejudices.

Coda: The Phenomenology of Embarrassment

As it happens, Vallelonga (1986) produced a little-known dissertation on being embarrassed and being ashamed that supports some of the conclusions presented in this chapter and offers much in terms of correctives and clarifications to the psychology of embarrassment. Already in 1986, Vallelonga was able to see that the literature on embarrassment was being unduly influenced by the observer's (third-person) perspective, which he called "deficient empiricality" (p. 158). This deficiency was discussed above as part of the limitations of sense-empiricism and the objectivistic, natural scientific impetus to contain and filter subjectivity. As a result, conventional embarrassment research was likewise seen as suffering from a failure to articulate a lived structure with lived temporality, an inability to agree on the essential meaning of the phenomenon, and an inability to provide a decisive account of its typological variations.

Vallelonga produced multiple general structural descriptions to compensate for the shortcomings of the embarrassment literature, though they are too numerous and robust to discuss in detail. His dissertation is a whopping 1,553 pages! But to give the reader an idea of his virtually unknown contributions to the psychology of embarrassment, he derived the following schematic of the phenomenon's typological variations from data analyses using the Giorgi method:

I. Exposure of Secrecy (the potential or actual violation of psychological privacy)
    1. Being embarrassed over potential exposure and potential disesteem (being self-consciously embarrassed)
    2. Being embarrassed over probable exposure and probable disesteem (being anxious in the face of the likely possibility of becoming embarrassed over actual exposure)
    3. Being embarrassed over actual exposure and actual disesteem
        a) Being embarrassed *before* an other
        b) Being embarrassed *over/at* an other with whom one is identified
        c) Being embarrassed *by* an other (includes being humiliated, put down, etc.)
        d) Being embarrassed *for* an other (experience of sympathy for one who is embarrassed)

II. Intrusion into Privacy (the potential or actual violation of bodily privacy)
    1. Being embarrassed over potential bodily exposure and potential disrespect (a form of being self-consciously embarrassed)
    2. Being embarrassed over probable bodily exposure and probable disrespect (a being anxious in the face of the likely possibility of becoming embarrassed over actual bodily exposure and disrespect)
    3. Being embarrassed over actual bodily exposure and actual disrespect
        a) Being embarrassed *before* an other
        b) Being embarrassed *by* an other (being humiliated or forcibly intruded upon)
        c) Being embarrassed *for* an other (experience of sympathy for one who is embarrassed)

In the light of his findings, Vallelonga saw the various theories of embarrassment as identifying certain legitimate aspects of the phenomenon piecemeal, some more accurate and/or robust than others. A similar conclusion was reached more recently in a phenomenological study that repeated the structure of type I.3a (see Robbins and Parlavecchio, 2006).

Key Terms, Concepts, and Themes

- Textbook science
- Essential intuition/Wesensschau
- Dramaturgical perspective
- Situational self/social identity
- Self-interpretations
- Personal identity
- Perceived self-esteem
- Situational-subjective-public-esteem
- Embarrassability
- Confirmatory bias
- Agency
- The autobiographical self
- Structural invariants
- Definitions and prototypes (as approximating general structural description)
- Embarrassment as prosocial
- Public and private typologies of embarrassment
- "I–Thou" experience
- Empirical variation
- Imaginative free variation
- Epoché
- Deficient empiricality

Part II:

Perspective

Chapter 5

Existential Phenomenology and the Landscapes of Living-Experience: Descriptive Exemplars in Five Domains of Human Being-and-Becoming

As we have seen, in the naturalistic attitude, subject and object are partitioned. Terminological and conceptual priority are routinely given to the latter. All that appears in time and space is deemed a segment of measurable, geometric reality. Existential–phenomenological thought does not operate in this style or within these strictures. As we have also seen, the basic task of existential–phenomenological psychology is to practice psychology in a manner that circumvents the objectifying, dehumanizing tendencies that mind–body dualism and the more general subject–object dichotomy have unleashed on the discipline at large. For existential–phenomenological psychology, this involves the dedicated study of human experience in its living form. To review, living-experience is experience that has not been preemptively filtered through conceptual abstractions and repackaged in objectivistic terms. Living-experience is always a meaningful, relational unfolding embedded in a person's being-and-becoming-in-the-world, thus implicating one's history, present concerns, and future outlook.

Existential–phenomenological psychology seeks to investigate, elucidate, and accurately portray living-experience with the intellectual humility required for such an ambitious undertaking. After all, one must repeatedly break from the flow of living-experience to be able to reflectively reengage it for the purposes of scientific work. Indeed, this task is quite challenging given the lack of precedent for such a psychology. A radical redirection is required of the psychologist, which brings us back to the difficult task of operating under the auspices of the epoché. But the results that it yields cannot be summoned by a sheer act of will. Phenomenological research requires practice, buttressed by training that facilitates a metapsychological (i.e., philosophical, theoretical) and perceptual reorientation of the researcher (Morley, 2010). The naturalistic worldview is so sedimented in collective consciousness that a researcher who has no existential–phenomenological background cannot simply bracket naturalism and proceed effortlessly into human scientific descriptive analysis. Thus, this chapter takes a closer look at the nature of living-experience as a central theme of existential–phenomenological psychology.

The chapter offers a sampling of some of the ways that existential phenomenology approaches the various domains of human psychological life outside the strictures of naturalistic objectivism. It will present a small selection of topics to represent the cognitive, bodily, affective, conative, and social domains of human being-and-becoming. A small selection will have to suffice, as each area is vast. The cognitive domain can serve as a brief illustration. In psychology, cognition refers to a wide array of phenomena involved in the acquisition and transformation of knowledge, including attending, perceiving, reasoning, judging, imagining, conceiving, understanding, problem solving, and remembering. To speak to all these phenomena would require far too much space to deal with here. The same can be said of every other domain, so the aims of the chapter must be modest.

Living-Experience in the Cognitive Domain

In conventional natural science psychology, the mind is the proverbial "ghost in the machine" (Ryle, 1949, p. 17), be it the feeble epiphenomenal backwash of sense-empirical psychologies or the computational homunculus of intellectualist psychologies. Historically, natural science psychology has vacillated between ignoring and/or demeaning the power of the human intellect and making it over in its own image (see Murray, 1986). When engaged in the latter, natural science psychology envisions thinking in highly detached, hypothetico-deductive terms, reflecting the natural scientific procedures involved in formal hypothesis testing (a trend that became increasingly popular after the so-called cognitive revolution). This kind of thinking approaches all that comes before it as a problem to be solved through abstract argumentation and, wherever possible, the use of mathematics. It is sometimes described as *computational thinking*. Jerome Bruner (1986) called it *paradigmatic thinking*. Paradigmatic thinking emphasizes formal logic and categorization, as well as explanation by empirical generalization. Paradigmatic thinking is "convergent" in nature (Guilford, 1950), meaning that it demands consistency to arrive at "the" correct answer, from obeying the law of non-contradiction to following the rules of disciplinary convention (i.e., the prevailing paradigm). It revolves around analytic breakdown. That is, its sense-making strategy is to divide and conquer, focusing on the isolated pieces or parts of what it studies. Martin Heidegger (1966) called this *calculative thought*, which is the term more commonly used in the phenomenological tradition.

Phenomenological psychology is rooted in a philosophical heritage that has long questioned the primacy accorded to thinking as defined by the assumptions and methods of the natural sciences. Husserl (1965), for example, asserted that science always operates naively, without ever reflecting on its most basic assumptions or their ramifications. Heidegger (1966) extended Husserl's critique, noting that calculative thinking never stops to reflect on the meaning of its method or the nature of the things that its calculations refer to. The critique is not that scientific abstractions have nothing to offer, but that they do not pull themselves up by their own bootstraps; nor do they exhaust the human potential for thinking. More importantly for our purposes, this critique is not restricted to philosophical debates over the nature of the science-making process. It radically reorients the existential–phenomenological psychologist to the intellectual life of those whom they study.

Existential–phenomenological psychologists do not proceed from or restrict themselves to the assumption that this kind of thinking is characteristic of everyday life. Their conviction is that psychologists operating in the naturalistic attitude get so caught up in their own abstractions that they are perpetually one step removed from the thinking life of persons. The psychological scientist projects a conceptualization of cognition onto their subject matter from without, unduly limiting their range of vision by self-imposed strictures. In day-to-day life, people may think in ways that are reminiscent of a fledgling scientist, and our scientized culture has furnished plenty of vocabulary to facilitate this tendency. But the person-as-aspiring-scientist model is a theoretical contrivance of the scientist. If it were bracketed as per the epoché, one would discover thinking as it ordinarily operates in the natural attitude that permeates the world of living-experience, which Husserl (1970) refers to as the lifeworld. The lifeworld is the wider (i.e., pre-scientific) cultural and historical world of sedimented, taken-for-granted understandings (Moran, 2005; Strasser, 1986).

Thinking in the World of Daily Living: "Commonsense" Thinking

Widening its scope beyond the parameters of calculative thought, the phenomenology of thinking has moved in two directions. In one direction, the one already noted in connection with the natural attitude, phenomenology digs "below" calculative thought. Edward L. Murray (1986) referred to this domain as that of *commonsense thinking*. Following Heidegger (1962), Murray spoke of it as the kind of thinking that typifies the world of average everydayness lying "beneath" the formalizations of natural science. Here, thinking is not driven by abstract theoretical reflection. Day-to-day thinking is immersed in affect, value, and practical action. It has a personalized intertest in the world rather than approaching the world as a spectacle for the detached intellect. This kind of thinking involves everything from mundane to mythical interests and routines (Husserl, 1970). This is not to say that no one ever experiences an accidental interruption or deliberately interrupts their habitual involvement in the world. Heidegger, for example, distinguished between practical absorption in a task, the interruption of practical absorption, and a disengaged presence that admits of different magnitudes of decontextualization, abstraction, and reflection (for which he used the terms *ready-to-hand*, *un-ready-to-hand*, and *present-at-hand*, respectively). When reflection does occur in the domain of commonsense thought, it is rarely formal:

> Unlike the sciences, common sense is a special development of intelligence in a very earthy domain with very little of the abstract and less of the theoretical. Often it appears to argue from analogies or similarities, but they often escape logical formulations. It has little recourse to technical language or formal discourse. Its give and take between saying and meaning is often amorphous. Yet, like the sciences, common sense is the fruit of considerable collaboration with its homey share of tested results, imprecise though they be. The shared content of commonsense thinking . . . is part of what Heidegger sees as the human They–self. . . . Such thought . . . supplies for us the unseen skeletal structure with which we operate in life. (Murray, 1986, p. 5)

Phenomenologists and their kin (e.g., existentialists, hermeneuticists) are not alone in having sensed the importance of recognizing a domain of pre-scientific intellection. One can find resonances of it in Wilhelm Wundt's (1917) *Völkerpsychologie,* Jerome Bruner's (1990) folk psychology, and in cross-cultural research on problem solving (e.g., Scribner, 1979). As noted in Chapter 1, research in the area of 4E (embodied, embedded, enactive, and extended) cognition has been tapping into this domain of experience. It is also worth noting that Dorothy Dinnerstein, a feminist, humanist, and Gestaltist, developed a virtually unknown approach to cognition that was ahead of its time, appearing around the same time as Hubert Dreyfus's (1972) phenomenological critique of cognitive computationalism. Dinnerstein never got the chance to write about her ideas, as she was killed in a car accident. One of her former students, John Iuculano, related, "She did express to me at a Christmas party that one of her students should take on the project. She had seven key features: cognition is motivated, flexibly focused, structured, layered, affectively tinged, self-reflective, and social" (Iuculano, personal communication, May 26, 2004). In various ways and to various extents, these currents of thought all deviated from conventional psychology's dominant model of the mind. For all of them, leaving the confines of the computational model is tapping into living consciousness, animated mind, cognition that is immersed in the flow of human becoming.

Imaginative Thinking

Existential-phenomenological psychology occupies a special place among these streams of thought in that it assigns a central importance to the imagination in the psychology of thinking. The imagination is considered the most fundamental form of cognition (Bolton, 1982). It is seen as the core integrative power that undergirds all forms of discourse (Murray, 1986). Existential-phenomenological psychology also recognizes the human potential for thinking that brings the imagination into focus as its own specialized kind of thinking, not as mere fantasy but as a manner of productively engaging the real. Murray (1986) called this *imaginative thinking*, and it represents the second direction in which existential-phenomenological psychology moves beyond the bounds of calculative thought.

As described by Murray, imaginative thinking has several major characteristics:

- Imaginative thinking opens human beings to the sense of possibility. By an implicit (prereflective) or explicit (reflective) *epoché*, it refuses to confine itself to conventional wisdom as defined by common sense or science. It is thus receptive to "divergent" thought (Guilford, 1950).

- Imaginative thinking welcomes perceptual and conceptual ambiguities, even paradoxes and contradictions, as places from which new possibilities may emerge.
- Imaginative thinking is highly synthetic, specializing in the elucidation of relations among parts, especially as these elucidations clear a path for the generation of new integrative syntheses.
- Imaginative thinking is originary in orientation, seeking to render the familiar unfamiliar and fresh.
- Imaginative thinking is the power to conceive of and realize possibilities related to one's own being-and-becoming. As Merleau Ponty (2010) once noted, "Our connection to the imagination is not a relation of knowledge, but rather a relation of existence" (p. 178). Imaginative thinking holds the key to personality integration, what Murray (1986) once described as "the imaginative integration of the worlded me" (p. 206).
- Imaginative thinking appreciates and embraces the art of rhetoric, not in the pejorative sense but as a power of persuasive interhuman discourse that extends beyond the strictures of logical deliberation. It taps the fecundity of metaphor, symbol, and myth and places it in a dialectical relationship with literalism and logic.
- Imaginative thinking recognizes the power and value of the aesthetic, poetic, and creative dimensions of human existence.
- Imaginative thinking potentiates appreciative, contemplative, meditative thinking or *dwelling*, as Heidegger (1971) called it.

The last four of these characteristics implicate imaginative thinking in its most personal and interpersonal forms, wherein its inherent connection to narrative makes itself felt with considerable force. The integrative power of the imagination is maximized where language is recruited for the purpose of bringing narrative structure to experience. Adler (2008), echoing the psychology of Jerome Bruner, once noted that good narrative thinking "meaningfully captures the shifting contours of lived experience" (p. 423). Through the medium of narrative, imaginative thought allows human beings to consolidate the unfolding stories of their lives.

Crucially, imaginative thinking is not diametrically opposed to common sense or calculative thought. It is rather a more multifaceted, flexible, synoptic outlook than common sense or calculative thinking taken on their own. Murray (1986) observed:

> It is a proper human accomplishment to live both logically and imaginatively, and it may well be that the greatest human achievement of all lies in the experiential realization of genuine poetic living, thus optimizing the strong presence of both kinds of thinking in human existence. (pp. 36–37)

Abraham Maslow (1971) made an analogous observation from within humanistic psychology when he characterized the ideal typology of being-cognition as tending toward *unitive consciousness*. In unitive consciousness, the person transcends the strict bifurcation of pragmatic deficiency motivation (D-needs) and appreciative being-values (B-values) in perception and cogitation (i.e., the bottom and top ends of his famed hierarchy).

Living-Experience in the Bodily Domain

Operating under the auspices of strict mind–body dualism, conventional (i.e., natural science) psychology characteristically passes over the distinctive humanness of the body as an integral feature of psychological life. It is disavowed in favor of an interpretation of the body as a collection of depersonalized causal mechanisms made of tissue. In the process, the bodily character of human existence is itself covered over. As Gabriel Marcel (1965) once noted, human beings live as a bodying forth in the world. Naturalism hides this corporeal manifestation of subjectivity. Indeed, to identify oneself with the objective body of natural science would obliterate subjectivity. As a response to this threat of obliteration, intellectualism fairs no better, as it merely posits consciousness as the objectifying agent of the body by fiat, by theoretical "sleight-of-hand" (p. 156). Marcel thus admonished that the phenomenology of the body must turn its attention to incarnate subjectivity. Similarly, Merleau-Ponty (1962) insisted that the human body is neither an object nor a mere mental construct or concept. As experienced directly, it exists in a "vital zone" of meaningful world engagement (p. 180). Unprejudiced description shows that the body offers itself to consciousness as residing "somewhere between automatic response and representation" (p. 180). To access the living human body, the psychological investigator must widen their viewpoint to include more than biological and chemical causation and consider how the human body (unique to each of us) figures as part of the setting and occasion through which human existence unfolds. As Buytendijk (1974) framed it, the ensouled body undergirds the total structuration of human being-in-the-world.

The move to turn one's attention toward the living body does not mean that phenomenological psychology glibly jettisons the insights of traditional, naturalistic viewpoints on the body. Rather, the more experientially distanced, mechanical interpretations of anatomy and physiology are duly complemented by investigations of the body as oriented, intelligent, animated into action, felt, expressive, and "owned" to various extents depending on the circumstances. The phenomenological psychologist, in other words, is not forced into a self-perpetuated myopia. Nowhere is this better illustrated than in the work of Erwin Straus. Phenomenological philosophers, beginning with Edmund Husserl, confronted the problem of embodiment at its highest levels of analysis (i.e., at the conceptual level of mind–body dualism itself), accompanied by rich descriptions of bodily living. But they did not always agree on how to conceptualize the relationship between the living body and the body of natural science. Sartre, for example, was more adamant than other phenomenologists (including Husserl) about drawing a conceptual line in the sand between the objective body and the living body. Erwin Straus's work fills an important gap in the phenomenology of the body because he took a detour through the world of conventional anatomy and physiology in the process of establishing his approach to phenomenological psychology. His approach can be described as follows.

A certain distance founds the distinctly human capacity to be present to the world. Human beings are physiologically accommodated to actualize this capacity by the ability to stand upright. We stand upright because our spines, rather than being straight, are curved in just the right places. As anthropologists have long known, this difference has massive implications for humanity. In phenomenological psychology, Erwin Straus (1966) has observed that the developments brought about by upright posture transform the entire structure of human experience and human existence. Standing upright increases the relevance of facial expression. Being vertical (as opposed to being on all fours) creates a distanciation that clears a space for both imaginative curiosity and the rational striving for objectivity. Being upright frees the hands, so that our opposable thumbs can be used for tool use. Of course, other animals use tools but not nearly to our degree. Human beings make tools to create still other, more powerful tools. As a human child begins to assume an upright posture, Straus observed that the importance of exploratory touch with the hands becomes increasingly evident:

> Anatomy and physiology relate the body as a whole and its parts to neutral space—as the frame of reference. In experience, however, I experience my hand as an organ in relation to the world. . . . In upright posture, the hand becomes an organ of active Gnostic touching—the epicritic, discriminative instrument par excellence. As such, the hand now ranks with the eye and the ear. (Straus, 1966, p. 150)

Moreover, the developments brought about by upright posture make it possible for human beings to communicate in a *symbolic* fashion (i.e., to use language in the proper sense of that term):

> The mark of the jaws is brute force. The muscles that close the jaws, especially the masseter, are built for simple, powerful motions. Huge ridges and crests . . . encompass the skull of the gorilla. They disappear when the jaws are transformed into the mouth. The removal of these pinnacles permits the increase of the brain case while, at the same time, the reduction of the mighty chewing muscles permits the development of the subtle mimic and phonetic muscles. The transformation of jaws into the mouth is a prerequisite for the development of language but only one of them. (Straus, 1966, pp. 162–163)

As is obvious, observations such as these set the stage for a radically different kind of discourse about the significance of the body. The language of this discourse was established in the pioneering work of Husserl, especially in the second volume of his *Ideas* series (Husserl, 1989), and extending into the era of *The Crisis of the European Sciences* (Husserl, 1970). Husserl's views on the body figured prominently in Edith Stein's (1989) dissertation, *On the Problem of Empathy*, which he directed. Jean-Paul Sartre would soon thereafter take up the project of elucidating the living body by performing a creative synthesis of themes from Husserl's work with certain others taken from Heidegger's *Being and Time* (1962). Sartre introduced basic themes that would then play a central role in Maurice Merleau-Ponty's (e.g., 1962) many discourses on embodied subjectivity, such as the body as expression, for example. Merleau-Ponty (1962) held that every bodily event has a psychic meaning. The body and the mind exist in a relationship of "mutual expression" without the body being wholly transparent to the mind's discerning eye (p. 160). Regrettably, Merleau-Ponty's work in this area has gone on to become well known, while Sartre's phenomenology of the body has been mostly overlooked. As Moran (2011) observed, "Sartre, even more than Merleau-Ponty, is the phenomenologist *par excellence* of the flesh (*la chair*) and of intersubjective intercorporeity" (p. 263).

Edmund Husserl: *Körper* and *Lieb*

Edmund Husserl's phenomenology of the body distinguishes between *Körper* and *Lieb*. *Körper* refers to the body interpreted as a mere physical thing of the natural world, encompassing everything from the body of anatomy and physiology to corpses. On this view, the body is pure matter, a collection of biomechanisms. *Lieb* refers to the ensouled, animated, living body. Husserl founded the distinction between Körper and Lieb based on the fact that the human body has both an "exteriority" (i.e., an exterior that can be viewed "at a distance," as one perceives everything else in the natural world) and an experiential "interiority." The body in its living form (Lieb) brings the latter into focus. The living body presents itself to consciousness differently than objects of the world and the bodies of other people. One's own body does not present all its sides and profiles to oneself the way "external" or "outer" perceptions do (e.g., I cannot examine my own back or retreat to observe my own body as a visual Gestalt. I must instead rely on devices like mirrors and photographs; Stein, 1989).

One should not mistake this talk of interiority and exteriority as setting up a false dilemma. The body can appear as either Körper and Lieb for one and the same person depending on one's approach. In this sense, the body has a quasi-dual nature as opposed to the Cartesian image of free and rational consciousness running merely parallel to a mechanistic body. That said, the body as lived firsthand does not originally or typically appear to human experience as nothing but a thing. According to Husserl, the living body is primordial and is always present as figure or ground in the field of consciousness. The living body and its organs of perception are not typically in focal awareness in our daily rounds, but neither is the living body ever totally absent from the perceptual field. It is the ego's continually operative sensorimotor medium for world engagement even if it has not "caught" one's attention.

For Husserl, the primordiality of the living body is founded on its tactile–kinesthetic senses, which is where its distinction from the exterior or "outer" perception of things manifests most prominently. One "feels" one's body and its movements immediately. There are those movements of one's body, externally perceived physical movements like reflexes, that could be attributed to virtually any other kind of moving body in the world. But there are those movements that are more closely allied to subjectivity and therefore cannot be attributed to other physical bodies. The human body thus has a two-sided character: externally perceived physical movements and firsthand, kinesthetically experienced movement, best expressed in the form of "I move" and "I do" (Husserl, 1970, p. 161). Living bodiliness or experiential bodying forth in the act of world engagement is a first-person human experience of "holding sway" in a body, which means that one's body emanates feelings that convey the sense of willing self-movement. One's immediate experience of holding sway in one's body makes possible the perception of other living bodies as participating in the same kind of ownership experience (Husserl, 1970, p. 217).

In its living form, the body is the center of one's experiential viewpoint on the world at any given time. It is a dynamic locus of orientation (i.e., up, down, left, right, etc., make sense only through the orientation of the perceiving "I move" and "I can" of the person; Husserl, 1970, p. 331). The living body senses an ever present "here" from which all else is positioned "there." This is sometimes referred to as the null point or zero point of orientation, but the meaning of these phrases is not mathematical, not geometrical. Rather, it is actional. The living body is a self-generating (moving, exploring, searching, attending) locus of oriented activity that founds living space. This is the space of possible action as envisioned from within the context of one's meaning-laden relationships and projects. Living, actional space is permeated with felt qualities of distance and closeness that are not strictly isomorphic with measured space.[1] Kurt Lewin (1935) referred to it as hodological space and, more simply, *life space*, meaning a space of possible movement or

---

[1] Firsthand experience continually bears this out. When you are tired or disheartened, traversing a short distance can seem daunting. Conversely, someone sitting right next to you can feel far away. Though we may pass this off as merely figurative, phenomenology does not.

potential action from the viewpoint of the individual person's experiential reality (see also Sartre, 2018).

To speak of possible movement implicates time perception. The living body plays an equally important role in the genesis of living, experiential time. The way the body is disposed and responsive in a situation depends on the given circumstances of the physical environment but not in the manner of blind, natural causality. The body–world interface is not a totally passive relation, but an intelligent one responding to present circumstances in light of unfolding, intentional involvements. "Circumstances" are actually co-constituted by ongoing bodily participation. The living body is physically attuned to its surroundings as belonging to a feeling, motivated (needing and desiring), meaning-forming being-and-becoming-in-the-world. Lieb thus plays a role in establishing how circumstances are present to the person. The living body is the incarnate orientation of one's "here-and-now." The living body co-constitutes a total sensual–kinesthetic field (partly shared, partly unique to each of us) that guides the ongoing, temporally unfolding interests and truth-verifying intuitions of a person's daily rounds (Husserl, 1970).[2]

This self-organizing, self-orienting is a continually unfolding process. Sensations, as belonging to a senser, are amalgamated into a unity of flowing perceptual reality, a streaming, living presence. One moves one's body to enact an apperceptive grasp and workable engagement of one's surroundings. In this way, the very worldhood of the world, its experiential configuration, is founded upon the meaningfully attending, exploring movement of one's sensing organs (Stein, 1989). Thus, Husserl (1970) held that the living body affords a "privileged status" to perception in cognition (p. 161). The result is that the experience of one's own body is central to the experiencing of all bodies. Bodily orientation toward things (including one's affective attunement, "holding sway," activity, and habituality within the environment) plays a role in determining how the things of the world are synthesized into objects of perception and present themselves as the facts of one's situation. As Husserl described it, thing-like experiences are correlated with kinesthetic experiences in the form of

---

[2] Husserl's interest in securing a firm basis for truth claims pervaded his works. It contrasts with the looming sense of doubt that was engendered by the Cartesian worldview (i.e., Descartes method of systematically doubting beliefs and experiences in hopes of arriving at certain truths). His interest in truth-verifying intuitions also contrasts with what he saw as the groundlessness of sense-empirical thought and naturalism in all its forms.

the enacted temporal structure: "if…then." For instance, *if* I grasp the handle and apply upward pressure, *then* the gallon of milk will rise for me to pour. This is the intentional background of every "straightforward ontic certainty of a presented thing" (Husserl, 1970, p. 162). Where an inexplicable break in this structure occurs, something then appears as "wrong" or illusory. Husserl further demonstrated how perception is primordially amodal in the co-constitution of the world. In stark contrast to the sense-empirical depiction of self-contained sensory modalities, one can "see" the firmness of the gallon full of milk as well as its "hollowness" when emptied.

Jean-Paul Sartre: The Living Body as Contingent Possibility

Another landmark phenomenological contribution to the study of embodiment was Jean-Paul Sartre's chapter on the body in *Being and Nothingness* (2018). Sartre began his analyses of the body in much the same way as Husserl. According to Sartre, in the naturalistic attitude, the body is posited as an entirely constituted object (rather than one in which we each play a role in co-constituting). Of course, the body is always already constituted to some extent (it is not a mere creation of the subject), but never fully and finally so, as if it were nothing more than another object in the world. The body as Körper is conceptualized from without, from an externalist, third-person viewpoint. This contrasts with the body as experienced firsthand. The externalist body is not *my* body. It is, in effect, the body of the other (i.e., a "textbook" body or a corpse). This is the standard view of sense-empirical psychology. Sense-empirical psychology has always upheld a mind–body dualism that objectifies the body and its functioning, beginning with the process of sensation. From the earliest days of psychophysics, sensation was deemed a relation between two sets of objectivities, those of physics and biology. By default, the subject became an afterthought. On this view, the mind "undergoes" or "suffers" sensations as a series of mere impressions produced by neuroreceptors. Conceptually filtered through the lens of anatomical abstractions, human experience came to be perpetually one step removed from the world. One no longer has immediate access to the actual green of the notebook in the world, for example. Instead, the notebook is cast as merely capable of producing the sensation of green inside the cranium (see Sartre, 2018, p. 424).

When confronted with the fact that we each possess the power of self-reflective awareness, natural scientific psychology (especially in its more intellectualist forms) has tried in vain to reattach consciousness to the objectified body. There arose an effort to reinterpret the body as a tool-like mechanism to be commanded by an onlooker consciousness. But the argument for such an interpretation falls into infinite regress, always requiring another onlooker to found the truth claims of every prior observation of the object-body. To end the regress, there must be a *body-subject* (see Merleau-Ponty, 1962). At some point, one must contend with fact that no one can take a purely objective point of view regarding their own body (see Sartre, 2018, pp. 431–441). One must contend with the hard and ambiguous reality of firsthand bodily experience. Being-for-itself, consciousness, the life of human awareness (as opposed to all that is experienced as existing in itself) must "be" its body, must be bodily on a firsthand basis; otherwise consciousness reflects little more than a pale caricature of human psychological life. Sartre never denied that we can (and sometimes do) interpret our own bodies based on their object qualities. Nonetheless, he held that when one relates to one's own body in its object qualities in daily life, it is for the purpose of transcending it toward one's possibilities for being-in-the-world (e.g., touching one's leg to make those adjustments needed to put on one's pants; see Sartre, 2018, p. 411).

Like Husserl, Sartre held that the living body is not a collection of mechanical motoric apparatuses (muscles, bones, joints, tendons, cartilage, ligaments) but a total moving, acting, sense-making structure (Sartre, 2018). One does not body forth by dispatching this or that discrete part into an isolated segment of the world. The living body is engaged holistically in a perpetual surpassing of itself toward the ends and goals of one's various involvements (Sartre, 2018). Every involvement issues from a null point, which is not a literal or reified point in geometrical space. One's living body is just as much "over there" at the directionality of one's actions as it is "over here." Yet, both this particular "here" and "there" are constituents within a unique living locale or relational milieu (incarnate being does not have access to an abstract view "from above" or God's eye view). Similarly, sensation does not refer primarily to a collection of mechanical sensory apparatuses. Phenomenologically, sensing is one's general orientation within a relational milieu. Sensing forms the backdrop within which things in the environment are co-constituted and take on their respective meanings. The way one senses exposes the stylistic form of one's being-in-the-midst-of-the-world (Sartre, 2018, p. 429).

More so than Husserl, Sartre emphasized the body's typical absence from focal awareness. In our daily world-involvement, the body does not ordinarily announce itself as a figure. Rather, it is characteristically a ground phenomenon. According to Sartre, one only experiences the body as the "constant evanescent reference" of one's practical activity (e.g., my hand, in the act of writing, vanishes from focal awareness) (Sartre, 2018, p. 434). Consciousness is at and with the writing itself rather than the hand of the writing. Anyone who has suddenly become self-conscious during an activity or performance knows this well. This accentuation of the world-pole of intentional activity demonstrates the influence of Heidegger's existential phenomenology on Sartre. Drawing on Heidegger, Sartre described the way in which the living body is always already involved with things as a meaningful ensemble of equipment. In our daily rounds, prior to reflective contemplation, things are disclosed through immediate, direct, practical activity, which Heidegger (1962) called ready-to-hand (note the reference to the hand of the living body). In daily living, things tend to take on their meaning and form against the background of non-thetic (i.e., as yet unarticulated) projects that are lived out with intentionally directed, bodily intelligence before reflective or theoretical activity commences (Sartre, 2018).

Other Heideggerian themes that appeared in Sartre's phenomenology of the body included *thrownness* (i.e., our being born as a being "thrown" into a seemingly arbitrary set of circumstances), *facticity* (i.e., beginning with our thrownness, the given "brute" facts of our world-situatedness), and *finitude* (i.e., the inherently vulnerable, limited aspects of human existence). Sartre spoke of thrownness and facticity in terms of the contingent nature of one's body. No one had to be born into their particular body. The living body is a contingency at the heart of one's being that can never be eliminated, only appropriated and assimilated in some way. Still, this assimilation never occurs by mere fiat. Sartre observed that the for-itself (i.e., consciousness) is not its own foundation. Recall that for Husserl the body is our presence in a field of potential (future) action. For Sartre the body is just as much if not more the bearer of one's past; our point of view is always already established, only to be discovered retroactively. Every human body is the bearer of a birth and all that this birth implies given one's situation in life (e.g., gender, race, relative beauty, ability, disability, social class, etc.; see Sartre, 2018, p. 459). One perpetually finds oneself already affectively attuned to any given situation, which is a living bodily experience. Finally, Sartre noted the always already intersubjective nature of bodying forth, observing that one cannot learn to see and move as others do without being a visible body participating in a culture (see Sartre, 2018, p. 427). The living body is a mobile center of sensing in-the-world simultaneously sensed by others with similar powers of observation.

For Sartre, even more so than Husserl, the body interpreted as a thing among things cannot be that through which things are disclosed to a subjectivity. Körper and Lieb represent two incommunicable levels of existence. In this sense, Sartre's viewpoint was more paradoxical than what one finds in Husserl. For Husserl, paradoxical relations were issues to be overcome by way of more penetrating analyses, whereas Sartre (being more "existential") was more oriented toward the tragic, inexplicable dimensions of human limitation or finitude. For Sartre, the factical body exposes human finitude (Sartre, 2018, p. 440). To Husserl's insight that the resistances and adversity that things pose to the living body play an important role in the co-constitution of reality, Sartre admonished that this adversity bespeaks human vulnerability. Human beings live an endangered body, capable of pain and injury, by necessity (Sartre, 2018, p. 436).

Sartre was not a fatalist, however. Far from it. He did not view the for-itself (human consciousness) as incidental to one's total situation, as in the objectivism of sense-empirical psychology. The relationship of consciousness to the living body was deemed as residing somewhere between contingency and possibility. It is *contingent possibility*. The body's givenness notwithstanding, the living body is not a mere hindrance, a subliminal screen occluding one's access to things. It is the contingent individuality of one's original relationship with the world as a meaningful ensemble of equipment (Sartre, 2018). The living body is a contingency at the heart of one's being that is continually surpassed. It is a non-thetic structure of consciousness. One does not experience the effort of one's world-spanning engagements until met with the resistances of the world. The living body is characteristically "passed over in silence," lived as that which is perpetually transcended by one's projecting oneself toward possibilities for being-in-the-world (Sartre, 2018, p. 442). Its felt modalities form the background of our intentional directedness toward the world.

Living-Experience in the Affective Domain

It is of special significance that the living body is a feeling body. The way that the whole of one's feeling–sensing body meets the world marks the inception of a field of meaning. As Stein (1989) observed, the living body makes possible the experience of non-specific sensual feelings (e.g., feeling sluggish), directed sensual feelings (e.g., the pleasantness of a savory dish, the comfort of a soft garment), moods (e.g., cheery, melancholy), and what she called spiritual feelings (e.g., aesthetic values, joy, psychic pain). These manifestations of feeling can give rise to acts of reflection, making them the "objective" foci of perception and contemplation (enacting the cognition domain). They can also motivate volitional, meaningfully oriented behavior (enacting the conative domain). Finally, feelings terminate in expressions that release them unto the world-with-others (enacting the social domain).

This integrative viewpoint contrasts with what one finds pervasive throughout the history of natural science psychology. In the naturalistic attitude, emotion is approached with the assumptions of dualism, giving rise to a range of perspectives that side with the anatomical body or the intellect. Emotions are seen as the residual side effect of either physiological (i.e., "arousal") and/or cognitive (i.e., "appraisal") mechanisms. As Maurice Merleau-Ponty (1964) once put it:

> The psychologist tries to see how man [*sic*] works out . . . responses to certain situations and stimuli, and to discover the laws which rigorously bind together such and such a group of stimuli with such and such reaction. We must not give an ontological—that is, an ultimate weight—to this way of thinking, for it is naive and unreflective. In earlier times psychology noted vaguely that emotion was both a 'psychic and a physical' state and sought to determine which was the cause of the other. Phenomenology will remain neutral before this issue, and without assuming that emotion is either psychical or physical it will simply ask what emotion means and towards what it is tending. (pp. 57, 61)

Perhaps no phenomenologist has contributed more to the study of the feeling life than Stephen Strasser in his *The Phenomenology of Feeling* (1977). In line with the perspectives of Stein and Merleau-Ponty, Strasser noted that sense-empirical psychology and intellectualist psychology have disproportionately concentrated on *bios* (as Körper) and *logos* (as calculative thinking) respectively in their approaches to feeling. This has resulted in a kind of ontological excluded middle that diminishes the significance of the pathic dimension of human experience (*pathos*). Due to their artificialism, neither sense-empirical psychology nor intellectualist psychology has brought the distinctly human nature of feeling into view.

Strasser proposed a phenomenological alternative to natural science psychological approaches to feeling, which consisted of a structural explication of feeling in terms of the following three constituents.

1. *The Experience of Being-Disposed (i.e., Affective Disposition)*: The phenomenological origins of human experience emerge from an undifferentiated world orientation that is felt in a sensing body. This pre-intentional state implicates the whole self–other–world complex (i.e., a person's total situation). Acts take their lead from these prior states of affect-laden tending-toward. They become the *motus* or motivation that attracts one toward this or that in the world.
2. *The Experience of Being-Underway*: When globally felt states provide the impetus to action, behavior can remain unorganized and pre-intentional or it can become intentionally directed. If it becomes intentionally directed, it can nonetheless regress back to pre-intentional governance at any given time in an experience of becoming overcome with emotion. Felt states can also undergo a progressive transformation, becoming meta-intentional acts oriented toward self-transcendent purposes.
3. *The Experience of (Temporary) Termination*: Feeling actions ultimately tend toward the achievement of an end state or terminus, which would (if deemed successful) signify the fulfillment of their expression. The behavior that results is always only temporarily (and thus partially) fulfilled, playing out in states of relatively satiated or unsatiated termination. This is characterized by momentary inactivity, a lingering with the results of one's actions. Where there is a feeling of temporary completion (i.e., where the feeling-governed activity is experienced as successful), the prior tension between one's sense of actuality and ideal-possibility gives way to a lessening of tension and a feeling of satisfaction. Where there is a feeling of temporary incompletion (i.e., of failure), there is also a relative lessening of tension, but it is experienced as a form of disappointment (e.g., sorrow, sadness, grief, etc.).

None of these phases are merely mechanical; nor are they governed by "logic" per se. The feeling life does not just explode onto the world (at least not under normal circumstances); nor is it perpetually dependent upon contemplative acts. It is part of the self-engagement of an embodied, situated subject with their world. The pathic dimension of human experience acts as the connective tissue between bios (Körper and Lieb) and logos (as more than calculative thought, as "spiritual," which refers to the irreal life of meaning, value, and purpose). Human beings participate in an ever-unfolding developmental dynamic of self-realization that involves the constant interaction of bios, pathos, and logos. In Strasser's view, feeling governs human acts at the point of inception, but feeling alone cannot bring about the completion and fulfilment of human behavior. Throughout development, varied forms and extents of felt presence to one's situation are at play. Human being-and-becoming is a stratified whole wherein the "bottom end" (i.e., the pre-given, pre-intentional, dispositional level of feeling) provides a factical subsoil for the "higher end" (i.e., the intentional and meta-intentional life of consciousness). The higher end of consciousness provides orientational trajectory and meaning to the lower. Over the course of development, intentional and meta-intentional manifestations of feeling come to play an increasingly prominent, salient role in the process of becoming. The experiential strata of the feeling life look as follows.

Pre-Intentional Being-Disposed: Primordial Attunement

Akin to what one finds in Heidegger's *Being and Time* (1962), Strasser held that the most fundamental and pervasive dimension or subsoil of the feeling life is pre-intentional, beginning with being disposed. Pure disposition (also sometimes called state of mind, being in a mood, or attunement) is a kind of twilight consciousness wherein life first crosses over into experience. Here, the differentiation of self and world is at a bare minimum. Pure being in a mood (e.g., being in a self-assured versus insecure mood, feeling inward and private versus lively and open, etc.) is always present even when we are without directed feelings. It is free-floating and bears no conscious apprehension of motive (e.g., feeling as being in a "lively" mood is not "of" "at" or "about" anything in particular). Whereas many currents of phenomenology emphasize the primacy of perception in their descriptions of conscious life, Strasser maintained that feeling disposition is the elementary foundation of experience. Perception presupposes object directedness with some degree of salience and articulation, manifesting figures against grounds. Disposition is pre-intentional. There is no clearly identifiable "object pole" of experience.

Being disposed can give rise to determinate modes of perceiving and acting, but taken on its own, it is a dimension of experience where intentional poles dissolve and bleed into one another. That is, what is apprehended is a supra-personal totality that precedes the positing of subject and object. It is trans-objective and trans-subjective. Disposition is the pre-predicative, pre-intentional feeling of the "All" of one's life that acts as the broadest horizon of worldly exchanges. Though it has not yet been personalized by acts of reflection, it is not *im*personal either. It does pertain to one's life, making it pre-personal. Moreover, being-disposed is neither mechanical nor "illogical" (as it would be cast by conventional psychology). It is pre-thematic and not yet recruited into the rhetorical domain of the "logical" (in the many senses of that term). Being-disposed is to be turned toward the infinite horizons of the trans-personal and paralogical (see Giorgi, 1993).

Disposition can also be a being-disposed toward the total experience of a specific set of circumstances, which is more likely to propagate or facilitate a series of intentional acts at a given time and place. But even here, being-disposed remains a sense of the whole of one's being-in-the-world, only in a somewhat more situationally delimited fashion. Being-disposed remains the undifferentiated subsoil that undergirds the emergence of intentional directedness. All personalized acts have their source in embodied pathic life beginning with disposition, but not their termination. The pathic life of feeling expresses itself in higher (intentionally directed) acts without ever being exhausted in them due to the fundamental incompleteness of perpetual human becoming. This will be revisited in Chapter 6.

Intentionally Directed Felt-Responsiveness: From Affect to Action

The pre-intentional level of feeling overlaps with the intentional, precluding the possibility of there being a discrete geological-styled "layer" of biochemical functioning impervious to "higher contents" of the mind. In other words, the phenomenology of feeling does not support a dualism of physiological arousal mechanisms set against an onlooker consciousness. There are intersections wherein the factical pre-orientation of feeling (disposition) is bequeathed with form (perceptual, cognitive, and behavioral) and then completed (albeit temporarily) by consciousness. The crossover from the pre-intentional into the intentionally directed level of feeling is marked by the perception of a double value in the experience of feeling governed action (Strasser, 1977). Concretely, a double-value perception indicates that perceived goods are experienced alongside other competing goods, not to mention perceived obstacles, dangers, and/or evils. That which is seen as desirable (i.e., a perceived good) is always apprehended from within a situation that would have to be managed and traversed by the discerning intentional activity and decision making of the subject.

Thus, secondary governance by feeling, which is intentionally oriented by organized movement toward a *goal*, develops from out of the pre-intentional level and ultimately transforms it. Intentional, goal-directed felt-responses reside on a continuum, ranging from the vague attraction to a person, object, or situation to felt-responses that present perceived goods (or evils) as articulated Gestalts. The most evolved (more articulated) manifestations of the latter end of this continuum are where the distinctly personal aspects of the feeling life make their appearance. Here, insights are added to feeling in such a way as to transform the pre-predicative comprehension of one's situation in a specific way: Goals and potential pathways to them become salient in consciousness. A new way of being, one that involves imagining, planning, willing, creating, and actualizing meanings emerges. In the process, *purpose* is added to goal-seeking. The ways to a goal are pre-given by conditions, but purposes are more open in terms of "way," more amenable to decision making and selection. For distinctly human willing to emerge implies that purposes must be able to precede goals. Subordinating goals to intended purposes transforms things in an environment to objects of a human (cultural) world.

The subordination of goals to intended purposes gives human beings greater freedom (in comparison to non-human animals) to design their worlds as they see fit. This is part of what it means to be a "spiritually ensouled organism" (Strasser, 1977, p. 243). Again, however, there is no assumption of geological layers here. Dynamic interaction is the rule. On the one hand, Strasser observed that the rationality of human functioning pervades areas of life far "below" what is normally considered "rational," be they bodily, social, artistic, or religious. On the other hand, even though technical, practical, and theoretical reason has freed humans from the leading strings of governance by feeling, this does not mean that feeling is incidental or altogether mute. The mutual influence of pathos and logos is a default condition of human existence. Technological and technocratic attitudes may diminish the felt governance of behavior, deliberately neutralizing feeling to focus clearly on categorical intuitions, but feeling remains the point of departure for the acting person. The goal that is pursued by the person is saturated in the felt impulses of an historical group. It represents the passion and imagination of a social group in a given historical epoch.

A Regressive Process: Becoming Overcome with Emotion

The eidetic structure of becoming overcome with emotion (sometimes referred to as "becoming emotional") illustrates the dynamic shift that can occur between the levels or strata of feeling. In a composed state, one has a pre-predicative grasp of one's situation. One can freely and spontaneously see ways and means to chosen ends, which potentiates organized, directed, intentional involvements with the world. This is a forward-looking orientation of existence. But a regressive transition from feeling-governed behavior to becoming overcome with emotion can also occur. For that to happen, the following must transpire.

1. In a given situation, one cannot or can no longer perceive clear possibilities (way and/or means) for achieving one's ends.
2. The perceived impossibility of acting in an organized, meaningful, composed manner gives rise to the cessation of directed activity. But one still feels the need to act in an organized, meaningful way.
3. In the face of this quandary, one's intentional orientation eventually comes undone. The situation is thrown into relative disorganization and disconnect. Acting starts to become reactionary, looking more blind, irrational, panicked, flustered, groping, and so forth.
4. In place of the total situation perceived as a Gestalt, the world takes on the character of a massive, looming, concretely experienced good or evil that grips the person and totalizes their consciousness.
5. Emotional expressions explode onto the world, the nature of which display the undifferentiated absoluteness of a general, all-consuming experience of longing for a good or to vanquish an evil. This flailing absoluteness looks just like a pre-intentional performance. Archaic, primary affective functioning erupts, holding secondary (intentionally directed, organized, self-governed) affective functioning in a suspended state.

Importantly, the total personality does not suffer a wholesale collapse upon becoming overcome with emotion. Its very existence is what underlies the emergence of the phenomenon. The self-governance of feeling is merely lost for the time being. Moreover, the emotional experience of being at the mercy of the situation corresponds to the "ultimate" intention: the intention of the neglect of all intention. Ironically, this is a "higher," secondary process: the process of letting oneself go. But when one is overcome with emotion, it is temporarily stripped of its progressive potentials. In Strasser's (1977) words:

> Only a being gifted with spirit is capable of violent emotion, of hopelessness, of shame, of remorse, of catharsis, and so forth. The eruption of emotion is to be characterized as an unspiritual phenomenon, but one that is completely conditioned by the spirit. (p. 274)

Non-Regressive (Potentially Progressive) Processes: Governance by Feeling in Daily Living

Becoming emotional as described above depicts a regressive event in the life of feeling. But this is not what typically presents itself in day-to-day living, and we have yet to turn toward those aspects of felt-governance most indicative of the self-realization process. Between pre-intentional and purely intellectual (theoretical, calculative) forms of activity lie the main forms of felt self-regulation: attitude, conviction, comportment, and basic comportment. An attitude crystallizes from a felt experience that is given form by a cognitively mediated motive. A projection of purpose is added to a primordial felt experience of attraction with a positive and/or negative valence. Attitude is the least stable of this group of phenomena, as it can change in a moment with a change of circumstances.

More stability is found in *conviction* and *comportment*. Conviction is composed of intentional (world directed, oriented) feeling, depth of feeling in terms of personal significance, and spiritual acts of devotion motivated by these deep meanings. Conviction is more stable than attitude because it is underpinned by motives of a theoretical, axiological, and/or practical sort. It is also more socially charged and thus more intimately connected to the realm of value, identity, and character. Comportment lies between attitude and conviction. It is innate, like temperament. It thus has no specific content bound up with it. It has the stability of predisposition but, says Strasser (1977), modes of comportment are not reducible to anonymous laws of nature. They are rather ways of porting oneself, or self-porting. In other words, comportment refers to ways in which one gradually accustoms oneself to the environment and world. Finally, basic comportment refers to the structure of a person's attitudes, convictions, and modes of comportment expressed as the total style of personality.

The Meta-Intentional Life of Feeling: Passion

Passion provides an exemplary illustration of the way felt intentional directedness is involved in the self-realization process. Passions can have a profoundly formative influence on basic comportment (i.e., personality) because they are highly invested attempts to bestow meaning on one's existence (Strasser, 1977). Passion refers to a fundamental directness that is more than intentional directedness to an object. Passion is meta-intentional, representing the coalescence of personal feeling with self-transcendent purpose. When it is genuine, it bears the characteristics of what Abraham Maslow would call self-transcending self-actualization (see DeRobertis, 2021b).

As Strasser observed, human beings are metaphysically needy (and vulnerable) beings. With mortality salience comes the knowledge of the unique unrepeatability of one's existence and, with that, not only the threat of physical death but an even greater threat: living an agonizingly meaningless existence. Thus, human development, at every new level of growth, seeks greater freedom, versatility, and world-governance. Optimally, the world is subject to our placing it in service of purposes and ideals against a field of horizons bearing infinite possibilities. Human development "intends" something more than the mastery of the mundane. It perpetually desires to transcend the boundaries of the technical, social, and cultural world (e.g., see Maslow, 1961, 1971). Passion arises when an underlying mode of felt readiness is transformed into a heightened capacity for emotional abandonment (a letting oneself be turned over) to that which is deemed valuable in this pursuit of ideal purposes. Passion thus has incredible organizing power. It can rearrange one's total personality structure and give it resolve.

Having said this, Strasser also noted that not all basic comportment is transcendent in the manner just described.[3] There are many ways

[3] Strasser is speaking of the transcendent here to refer to the higher reaches or higher level fulfillment of the transcendent aspect of human existence. This is a self-transcending orientation, which brings the notion of transcendence in this context closer to what Viktor Frankl refers to when he speaks of self-transcendence as the will-to-meaning.

that a person can be engrossed in or absolutize a certain mode of world engagement to create meaning in life or obtain intense feelings of satisfaction. Passion can be misguided or totally irrational, being little more than a perversion of transcendence. There can even be all-out inversions of transcendence that are highly deluded and ego-centric. Transcendence is a perpetual developmental task of human becoming, but there is no blueprint afforded to humans to guarantee its fulfillment. With the freedom to comport oneself comes the possibility of erring in the process, of imprisoning oneself rather than realizing the heights of transcendent living.

Living-Experience in the Conative Domain

The *APA Dictionary of Psychology* defines *conation* as "the proactive (as opposed to habitual) part of motivation that connects knowledge, affect, drives, desires, and instincts to behavior." The adjective *conative* is defined as that which *is* "characterized by volition or self-activation toward a goal" (American Psychological Association, n.d.-b). While it is heartening to see conation represented in this official manner, psychology has had a long, conflicted history of dealing with the conative dimension of human existence, especially as concerns the possibility of freely willed behavior. To illustrate, Albert Bandura (2008), ranked the fourth most eminent psychologist of the 20th century (Haggbloom et al., 2002), has referred to the notion of freely willed behavior as an antiquated relic of medieval philosophy. Bandura, who spent the better part of his career studying "agency" aspects of personality, nonetheless deemed free will unscientific based on the fact that people act from within a nexus of environmental conditions (which is, of course, a straw man argument). Psychologists of varied backgrounds have found themselves having to confront the conative aspects of psychological life, but the notion of "willing" incites the fear of an invasion of philosophy in psychological matters.

Existential–phenomenological psychology has never succumbed to such fears; nor has it approached human willing as the byproduct of calculative intellection unfettered by the tethers of bodily, feeling being-in-the-world. The "free" in free will has never been cast as in any way arbitrary. Rather, the phenomenon of willing is situational, founded upon a person's limited openness to the world, and thus finite. Developmentally, the will must evolve and emerge. It must be set free by and for others (Erikson, 1961; Knowles, 1986; May, 1969). The ability to transcend any current fixity to varying extents is a fact of the for-itself life of consciousness (see Giorgi, 1992; Maslow, 1971), but the freedom of the will is relative to developmental level, the relative health of the individual, and the nature of one's total circumstances (see DeRobertis, 2011, 2021b).

Alexander Pfänder and the Phenomenology of Willing

Alexander Pfänder's (1967) work in the conative domain is fundamental. Pfänder observed that human living is embedded in a field of needs and wants that give rise to strivings (and counter-strivings where avoidance or escape is deemed necessary). The emergence of strivings takes place from within a preexisting prereflective centrifugal consciousness directed away from one's embodied null point in space out toward the world. Centrifugal consciousness consists of phenomena like attending, perceiving and apperceiving, questioning and pointing out, projecting, asserting, and so forth. If something in the world-pole evokes striving in the ego- or self-pole of the self-world relation, a marked centripetal activation then accompanies centrifugal consciousness, wherein one now feels inwardly impelled by a force of attraction (or repulsion in the case of a counter-striving). Valences (i.e. experiential forces of attraction or repulsion) come to the fore in the perceptual field. As a result, a newly transformed, ego-affected centrifugal aiming at the world has arisen (i.e., a striving), but it is as yet blind. It is not yet guided by consciousness of a goal.

Importantly, Pfänder noted that when centripetal activation occurs, it grips but a part of the ego-pole, not the whole of it. The ego-pole does not simply "collapse" into the world-pole. A certain distance remains, no matter how small.[4] Thus, each striving has an "inner" experienced duality: a centrifugal (world-directed) current fused with a relative degree of inner resistance to maintain the integrity of the ego-pole. This gap is the kernel of human world-openness. It reserves the potential for ego-governed, agentic comportment. The resistance of the ego to the

---

[4] It may be helpful here for some readers to be reminded of Viktor Frankl's (2006) psychiatric credo. Frankl asserted that there is no specific diagnosis or general form of psychopathology that would so condition a human being to leave them without the slightest freedom. Even in cases of psychosis, the innermost core of a patient's personality is untouched. A residue of freedom, no matter how small and limited it might be, is left. What is decisive is whether a person can recognize what freedom is available to them so that it can be mobilized agentically. "Freedom from" is realized in "freedom for" or "freedom in order to . . . ."

positive (or negative) evocations of the world produces an experiential tension between self and world. So long as it remains, it is the person's resistance to impulsive, blind reactivity (which may prove to be manageable or become totally out of one's control as a matter of course).

Pfänder's description thus far has not crossed over into the experience of willing, however. The reason pertains to the nature of the ego-pole's involvement. The ego-pole has a twofold structure, consisting of ego-body (Leib) and ego-center. Strivings (and counter-strivings) do not always affect both aspects of the total structure, at least not to the same extent. What has been presented thus far primarily implicates the ego in its prereflective bodying forth, where striving affects the ego-body more so than the ego-center. If the striving of the ego-body is powerful enough, it can make one feel a sense of compulsion, as if one is powerless in the face of the valences emanating from the world-pole. But where the experience of one's participation in the world is mediated by the ego-center, a different picture emerges. Here, striving is no longer fundamentally or exclusively centrifugal, but subject to centripetal evaluations of an agentic sort. This opens the door to the possibility of genuine willing. Compared to the mere victory of the strongest striving, the act of willing is completely new. The subject is no longer involved as the mere origin of acts in the broad, general sense. The subject becomes the experiential *originating source* of said acts. Here, the act is precisely *not* experienced as an occurrence caused by a different source or external agent. Behavior is no longer blind. Rather, it contains a consciousness of what is willed. The residual duality noted at the level of basic striving is transformed into a duality negotiated by seeing acts (i.e., by insight).

Yet, Pfänder was careful to note that willing is not theorizing. Mere theoretical affirmation or negation is not willing because there is no practical intent involved. Nor is willing mere wishing or hypothetical willing, which are, at best, examples of "virtual" will. In willing, the ego proposes to itself the "to-do" or "not-to-do" of a project. In other words, the emergence of an act of willing is founded upon real intent, the burgeoning consciousness of a project to be carried out some time in the future. Pfänder described this as a practical act of proposing this or that activity filled with an intention from the ego-center (i.e., from the self). It constitutes an act of self-determination wherein the ego is involved as both the subject and object of the act. The act of choosing is a special case of willing involving reflection on mutually exclusive projects, weighing "oughtness," considering the possibilities and values implicated in each potential project. Unlike striving and counter-striving, in willing, one can decide in favor of some striving inclination in spite of a stronger counter-striving. Moreover, there can be willed acts without any obvious strivings or counter-strivings, as in those acts based on calm consideration and insight.

According to Pfänder, acts of willing are founded upon *motives*. On his view, a practical questioning attitude pervades human psychological lives. Each of us, at every turn in life, lives out the question, "What should I do?" However, even when some "oughtness" is perceived, an act of willing has not yet been initiated. The ego-center must place resolve upon what is perceived as demanded by the experience of felt oughtness. That is, the ego must grant approval, consent, and engage in a subsequent move to perform acts. The oughtness thereby becomes a "motive" that grounds willing in a situation. For Pfänder, when it comes to the phenomenological origins of experience, motivation is lived as an "in-order-to" rather than a blind causal mechanism (i.e., a causality that is totally external to subjectivity). Motives go beyond any manifestation of mere attraction and repulsion (striving and counter-striving). Strivings are real, factual (centripetally impinging) contingencies, whereas practical demands (the stuff of motives) are non-real/irreal, ideal "pointers" shedding light on a world of human possibilities (Pfänder, 1967, p. 31). As Pfänder put it, the arousal of strivings affects the body of the soul. The making of a demand in motivation addresses the spirit of the soul, the dimension that is able to "hear" these demands in an agentic, self-governing way (though it does not have to listen; nor is it always able to).

Given this description, it should be obvious that Pfänder's account of motivation is more restrictive than what one usually finds handled in most psychological literature on the topic (which extends past the phenomenal field to include natural science perspectives on that which "moves" an organism). Being moved to action as an involuntary "push" by drives or "pull" by incentives makes no practical demand and is not a conscious support for an act of willing. These unconscious "motives" are not *true* motives. True motives do not cause behavior as a force that compels. Rather, they supply grounds for the ego-center's impetus to act. The ego-center wills spontaneously in a certain manner and is the relatively free agent, not the mere sufferer, of willing.

Willing as a Paradoxical Phenomenon

Since the time of Pfänder's work, various phenomenological psychologists have extended his insights, building on the notion that human willing is a phenomenon that is distinct from both arbitrariness and causality. Of note is the often-overlooked work of Richard Knowles (1986), whose reinterpretation of Erik Erikson's (1961) psychosocial theory integrated the descriptions of willing offered by Adrian van Kaam (1966) and Rollo May (1969). Like Pfänder (though he did not cite him), Knowles observed that willing is neither impulsivity nor wishing bereft of the impetus to action. It is not control oriented, formal (theoretical, calculative, abstract) intellectual assessment. Drawing on van Kaam and May, Knowles further noted that willing is not to be confused with control-oriented notions of autonomy, sheer willfulness (sometimes dubbed "willpower"), or the compensatory mechanism of compulsivity. Knowles agreed with Rollo May (1969) that the "autonomy of the ego" tends to appear in natural science psychology as a Cartesian homunculus masking as a genuine ego-center or proprium, to use Allport's (1955) apt term.

Positively speaking, Knowles agreed with van Kaam (1966) that willing is experienced as the smooth, harmonious pairing of a person's basic world-openness with their executive functioning (i.e., attending, intending, judging, organizing, selecting, deciding, etc.). Similarly, Knowles's view was commensurate with May's (1969) description of willing as an unfolding dialectic between wishing (as imaginative–creative *élan*) and the capacity for deliberately self-organizing self-direction. According to Knowles, willing is best understood as a kind of paradoxical presentation, a smooth dynamical responsiveness capable of a range of responses from letting go to taking control depending on one's total situation. To be sure, phenomenological descriptions from thinkers as diverse in orientation as the above-noted Edith Stein (1989) and Jean-Paul Sartre (2018) have converged in observing that willing has a twofold structural essence. On the one hand, it is spontaneous, co-constitutional, and creatively disposed. But an act of will does not pick itself up from its own bootstraps. Willing is situationally dynamic, bodily, and affective. Given the fluid, paradoxical nature of willing, it is no wonder that conventional psychology, with its emphases on formal theorizing and mathematical precision, has been unable to disambiguate its structure. Even the more contemporary notion of reciprocal causation cannot penetrate its essence.

Living-Experience in the Social Domain

In natural science psychology, the social dimension of human existence has been subject to two extremes: relative neglect and overemphasis. Its relative neglect has resulted from an internalist bias. This has been expressed in a host of ways, ranging from the effort to explain away human behavior based on an individual's unique set of genetic codes and internal neurological processes, to their unconscious mental processes and associated defense mechanisms. Currents of thought within conventional psychology eventually began to cast internalist explanations as committing an individualist or individualistic bias, pointing out its presence in much of the discipline's classic theory and research (e.g., the now famous Vygotskian critique of Piaget, its controversies notwithstanding). In response, culture-oriented forms of psychology (e.g., cultural psychology, cross-cultural psychology, multicultural psychology, indigenous psychologies, and even social and cultural forms of neuroscience) have come on strong, especially since the 1990s. However, in its many reactions to internalist explanations, psychology has too often advanced merely to the point of tacking on externalist explanations to internalist explanations (e.g., "this is your brain on culture"), offering no fundamental challenge to the scientific establishment. Alternatively, it has gone to the other extreme and embraced social, cultural, and/or historical determinism (a problem that we saw in the embarrassment chapter). The vacillation between these two extremes led a dissatisfied Abraham Maslow (1961) to once admonish that psychology cannot be completely subsumed under the auspices of biology and sociology. As he put it, psychology "has its own unique jurisdiction . . . that portion of the psyche which is not a reflection of the outer world or a molding to it. There could be such a thing as a psychological psychology" (p. 6). Sympathetically, phenomenologists have long sought to accurately portray human sociality without succumbing to either of the extremes noted here, both of which precipitate forms of psychologism. In phenomenology, the internalist tendency commits various forms of biologistic psychologism and heads in the direction of solipsism. The externalist reaction commits sociologistic, anthropologistic, and/or historicistic forms of psychologism depending on the nature of the explanations involved.

Human Existence is Co-Existence

In their philosophical introduction to existential phenomenology, Luijpen and Koren (1969) began their chapter on intersubjectivity by noting, "existence is co-existence" (p. 145). By using the term *existence*, Luijpen and Koren were making a supra-empirical assertion. They were not simply noting the obvious empirical fact that every human being happens to live among other human beings. How one *exists* implicates how one's life matters or is "at issue" for a person. Thus, the language of existence draws one into the realm of living-experience. The living meaning-making activity of every human being is interpenetrated with the meaning-making activity of others. On the one hand, Luijpen and Koren (1969) held that the mental life of other persons cannot be subsumed under the meaning-bestowing activity of one's own projects. On the other hand, the "I" is not the sole creator of its own world or the wider cultural world of which it is a part.

Crucially, the relation of existence to co-existence is not incidental. Human being-and-becoming are, in all the major dimensions of existence, being-and-becoming-through-others. This is so much the case that one always finds oneself always already having been involved in the life of others before "taking hold" of one's life as one's own. Each one of us lives in and through a social body, an interpersonal intermediary that is both organic (e.g., entering the world of smoking by learning smoking behavior from others) and inorganic (e.g., living in a world of interhuman instrumentalities like tools, canals, roads, planes, schools, etc.). The living body, because it is not a mere thing of nature, allows the "we" of intersubjective experience to emerge. Stated differently, because the living body is sensitized and resists total objectification, it opens a space for intersubjective life. Our feelings, moods, and values all reflect our time and place in a larger interpersonal theatre of family, culture, and history. Similarly, the relative freedom to act (or lack thereof) depends on the affirming acceptance afforded to the person through their group affiliations, as well as the foundational supports provided by their sociocultural milieu. Cognitively, already at the level of perception, what one senses, localizes, interprets, and identifies from the environment reflects the social world in which one lives. Thus, Luijpen and Koren (1969) observed, the Papuan would not see a "poker," but someone from a culture with fireplaces would because of their social affiliations (p. 148). Here, Luijpen and Koren were building on the work of Remy Kwant (1965).

Remy Kwant on the Interhuman Foundation of Existence

Kwant (1965) began his phenomenology of the social domain by noting that psychology has characteristically treated people in a thing-like fashion since its inception. Even as Wilhelm Wundt, in the founding days of psychology, recognized that consciousness was different enough from objects to require its own research methods (e.g., introspection), he went on to treat consciousness atomistically (e.g., the emphasis on identifying the elements of consciousness). This was due to the influence of the physical sciences upon his approach and the analytic impulse inherent in them. This impulse extended well past Wundt, of course. Behaviorism went even further, and all forms of naturalism in psychology (and the social sciences at large) similarly afforded a primacy to thing knowledge over person knowledge.

Kwant, taking a lead from Husserl (1970), held that the object-primacy of psychology can be traced to the natural attitude. In the natural attitude, the things of the world do not seem capable of hiding any secrets, at least not in the same way or to the same extent as human beings. Unlike people, things can be mastered given enough time. In practical affairs (with the help of science and technology), human beings have been gaining increasing mastery over aspects of the environment. There are exceptions, of course, not the least of which being the current environmental crisis. But these exceptions do not alter the more fundamental sense, pervasive in the natural attitude, that things have more transparency than human beings. The natural attitude tends to hide the world as socioculturally co-constituted by way of interhuman communication. It is to the credit of science that it made the world a problem again, demonstrating that it can expose and unlock nature's many secrets. But science did not make a radical break with the natural attitude and address the foundational issue of constitution. Science (including and especially psychology) took up the constitutional blindness of the natural attitude and, the rise of cultural psychology notwithstanding, has proven itself incapable of fully confronting the interhuman world. Even cultural psychology has yet to look seriously at a methodological alternative properly suited to human psychological life.

The naturalistic attitude also adopted the natural attitude assumption that one can only infer knowledge of other minds from one's own experience. We can call it the *inferential hypothesis*. It states that the possibility of direct, immediate, embodied, intuitive knowledge of others is precluded in advance by the presumption that human beings live behind their eyes, deep within the recesses of the brain. This became the most fundamental expression of the presupposition that object knowledge has more clarity and transparency than intersubjective knowledge in psychology. Kwant offered six refutations of the inferential hypothesis.

1. Kwant noted that this assumption would preclude the possibility of infants, with their fundamental lack of familiarity with the world, from getting to know others or understanding other human beings. They would have nothing to go on.
2. The same kind of problem presents itself with respect to how an older child or adult would ever come to know and understand those who were different from them.
3. Kwant observed that the "inner" and "outer" manifestations of consciousness (thanks to the expressiveness of the living body) are so intermingled that a totally objective comparison of the two would be impossible. As an example, he noted from the psychology of emotion that the suppression of the behavior of joy suppresses much of the joy itself (intimating the James-Lange theory of emotion).
4. Freud and the entire tradition of psychoanalysis has repeatedly demonstrated that other people often know us better than we know ourselves.
5. Heidegger (1962) has similarly shown that the existence of a self-alienated "they" characterizes human comportment in its average everydayness, preceding its modification to become an authentic taking up of one's "ownmost" possibilities (e.g., see pp. 299–311).
6. The spontaneity of human relations excludes the thesis that discursive reasoning lies at the heart of all human interaction. Thinking is first and foremost intelligent behavior before it is thinking put into words, concepts, categories. Theoretical knowledge is a vestment of prereflective and practical behavior and language, making it already social through and through.

Given these refutations, Kwant concluded that the assumption of greater familiarity or clarity regarding objects is unfounded. Psychology developed this unfounded assumption through an intersubjective (interhuman) process: a mutually consenting dialogue among a community of scientists. Kwant further asserted that the interhuman is primary in the constitution of knowledge in general, not just in science. While it is true that humans can engage in deception and are infinitely more complex than the things that surround them, they are nonetheless fundamentally more familiar than objects. To show this, Kwant turned to the issue of meanings' co-constitution. Sense-empiricism has long sought to explain the emergence of meaning in the life of human beings by reducing it to its material bases, blinding itself to the substantive contribution of reason beyond its natural conditions. Meanwhile, the traditions of thought that are commonly labeled rationalistic, idealistic, or intellectualistic have posited (conscious and unconscious) calculative thought as the constitutional source of meaning, overlooking the incarnate nature of human rationality.

Maurice Merleau-Ponty issued a challenge to these traditions by demonstrating how pre-personal, embodied relations with the world ground thought and the global meaning-making process. The pre-predicative engagement of the ego-body or body-subject is involved in the formation of meaning from within a specific historically unfolding sociocultural development. For Kwant, Merleau-Ponty's conception sits at the precipice of a breakthrough, but even his phenomenological investigations failed to expose the essence of the interpersonal in the co-constitution of meaning. In Kwant's view, sense-empiricism, intellectualism, and Merleau-Ponty all ultimately neglect (admittedly, in different ways and to different extents) the primacy of affectively attuned, real-time interhuman encounters lying at the center of the co-constitutional process. In Kwant's assessment, Merleau-Ponty placed too much emphasis on the pre-personal ego-body's historical sociocultural enmeshment in the co-constitution of meaning (committing a kind of inadvertent historicism). As Kwant put it, the culturally colored possibilities of the ego-body are knowable, understandable, and rational to the developing person in the first place because, as a child, they learned of them in ongoing real-life encounters with other persons in the presence of the here-and-now. These possibilities develop in and through affectively mediated, individualized intersubjective engagements, especially attachment relationships. Human beings understand what in their culture is deemed "the human world" because they have already come to understand culture-participating other persons in co-actualizing relationships fit with the loving care required to maintain world-openness, not vice versa (see also, DeRobertis, 2012b; Nameche, 1961; Strasser, 1969, 1986).

The Realization of Human Sociality

For Kwant, experientially immediate being-with-others is thus the origin of world meanings. In other words, while being-with-others can manifest in many forms, a certain kind of being-with-others is the alpha and omega of existence, the foundation and realization of human meaning-making. Kwant spoke of genuine *encounter*, which is embedded with subject-affirming affectivity. Luijpen and Koren (1969) also used the terms *presence* and *dialogue* to express the same phenomenon. When it comes to the living-experience of other human beings, one can gauge the degree of relative intimacy, depth and breadth of meaning, and creative potential involved by the extent to which one is open to the subjectivity of the other. In the mode of general indifference, the subjectivity of the other is leveled. This is a purely functional style of interaction that is affectively dulled. The other is reduced to their predicates without necessarily having to engage in total objectification. Total objectification is more characteristic of hatred. Hating the other is realized by the suppression and rejection of the other's subjectivity, as historical precedents (e.g., the Holocaust) have repeatedly shown.

Social interaction originates in pre-personal forms, but it can elevate to a highly personal level of interaction wherein one sees the other in the full light of their subjectivity. This elevation is realized in certain manifestations of love, but not love interpreted as a mere feeling. Love is realized through empathy and action. As Alfred Adler (1958) noted long ago, "love" means little when it manifests as mere permissiveness or acquiescence. Love is not indifferent to values. It is not indifferent to responsibility and accountability to others, even beyond the I–You dyad. Love points one in the direction of ethical behavior. It beckons a call to action. As Luijpen and Koren (1969) observed, the loving encounter implicates the other's appeal to one's subjectivity. A word, a look, a gesture beckons one to break with ego-centeredness. Love is ultimately a kind of creativity that is mobilized and committed in a way that is intended (consciously or not) to release the best potentials of both the lover and the beloved (May, 1969). It potentiates self-transcendence and mutual self-realization. Love is, to borrow Gabriel Marcel's (1964) term, an experience of *creative fidelity*.

Final Remarks

It is important to note that the material presented in this chapter is not meant to serve as some kind of shortcut for bypassing the rigors of the phenomenological method. The material is offered merely as an opportunity for the reader to develop a better grasp and a heightened sense of what explorations of living-experience look like. It significantly differs from the prefigured conceptualizations of experience that one regularly encounters in natural science psychology. What has been covered here should not be considered as received knowledge. This is why, at the outset of this chapter, I returned to the difficult task of operating under the auspices of the epoché. The epoché has been discussed (both in this text and repeatedly in the extant literature) as a means for phenomenological researchers to circumvent biases emanating from the natural attitude and its naturalistic derivative. But the reader is also reminded that before the epoché was discussed in this capacity, I noted (in Chapter 2) that phenomenological researchers wish to work from what is immediately given rather than from what is intellectually handed down, assumed, or projected into the data. This applies to the material of this chapter as well. The epoché asks the researcher to maintain a circumscribed ignorance, a disciplined openness that facilitates the process of immersing oneself in the worlds of one's research participants. One must resist the impulse to judgment. One must refrain from coming prematurely to conclusions based on what one has brought to the investigation. One must trust in the rigors of the research process. And though it is not typically discussed this way, the epoché also guards the originality of phenomenological description against uncritically taking the work of fellow phenomenologists as gospel. The reader is referred to the work of Sheets-Johnstone (2020, 2022) who, in recent times, has done an exemplary job of showing how this can happen.

Key Terms, Concepts, and Themes

- Paradigmatic/calculative thinking
- "Commonsense" thinking
- Ready-to-hand (practical absorption)
- Un-ready-to-hand (interrupted practical absorption)
- Present-at-hand (disengaged presence)
- Imaginative Thinking
- Divergent thought
- Dwelling
- Narrative thinking
- Unitive consciousness
- Upright posture
- Körper
- Lieb
- Bodily holding sway

- Null/zero point of orientation
- Life space
- Sensing (phenomenological conception)
- "If–then" structure in the co-constitution of things
- Amodal perception (in the co-constitution of an experiential world)
- The living body as contingent possibility
- Non-thetic projects
- Thrownness
- Facticity
- Finitude
- The pre-intentional life of feeling (the experience of being disposed, non-specific sensual feelings, moods)
- Double-value perception in feeling governed (intentionally directed) behavior
- Goals and purposes in the life of feeling
- The intentional life of feeling (the experience of being underway, directed sensual feelings)
- The meta-intentional life of feeling (spiritual feelings, passions, self-transcending ideals in the life of feeling)
- The experience of temporary termination
- Becoming overcome with emotion
- Attitude
- Conviction
- Comportment
- Basic comportment
- Conation/volition
- Willing
- Strivings (and counter-strivings)
- Centrifugal consciousness in striving and willing
- Centripetal consciousness in striving and willing
- Motives
- Willing as a paradoxical phenomenon
- Wishing
- Willfulness/willpower
- Ego-center/proprium
- Human existence as co-existence
- The living body as conduit to intersubjective experience
- The primacy of the interhuman in the constitution of knowledge

- Encounter (presence, dialogue)
- Love
- Epoché

Chapter 6

Standing on the Shoulders of Phenomenology: Living-Experience as a Stepping-Off Point for Existential Psychology

The history of existential psychology is built upon a phenomenological foundation. This was inevitable given the influence of existential–phenomenological philosophers on its development, including the likes of Martin Heidegger, Jean-Paul Sartre, Karl Jaspers, Max Scheler, and many others (e.g., see Binswanger, 1963; Boss, 1963; Frankl, 1969; Laing, 1990; May et al., 1958). These influences notwithstanding, it is also important to note that existentialism and phenomenology are two distinct philosophical traditions, and there have always been existential philosophers and psychologists who were not phenomenologists.

Some existentially-oriented researchers prefer quantitative analysis to qualitative research (e.g., see Greenberg et al., 2014). And in cases where existential psychologists place an overall value and emphasis on qualitative and phenomenological findings, they are not necessarily specialists in phenomenological research. In fact, existential psychologists sometimes object to what they consider too heavy-handed an emphasis on the reduction process in phenomenological analyses. This objection relates (once again) to the existential–phenomenological paradox mentioned in the Preface. Recall, according to this paradox, phenomenology depicts the typological and strives toward the elucidation of essence and the structure of consciousness. Existentialism wants to highlight the unique in its concreteness, expressing the situated reality of the individual.

Existential psychologists sometimes prefer to engage in what Friedman (1991) called "existential pointing to the concrete" (p. 547) in lieu of phenomenological analysis. This "pointing" (admittedly, a vague notion) shares with phenomenology the impetus to circumvent the abstractions of natural science or any other established system of concepts that prefigures the truth about persons in advance of direct, firsthand experience. But existential pointing to the concrete maintains a more concentrated focus on elucidating the experience of individuals as lived amid all the contingencies of their unique situational embeddedness. It resists, even more so, the phenomenological process of progressively stripping away idiosyncratic, incidental meanings as the researcher transitions from the idiographic to the nomothetic level of analysis. The typologies of phenomenological psychology can sometimes appear to existential psychologists as tending toward "essentialism." Yet, one finds a counter-impetus in existential pointing to the concrete that betrays this critical stance, and it is highly phenomenological in spirit (even if this fact is quietly passed over). Existential psychology carries out its analyses by regularly moving back and forth between the unique and "the human." The human condition in general, as a universal, is "reduced" and extrapolated from diverse experiences. The idiographic level of analysis is thus put into dialogue with considerations of the essence of human existence, which is a phenomenological aspiration operating at a very high level of descriptive generalization. Here, I am speaking of existential psychology's characteristic emphasis on existential "givens" or fundamental human concerns.

Fundamental human concerns bring what might be termed the tragic and the ecstatic of psychological life into relief. They (the tragic and the ecstatic) very much exemplify the distinctly human world of experience. Third-force or humanistic psychology has always shared these interests, so they have remained points of convergence between existential and humanistic psychologies. But whereas much of humanistic psychology showed an overall preference (by no means exclusive) for shedding light on the largely overlooked "higher reaches" of human nature (e.g., the ecstatic side; see Maslow, 1971), existential psychology made its mark in large part by representing the darker side of human nature in the third-force movement. Existential psychology has thus become widely known as a branch of psychology that specializes in the study and treatment of challenges inherent in the human condition. This chapter will provide a general overview of select themes from existential psychology as illustrations of its approach to living-experience. Historically, death has figured prominently among these themes. Accordingly, I will anchor the chapter in a phenomenological description of the emergence of death knowledge in human development.

The Unfolding Meaning of Death to a Developing Child

Psychology, under the influence of naturalism, has approached the development of death knowledge from a perspective that is both adultist and scientistic. The developmental study of death knowledge has long been dominated by the question of when children finally learn the "real" meaning of death, which is the meaning that adults ascribe to it. When the question arises as to what exactly that adult meaning consists of, death is framed in the concepts of contemporary biological science and is understood as an essentially biological event (Longbottom and Slaughter, 2018). The entire field of meaning emanating from the child's world is thus constrained in advance of study.

A phenomenological approach admonishes that a researcher must take children's experiences of death on their own terms without prejudgment. That said, the kinds of data collection procedures that have been discussed thus far are not always optimal or perhaps even applicable when studying children. The question of procedures depends on the specific nature of the topic of study and the age of the children under study. The observations of which I will be speaking were not conducted based on formal interviews or protocol writing. I could have collected natural attitude descriptions from adults about the way their children's understandings of death evolved over time. Note, however, that this may have posed the arduous task of negotiating the adults' natural attitude and naturalistic prejudices while always remaining one step removed from the children themselves.

Another strategy is to engage in direct interactions with children and somehow record these interactions for analysis in a non-obtrusive, non-interfering way. Ideally, the researcher would spend time with the children being studied in their day-to-day activities or in play, attending to death-indicative cues and expressions, looking for appropriate times to make relevant inquiries. Observations should be made in situations where children can interact spontaneously. This would provide the most effective avenue for accessing children's viewpoints on their own terms. But the avenue itself guarantees nothing. The epoché is needed to elucidate without distortion. For that matter, all the criteria laid out in Chapter 2 must be met if the research is to be deemed phenomenological. To review, the researcher must suspend judgment, adopting the attitude of circumscribed ignorance characteristic of the epoché. They must turn toward the irreal life of meaning with empathic attunement to the participants' intentional orientation. The aim is to describe the participants' worlds as lived without narrowing one's field of vision in advance by hypothesizing or creatively embellishing. The researcher must attend to the complex, multifaceted whole of the phenomenon under study, noting transformations in its unfolding, using real and imaginative variations to intuit and explicate essential meanings.

Phenomenological psychological research generally requires a minimum of three participants for deriving a general structural description that meets the requirements of good nomothetic human science. But phenomenological psychological inquiry can nonetheless begin before this minimum has been met. Giorgi (2018), for example, discussed the process of using oneself as a source of data, which is a sample of one. Moreover, over the years, he has done single-subject studies in the process of working out his method, the findings of which were deemed general descriptions of situated structures awaiting refinement by the integration of additional analyses (e.g., see Giorgi, 1975, 1985). To be sure, a one-subject study is well suited to the content of the current chapter given the above-noted discussion of existential pointing to the concrete.

In what follows, I will be presenting an observation of one participant: my daughter. The description will be more reliant on second-person perspectivity than usual. The participant is a child, which makes second-person description not only more crucial but also more challenging due to the relative differences between her worldview and my own (as an adult) and our respective ways of expressing ourselves and communicating. Thus, for a project such as this, the adult doing the describing extends themselves out as far as description allows. When points of seemingly impenetrable obscurity are reached, one must acknowledge them as part of the research process. One may collect more data. One may seek out theoretical models for guidance, or one may discontinue the description, offer signposts for potential interpretation, and/or offer one's own preferred interpretations (thus signaling what may turn out to be a decisive transition into hermeneutic territory).

Given the smallness of the sample, what is being presented might be deemed a phenomenological case study. At the very least, it can be considered a phenomenological pilot study. The study focused on approximately a year and a half of my daughter's life. I chronicled my daughter's awakening to the meaning of death from the time it took a spontaneous reflective turn several months before she turned 9.[1] After relevant interactions, I recorded and made working notes of my observations privately on my desktop. The observations stopped just about a week before her 10th birthday. Before presenting these observations, I will begin with a preliminary phenomenological reflection on relevant developmental events prior to that year. I am calling it a preliminary phenomenological reflection because I was not engaged in formal data collection at the time of these events. Accordingly, the description is retrospective.[2] The reader is free to judge the rigor of my description as a matter of course.

Preliminary Phenomenological Reflection

Death makes its presence felt, directly or indirectly, in the sense of vulnerability. The first time I witnessed vulnerability in my daughter was in the moments after her birth. My wife had a scheduled cesarean delivery, and as the doctor was performing the procedure, she exclaimed, "You're all baby!" By this, she was indicating that she was correct in her assumption that natural childbirth was not an option for my wife. She was too small, and my daughter was too big. My daughter, snugly embedded in the womb, was finally "freed" in my eyes. Being a bit claustrophobic, my initial reaction was a projection. I can remember looking at her hands and feet, seeing that they looked slightly contorted, and I wondered if there was a sense of relief on her part. This projection

---

[1] As an aside, Longbottom and Slaughter (2018) astutely observed that estimates of when children learn the "full" adult notion of death (which are based on aggregate data) will vary depending on the nature of the data collection procedures used, the way the data are conceptually analyzed, and what the children in the sample were exposed to in their family and culture. They observed that children learn the meaning of death piecemeal over time, culminating in a biological understanding of death "usually by age 8" (p. 2). Understanding the meaning of death as an abstract concept is estimated at around 10. Using these estimates, my daughter (who has a communication delay) struggled to achieve the same developmental accomplishments as a neurotypical child during the same period of the lifespan. While her early efforts seemed a bit behind the curve, by 10 this was no longer the case. Interestingly, her communication delay made her more vocal in her attempts to clarify meanings than the so-called "average" child, which was a distinct advantage in studying her experience. Phenomenological psychological researchers typically prefer participants who are more disposed to articulate their experiences in as much detail as possible.

[2] Technically speaking, most phenomenological research involves the analysis of retrospective accounts. That is what participants are usually providing in their interviews and protocols. Giorgi (2009) has spoken to this as a potential criticism of phenomenological psychological research and provided refutations of the criticism as damning. As a point of interest, Giorgi used terms like honesty, insight, sufficiency, and adequacy as criteria for judging the veridicality of a retrospective description.

ceased as I watched the nurses clearing her airways. As they slid a small tube down her throat, she was visibly disoriented and uncomfortable, but could do nothing but attempt to swallow and move her head back and forth very slowly. Her extremities moved but not with any great degree of coordination. To what would they be coordinated? The only support to her body was the examination table on her back as she lay there undergoing the procedure. The room was bright, her eyes were not open to see what was happening. I remember feeling distressed and anxious and wanting very much to offer support to her limbs and her body as a whole.

As they finished and started to clean her, the crying began. It made sense to me, transitioning from the warmth of the womb to this bright, cold environment where she was being physically "examined." She was calmed somewhat once gathered up and carried out by the nurse who invited me to accompany her. I did. They swaddled her and put her under a warming lamp. I went to her. The swaddle was calming, but only mildly so. She got an arm free, and I placed my finger in her palm. She grabbed hold, and I remained there for over an hour, speaking softly, finger in hand. From being manipulated rather than held, to then being swaddled, to being swaddled with a finger to hold on to under a warming lamp, her cries incrementally decreased in intensity and frequency, though not altogether.

What lay behind this need for supportive holding and affirming handling? (D. W. Winnicott used these terms, and it seems to me that the justification is self-evident.) Classic psychoanalytic theory called attention to the obtrusive nature of the post-natal environment, and I could see where that came from. But what was far more striking to me was my daughter's sudden separation from her mother and the concomitant loss of intrauterine life's structural integrity. My daughter and my wife were already forming a relationship in utero. My wife would read to her, notice when she would move and how. Toward the end of the pregnancy, my daughter would become active around 4 am every day. This would awaken my wife and she would be forced to get up and watch television. They were already establishing a pattern of intertwined physical functioning. Within moments after the incision, the entire structure of my daughter's embedded harmony was dismantled. The ever-present voice she had become accustomed to hearing was not there. The intertwining was undone. What her birth showed to me was that the original sense of human vulnerability and source of anxiety is the sudden loss of the animate, burgeoning, spatial dimensionality of intrauterine life. For a time, the only environment one has ever known (the intrauterine environment) has a special kind of dimensionality. Given its symbiotic form, it is more pre-personal than what has been previously described as living space in earlier chapters. It is about the quickening of interhuman relationality rather than existential projecting. It is a proximal space alive with sound, voice, movement, and a felt rhythmicity of which one is an inherent part. To be born is to transition to an environment that is unfamiliar, unpredictable, and colored by a loss of primordial form. It is to lose the constant presence of the original environment's animate qualities (sound, voice, and rhythmicity). This is compounded by the emergence of new feelings of discomfort and neediness, as the rhythms of the child's body and the mother's body are no longer "one." This is the situation that undergirds the neonate's first cry.

There is a lot here, and it is all related to dynamics involving the development of prereflective, living (bodily–affective) spacetime. The original meaning of death is the vulnerability of being separated from one's living physical source, the rhythmic, auditory origin of burgeoning spatial dimensionality. The structural dismantling is, metaphorically speaking, akin to the threat of being sucked into the vacuum of space. In existential literature, death has always been characterized as an experience of finitude. But, in its original manifestation, finitude is paradoxically experienced as the threat of a kind of felt infinitude: the sudden appearance of lifeless "infinite" (as in without bounds or boundless) space. The primordial sense of death is the threat of boundarylessness that accompanies the loss of intertwined bodily rhythmicity and the soothing voice that emanates from it.[3] Though it goes unsaid, the implicit awareness of the significance of this loss undergirds the practice of swaddling and the values of those who advocate for early and frequent skin-to-skin contact between mother and child. Neither can be explained away (à la biologism) as a mere release of oxytocin.

The human experience of death may transform in numerous ways as development proceeds, but this basic experience remains a possibility throughout life. In times when I have been lost, especially (but not exclusively) as a child, my anxiety has been incited by a perceptual shift wherein the environment suddenly feels terrifyingly "big" and impersonal. A more pronounced version is characteristic of kenophobia, and sometimes agoraphobics can have similar

[3] The etymological roots of the word "bound" carry connotations not only of the setting of boundaries but also of adjoining and of sound, resounding, and echoing.

experiences. It can also lead to profound, self-transcendent experiences of appreciation (enter the ecstatic). Just a few months ago, I went to see William Shatner speak at a live event. He was asked about his experience going into space. To the audience's surprise, he did not speak like Captain Kirk. Instead, he noted that what we tend to think of as "space," as influenced by books, television, and movie depictions, is wrong. He pointed upward and said, "That, out there, is death." He spoke of its complete blackness and deafening silence, and then recalled looking back at Earth with longing and sadness. He remembered realizing how special his home was, referring to the planet and its inhabitants as "specks." When he returned to Earth, he trembled and wept. He knelt and kissed the ground. He reflected on this moment by noting that this, our home, is an island of life in the void. But, he said, "It is in danger, and what can you do? What can we do? Goodnight."

Speaking of goodnights, the primordial threat of death would repeatedly resurface in my daughter's life every time the sleep cycle beckoned. She not only needed to be lulled into sleep by soothing contact, but she would not remain asleep if contact was broken. Sensing herself slipping away from consciousness or having already fallen into sleep, any sense that she was unsupported by another body would jostle her awake and she would cry. Then, just before her sixth birthday, my daughter started to show signs of being scared to go into a dark room or hallway. This was a curious development. The dark had not been experienced as a threat up to that time. In fact, there had been times when we found my daughter milling around in dark places in the house. She would sometimes invite me into the basement in the dark to play. And why not? The safety of the womb was a darkened environment. Something had changed. But what? How could one know? She would not have been able to speak to her situation.

From what I observed, two things were involved. First, she had just gone through numerous teachers at school (five in one school year, to be precise). Her teacher left for surgery, never returned, and they could not give her a permanent replacement, so it became a revolving door. It was constant change, repeated beginning attachment and separation. The rapid cycling of attachment and separation resulted in some acting out behavior, and the anxiety that it precipitated reactivated her original sense of vulnerability as the loss of intersubjectively mediated structure. And so, each time she was faced with the problem of going into a darkened room or hallway, she sought an intersubjectively mediated solution: "Daddy, will you come with me?"[4]

Second, her language abilities were advancing at that time, leading to increases in rational and imaginative thought (especially the latter). Cognitive advances turned her awareness more forward in time, yielding the living-questioning attitude of "What could be in there?" The development was still somewhat curious. She had never seen a horror movie or watched any form of media that scared her (my wife and I were diligent about monitoring what she saw). In fact, she was the child who was unafraid in Halloween stores, which made my wife and I so proud. She had experienced startles in her life and felt intimidated by things like energetic barking dogs now and then, but little more. Yet, as if on cue, she felt a newfound sense of vulnerability entering a dark place.[5] This is typically interpreted as a "fear" of the dark, but that is not quite accurate. To call it a fear seems justified in that a given darkened place is the objectified, worldly reference point (i.e., the certain "something" about a given locale) for the sense of vulnerability, which is even more salient in cases of phobia. This gives it the appearance of dread and uncanniness (see Heidegger, 1962). But the fact is that the darkness itself (as opposed to snakes, spiders, heights, etc.) is not what threatens. It is what *could* be in the dark that threatens, which is itself unknown, making this "fear" more an experience of anxiety (as we will see in more detail in Chapter 7). At times when I've asked my daughter what she thought was in the dark, her answer was always, "I don't know." When pressed, she would grope for answers, spanning her imagination on-the-spot for "scary things."

A Second-Person Description of a Transition: From "You're Dad Died?" to "Daddy, Please Don't Die."

Shortly before my daughter turned nine, my father came up in conversation. She had not met him because he died shortly before she was born. Realizing that she had met all her other grandparents, she

---

[4] Kopcso and Láng (2023) have recently observed that the fear of death through adolescence remains predominantly the fear of losing significant others. They found that the fear of the dark in adolescence reflected an experience of darkness that is loosened from interpersonal connectivity and is more about uncertainty in general. Nonetheless, they found fear of the dark and the fear of death (with its interpersonal character) continue to be moderately correlated in adolescence even after controlling for trait anxiety. Their findings thus converge with the current exploration.

[5] Aggregate data indicates that fear of the dark peaks between ages four and six (Orgilés & Espada, 2008).

asked, "Who is your Dad?" "He died before you were born," I replied. "Your dad died?" "Yes," I said. She sat in silence. My daughter never experienced a death before. No one in her life had ever died. It is safe to say that the notion of death, death as an idea, was foreign to her (she had not even seen any Disney films up to that time, which often introduce the notion of death to kids). She did not say anything, and we moved on. But the issue was not settled. She did not just pass it by and forget about it. The meaning of death was now an issue for her and, as I would find out, she was determined to understand what death meant. She would struggle to gain some clarity on the issue for some time. Upon seeing this, I set out to begin formal data collection.

I began when the issue resurfaced a couple of months later. A friend of mine had not visited in a long time, and when he came up in conversation, my daughter asked, "Did he die?" I was initially taken aback by the question. I realized she had been holding on to the issue of death, wanting some clarity of understanding. I answered in the negative and told her that he was just busy. The whole thing gave me pause. Could she have wondered if he had really passed away? I did not get that sense, but it was only an impression. Could I trust it? Did she employ the concept of death in those terms, or was this a beginning effort to grasp at its meaning? About a month later, it would be clear that the latter was the case. After an episode of acting out, during which she could tell my wife was upset with her, she and my wife patched things up and began to get on as usual. As they started to talk, my daughter interrupted and asked, "You're a new mom?" Caught off guard, my wife inquired, "What?" My daughter continued, "The old mom died?" My daughter was indeed in the process of striving to comprehend the meaning of death. But it did not have the meaning ascribed to it in textbooks. At this early stage in its development, the conceptual meaning of death was that of absence as a counterpoint to the characteristic fullness of presence. I wondered, did my prior interaction sow the seeds of this idea in her mind? It seemed inevitable. To the extent that I influenced her efforts at understanding, this was a concrete illustration of how the evolving meaning of death in human development is interpersonally co-constituted. Still, I would not take full credit for the evolving meaning as it emerged at that time. She had put two and two together, as it were. For my daughter, death was juxtaposed to life and the possibility of phenomena like revitalization, renewal, and rebirth. Death was part of a broader pattern of living interaction. It represented the outmoded, the not altogether left behind, the absent that lies behind the present.

Her questioning continued as she attempted to firm up the semiotic boundaries of death a bit. Watching a television show, she wondered where certain characters were during a particular scene and asked my wife and I, "Did they die?" The question has considerable force when posed to those who live with the "adult" meaning of death every day. My wife was taken aback. "What?! Nooooo." I felt the impact as well. I had to stop and ask myself again, does death simply mean to her that someone is not around or not coming around anymore, that they have simply severed a relationship, or does she believe that they are literally no more? I caught myself amid the event and returned to the attitude of the epoché. If I adopted an adultist posture and simply assumed that she was making errors, there would be nothing worthy of description.

I remained open and waited for death to come up again. A few days later, we were playing "dolls." At one point, she inquired about one of her older "LOL" dolls that was put away in another room in an LOL bin my wife created for organizational purposes. My daughter looked at us inquisitively and asked, "The old one died? The LOL dolls all died?" She was checking her meaning of death, seeking out feedback on whether she correctly understood death (as the absent counterpoint to full presence). The dolls, having human form, were an opportunity for her that would not have been afforded by other toys. Subsequent inquires focused on death as, first and foremost, a human phenomenon. One day, from seemingly out of nowhere, she asked, "Dead people don't talk?" "Correct," I answered. "They're all alone without their Mom?" "Yep." The conversation stopped. She moved on. I let it marinate. I reflected and returned to my working notes. What did she just reveal to me? Her inquiry demonstrated that for her human life is about having a communicative engagement with others, the ability to reach out and connect, to be heard. Death is *not* having a voice or the ability to connect to one's source, the life giver in every sense of the word: the primary caregiver (traditionally, "mom"). Here, the original meaning of death as articulated in my preliminary reflection returned, but with a modification. Rather than the mother's absent voice taking center stage, the voice of the one who has slipped into the void had come to the fore. The infant cry (the first voice) was outmoded by the word. The loss of this now-talking voice assumed salience over the loss of the mother's voice.

About a month went by and another attempt to apply her working notion of death emerged. This time the subject was not human. In play, certain dolls had pets, one named Rufus. She turned to my wife and me and declared, "Rufus, her dog, died! She went to the other home." Again, death was deemed a not altogether left behind absence that is counterpoint to the characteristic fullness of presence. Yet, days later she uttered an unprecedented kind of sentence. She noted that one of her dolls died and followed up with, "She's gone forever." It appeared to be her first effort to capture the essence of what we adults refer to as the irreversibility of death. She was trying to understand a new dimension of meaning by trying out a novel phrase in conversation with us (which I can only assume she heard somewhere, perhaps in a television show or movie). The process is quite unlike a formal hypothesis test. How could one derive evidence to support it? The doll still existed, so "hard reality" offered only disconfirmation of death's irreversibility. Yet, she would lend credence to this evolving notion based on an implicit faith in others. The whole process further illustrated the importance of the subject–subject relationship and dialogue in the evolving meaning of death.

For a time, my daughter lived with death as an ambiguous phenomenon, moving back and forth between death as a not altogether left behind counterpoint to presence and death as implicating an as yet to be determined "forever." While watching a cartoon, she noted of an absent character, "She died." My wife replied, "She didn't die." My daughter responded, "Yes she did; she just went to the other home." One day, while waiting for the school bus, I stepped on a spotted lanternfly. My daughter took an intense interest and said, "Daddy, make it deader!" Apparently, death was not an all-or-nothing phenomenon. Death could be graded, a conceptual marker of relative degrees of destruction. The less a being displays the form characteristic of its manner of presence, the more it is dead. On another occasion, I attempted to turn a dead horseshoe crab over with my boot. The tip of the shell cracked off and she said, "You're killing it!" My wife then said, "It's already dead," to which my daughter responded, "No, the shell. He's killing the shell." For her life and death did not have a strict either/or structure. A few days later, I discovered a dead baby bird on my lawn. My daughter was outside with me. As I picked it up to put it in the garbage, she was gravely concerned and exclaimed, "Oh no! She's dead! We've got to help her and bring her back." She pressed on with the notion of reviving the bird a couple of times before I got to the trash bin. Interestingly, the inquisitive nature of her interactions with me on the way to the trash and the ease with which she let the matter go once I got there made me doubt that she was merely unable to perceive the irreversibility of death. After all, living organisms sometimes die and are indeed revived. She and I had been watching a lot of animal rescue videos on the internet. Sometimes the rescuers were able to save the animals through careful and timely intervention, sometimes not. But the animals in the videos, admittedly in bad shape, were still alive. Sometimes they looked dead. They were sometimes listless. She knew this and attempted to apply what she had been watching to the dead bird situation. Still, life and death remained intertwined. About a week later, in play with her dolls, I overheard her note, "My mommy died; she went to South America."

I sat and mulled over my working notes. After the bird scenario, I sensed my daughter to be in a time of tentative transition in her as yet fluid notion of death. At this point, it seemed like the right time to make a pointed inquiry. I took a few days to think up strategies and finally decided to just come out and ask her the meaning of death in plain terms out of context. Up to this point, death had always come up spontaneously in real or fantasied contexts wherein it was relevant. I wondered what I would get if I made a pointed inquiry that was not context bound (knowingly risking the imposition of an adultist prejudice). One day during a lull in our play, I asked her, "Hey, what does it mean, "Somebody died"?" She answered, "They're not alive anymore." "What does it mean that they're not alive anymore?" "They're dead and turned into a zombie." Here again, there was evidence of a categorical distinction, but without crystal-clear, distinct boundaries. Deadness had a connection to life: the living dead or *un*dead. Zombies were a staple in the cartoon world that she was familiar with and represented death in quasi-living terms. For her, death was basically understood on life's terms, as a kind of counterpart to life. It represented a conceptual polarity that is not totally and completely other than life. Death was not a pure nil but the lessening of life-indicative phenomena. Still, it would not be accurate to glibly maintain that she was incapable of processing the finality and irreversibility of death. Later that same day we were watching *Frozen*. There was a "death" scene. She observed, "She got frozen and now she's dead." Knowing the tactics of Disney movies, I suspected that this might be undone by a kiss or some other form of magic, so I said, "Well, maybe." She snapped back at me. "No!" I was taken aback. It was as if she was irritated with me for contradicting the fruit of her intellectual labor. The character was indeed revived from the dead, and I felt bad for my daughter. How confusing this must be! But she was unfazed. Without my realizing it, her grasp of the distinction between fantasy and reality was firm enough to handle the discordant information (though I did wonder about younger children and how difficult this whole process must be).

Strangely enough, the inability to meet Bo Diddley became a significant pivot point in the unfolding meaning of death for my daughter. My daughter loves early rock-and-roll, and somehow or other, it was Bo Diddley above all other artists that captured her imagination. She always loved his music and videos more than any other musician. She would sit on my lap and watch Bo Diddley videos for an hour or more on a semi-regular basis. One day, she asked, "How old is Bo Diddley?" "He would be 95, but he died," I answered. "Well, I think he's alive sometimes," she replied. "What do you mean?" "Sometimes when I watch the videos, I joke with Bo Diddley!" For my daughter, his life force was maintained, meaning that it was made present by the combination of his virtual presence on the screen and her own living engagement of that virtual presence. The combination of her real presence to his virtual presence meant that he was not definitively dead and gone. I said nothing more. I watched the video and rubbed her back. She then asked, "Is Bo Diddley dead or alive?" I maintained that he died a few years ago. She replied, "I think he's gonna be alive, I'm gonna go to his house and rock out. He's the king of rock." This was a significant interaction because I could sense that she was feeling the hard reality of Bo Diddley being gone and not wanting to sit with the disappointment of not being able to ever see him in person. The very next day she heard his music emanating from another room in the house and she said, "That's Bo Diddley! He's my big brother, but he's been dead for a long time though." She was working on acceptance. She was in the process of managing the pain of inevitable death. It was not easy. A few months later she started forming a marked conceptual connection between aging and death. Over the course of that month she was becoming increasingly attuned to the lines in the faces of others (including my own). In a conversation with my wife, she exclaimed, "I don't want to get old and crinkly!" About a month later, in play, she narrated, "She got old and she died."

Three months before my daughter's tenth birthday her struggle to comprehend and accept the hard reality of death's closed-door policy came to a head. She asked again, "Is Bo Diddley dead?" "Yes," I answered. "But I want to meet him!" "I know. He's from a long time ago," I said. "Is he gonna turn into a zombie?" "No." "Just a skeleton?" "Yes." "But what if I get old and turn into a skeleton?" "We all do. Everybody dies eventually. It's just part of life," I said. Her image of death was still graded. Its relative manifestation was gauged by the perceived magnitude of deterioration apparent in a being's physical form and potential for reciprocating engagement with its surroundings. Emphasis was given to those characteristics that support sensation and movement (the most salient characteristics of animal life). When it came to these qualities, there was a hierarchy of functioning: first humans, then zombies, then skeletons. Death maintained a connection with the trace of material reality. The total invisibility and non-materiality of death was difficult to envision, both conceptually and emotionally. (It made me think of the process of discovering zero in mathematics.) Conceptually, there was the problem of holding "something" in mind (someone's death) that is conveyed through a slow, visible, physical process of deterioration but eventually results in the total negation of the person's presence. Emotionally, there was the problem of having to confront the suffering that is realized as this total negation is brought into view.

Almost a month later, her questioning about death started spanning the world of Bo Diddley's contemporaries. "Dad, how about Ronnie Dawson? Is he dead?" "Yes." "Little Richard?" "Yes." "Awww!" She was visibly upset. Death was clearly being lived as the impossibility of face-to-face encounter. The power of death was conveyed through the realization of those whom she would never be able to meet. My wife entered the room. She turned to her and said, "Well, if they are dead, I am not going to worry about it. Right, Mommy?" She clearly *was* worried, but she knew she had no choice but to figure out a way to persevere. A few days later, a potential solution emerged. She continued her questioning, only this time moving forward in history, away from Bo Diddley's contemporaries. "Is Devo alive?" "Yes." "Yes!" "How about Cheryl Crow?" "Yes." "Yes!" The power of death was contained by the realization that there were many other of her favorite musicians that she could meet.

Implicit in our dialogue was a mutual understanding of the unconditional nature of death. The only way to manage it was to focus one's attention on the possibilities of life (ironically, the very realities that had to be "overcome" to progress in her understanding of death). I was heartened by the thought, "My daughter is growing up." I saw great potential in this imaginative turnaround. On June 4, 2023, my daughter learned that when you get older, you can move out. To this, she had an interesting and revealing follow-up: "When you get old, are you going to die?" The "you" in this question was ambiguous. Was she referring to herself, to me, to people in general? "Yes, everyone does. It's just a part of life." June 5, snuggling up for bedtime, my daughter burrowed into my chest and said, "Daddy, please don't die." "Okay," I said.

A little over a week later (June 15), my daughter asked a question that supported what conventional research has suggested is the most difficult aspect of death for children to process: its biology (Sigelman & Rider, 2018). While walking along a waterfront, I noticed two large dead fish floating ashore close to the place we were approaching and pointed them out. "A couple of dead fish. See them?" She asked, "Do dead fish have ears?" "Yes," I responded. "Do they hear?" "No." In the naturalistic attitude, this question would be deemed nothing more than an error, an inability to properly grasp an organ's basis of operation. The fact that a dead ear cannot hear is biology 101. But this interpretation hides the world of the developing child. The interpretation presupposes that my daughter was asking about the function of a set of mechanisms from anatomy and physiology. But that conceptualization originates from the adult world, not that of the child. For my daughter, to "have ears" was to be able to hear. And, phenomenologically, is this not the case? As parts of the living body (Lieb), ears hear. Adults sometimes speak in ways that reveal the interpenetration of form and function characteristic of the living, sensing body, as in "I only have eyes for you." To "have eyes" is to see. Likewise, for my daughter, to have ears was to hear. Our interaction was a phase in the development of her understandings of both death and the body, and any natural science psychologist would agree, of course. But the naturalistic interpretation remains blind to the true nature of that learning. What the interaction with my daughter revealed was that understanding the "biological" aspect of death experientially entails learning to juxtapose Körper to Lieb. My daughter was not making an inquiry into the nature of anatomy and physiology from a place of sheer ignorance. She was asking from the perspective of one who lives the body. Our interaction was the beginning of a learning process, the result of which would be a more multifaceted understanding of the body's two-sidedness. Adding the relative truth of Körper (to see the body as a corpse) involved a differentiation from the more fundamental reality of the body directly experienced as living, as Lieb.

This exchange also marked what I considered to be a return to the material presented in the preliminary reflection above. My daughter's question was very specific, asked without hesitation, focused only on the ears, and when the exchange was done, she moved on. Nothing else about the body of that animal mattered. Why the ears? Animals cannot talk, and she knew this well, but they can nonetheless hear other members of their species. So, what was the meaning of this very pointed inquiry? Later that day, I asked my daughter why she asked about the ears of all things. Predictably, she could not say. My description reached a point of relative obscurity. If I were to thus end my description with an interpretation based on what I have observed (e.g., "They're all alone without their mom"), I would venture that the primordial meaning of death as related to sound was still with her: the absence of sound as the loss of a core medium for connecting to the (m)other.

A General Structural Description of the Evolving Meaning of Death to a Young Child

The sense of death is lived in a prereflective, bodily–affective way long before it is cognized. It begins not as the perception of a distinct possibility, but as the sense of vulnerability that accompanies a particular experience of loss and resultant disorientation. The original meaning of death is the vulnerability that accompanies having been separated from the living, burgeoning spatial dimensionality of the womb. Death is primordially the threat that issues from the loss of intertwined bodily rhythmicity and the soothing voice that emanates from that intertwining. Death is thus at its core a social phenomenon.

As a child becomes reflectively aware of death and attempts to clarify it, its initial meaning becomes that of absence as a counterpoint to the characteristic fullness of presence. Having learned about absence and presence in the context of a given childrearing environment, the evolving meaning of death is thus a matter of interpersonal co-constitution. The social aspects of death only expand and diversify as development unfolds. New meanings of death emerge. But the developing structure of the death concept does not progress in a linear way, as if through a stepwise series of discrete logical achievements, with each new understanding striking the former from the record so that a newer, more objective viewpoint can take its place. The structural meaning of death takes shape in a fluid, metamorphosizing, global/encompassing manner. Death, when seen as a distinctly human phenomenon, eventually becomes the possibility of not having a voice, of lacking the ability to vocally reach out and connect to the other who is deemed the source of life (i.e., the primary caregiver). This is an integrative reorganization of the above-noted themes of separation, loss, disorientation, absence, and especially, voice (the infant cry is transformed by the appearance of words).

A novel constituent is introduced when the child is eventually exposed to some notion of "forever." At first, they will be unable to grasp its full import for understanding death, but they will nonetheless trust in the fact that its meaning needs to be worked out as a reflection of their faith in those who have exposed them to the idea. The process is a further example of the primacy of the subject–subject relationship in the unfolding meaning of death. For a time, the child will live with death as an ambiguous phenomenon, moving back and forth between death as a not altogether left behind counterpoint to presence and death as implicating an as-yet to be determined forever. Again, nonlinearity is the rule. Death does not evolve on an all-or-nothing basis. In terms of the phenomenological origin of experience, death becomes a semiotic marker for relative degrees of the destruction of form. But life and death remained intertwined. The child lives with an ambiguous, tentative, or open-categorical distinction, one that does not have crystal-clear, distinct boundaries. Death is basically understood on life's terms. Life, the constant state of the child, has perceptual salience over death. As a result, in the child's world, a life force may be experienced with a more pronounced sense of reality if they invest their living presence to various indicators of virtual presence.

A change in the overall meaning of death will eventually occur as the developing child starts to forge a conceptual connection between aging and death. The beginning integration of the temporal process of dying gives death a more pronounced biological significance. Still, the image of death will remain graded to varying extents. Its relative manifestation is gauged by the perceived magnitude of deterioration apparent in a being's physical form and correlative potential for sensorimotor engagement with its surroundings. With the attentional turn toward the dying process, the child's attempts to understand death become a struggle to distinguish a corpse from the living body, what phenomenologists call Körper and Lieb. The latter is the primordial and paramount reality of the body for the developing child. (As adults who have learned to habitually reinterpret the body in objectivized terms, we tend to look down at the child's difficulty separating life from the body, but it is we who have unwittingly adopted a set of sedimented naturalistic meanings and are guilty of bias.) Again, in confrontation with the dying process, the social dimension of death's overall structural meaning remains essential. The power of death is conveyed through the realization that there are others who will never again be "fully" present, in the here-and-now, in the flesh. The most threatening, intimidating aspect of death becomes its now consciously recognized potential for permanent interpersonal separation.

Implications and Horizons

The above analysis displayed overlap with textbook accounts of death knowledge in the sense that issues like death's finality, irreversibility, universality, and biological aspects posed a challenge in the process of the unfolding. But the analysis also diverged from the conventional approach to death knowledge in its approach and results. Natural scientific psychology has recast the development of death knowledge as a series of select, discrete theoretical abstractions constructed from the researcher's vantagepoint. It then unwittingly projected them back into its investigations as its conceptual foundation, thereby marginalizing the perspective of its research participants. In contrast, the phenomenology presented here bracketed (not doubted or deleted) "accepted" meanings of death. The description showed that the evolving meaning of death is not reducible to the progressive amelioration of a series of logical errors. The results culminated in the elucidation of a coherent, dynamic structure (the yield of an eidetic phenomenological reduction) that contextualized conventionally accepted meanings of death in the experiential life of the developing person. The structure consisted of themes that may act as springboards for studies of death awareness in the context of living-experience. For example, one might study the various ways in which the sense of death is lived in a prereflective, bodily–affective way before it is cognized. One might examine how separation, loss, disorientation, absence, and voice play out in their relationship to death knowledge in varying contexts over the course of the lifespan. Themes such as these have, in fact, come up in various forms of existential (Greenberg et al., 2014) and existential–phenomenological research (e.g., Leone et al., 2013; Sánchez Guerrero, 2021; Weitkamp et al., 2016; Woodgate et al., 2021).

When reflecting on the above findings, it is interesting to note that early manifestations of the meaning of death do not vanish as development unfolds and death knowledge goes through metamorphoses. This is demonstrable in relation to the social core of the development of death knowledge, which I found striking during the research process. From the earliest days, death awareness was found to be tightly affiliated with separation, imbuing death with a meaning structure framed in terms of the absence of the other. Death came to signify relative absence as a counterpoint to the fullness of presence and then became a marker for relative degrees of deterioration in a life form. In these manifestations, death is not an absolute end. And even in the adult world, these meanings live on, though they contradict the biological definition of death. All one need consider is the importance that adults attach to both remembrance and notions of an afterlife. Regarding the former, human beings see themselves as living on through their life's work, their successors, and through their children. Correlatively, they place a high value on the remembrance of others, visiting graves, regularly observing Memorial Day, donning their automobiles with "9/11-Never Forget" stickers, waving POW/MIA ("You are not forgotten") flags, and so forth. Regarding notions of an afterlife, human beings throughout time have organized their lives around mythologies of a hereafter, reincarnation, and so forth. Seeing loved ones again is what gives a heaven its meaning. An afterlife of solitary confinement is no "life" worth living. It is not a heaven at all, but a hell.

Across the lifespan, the power of death is felt most prominently in the realization that there are others who will never again be "fully" present, in the here-and-now, in the flesh. The perceived potential for permanent interpersonal separation is the apex manifestation of death. Interestingly, the social dimension of death knowledge threaded throughout the above results became a point of controversy in existential–phenomenological philosophy, and it has yet to fully infiltrate the ranks of existential psychology. Influenced by the seminal work of Martin Heidegger (1962), existential philosophy and psychology have long maintained that human beings enhance the richness and significance of their lives by conscientiously recognizing its time-limited nature (i.e., being cognizant of one's inevitable death).

Given what we have seen above, this suggests that one would come to reverse the structure of death as it is lived in childhood, transitioning from an understanding of death-in-the-light-of-life to life-in-the-light-of-death. For Heidegger, the nature of this reversal involved appropriating death as one's ownmost possibility. Emmanuel Levinas (1969) took issue with this idea as harboring an individualist bias that betrays living-experience. For Levinas, death is so unlike everything else in the universe that it cannot be apprehended or appropriated as one of a person's distinct possibilities (something we saw in my daughter's struggles to understand the death concept). He thus shifted from speaking about death as the possibility of impossibility, to death as the impossibility of possibility. In line with the current results, death, for Levinas, is made meaningful as the loss of the other. Peperzak (1993) summarized Levinas's position as follows: "If death—and suffering—were a purely individual event, it would be meaningless; its having a place within the horizon of the metaphysical (i.e., intersubjective) relation saves it from absurdity" (p. 189). Delaying the death of the other and delaying one's own death for the sake of the other become the decisive factors in determining life's richness and significance (see also DeRobertis, 2021b).

Select Themes of Living-Experience in Psychologies of Existence

As noted, the threat of nonbeing is a central theme in existential psychology. Being and the threat of nonbeing, the awareness of life and of death, constitute a fundamental antinomy of the human condition. The specter of death perpetually looms behind the wonder of life, a situation that cannot be undone or "solved" as just another of life's many problems. It is a fixture of the human situation that "trickles down," so to speak, into still other antinomies or *existential dichotomies*, to borrow Erich Fromm's (1947) terminology. The phenomenological description presented above exhibited features that expose several of these. For example, the results simultaneously highlight the inherently social nature of human existence as well as the potential for isolation and loneliness throughout the lifespan. The unsettling, unwelcome feelings aroused in the process of learning about death and the strategies employed to offset these feelings (i.e., focus on the possibilities inherent in one's life situation) illustrate the fact that the joy of living always coexists alongside the human capacity for suffering. Implicit in the need for these strategies is the human need for a meaningful life, which is always lived amid the threat of meaninglessness.

The fact that possibilities are always tethered to one's specific set of contingent life circumstances illustrates yet another antinomy: freedom is limited, always existing within the context of a thrown situation, aspects over which one will have little to no control. As human development unfolds, these antinomies will give rise to more advanced existential issues, for which there was no analogue in the results presented here. For instance, with burgeoning freedom comes burgeoning responsibility for one's own existence and those valued others with whom one identifies. This implicates the struggles involved in forming an identity and envisioning a personal destiny. Here, another antinomy presents itself: Since the process of fulfilling one's destiny can never be completed once and for all, experiences of completion are always relative, occurring against the background of fundamental existential incompletion.

Isolation and Loneliness

The early history of existential psychology is closely allied to psychoanalytic thought. From Ludwig Binswanger, Medard Boss, and Viktor Frankl in Europe to Rollo May in the United States, existential psychologists have long been influenced by depth psychology. Erich Fromm, who was born in Germany and moved to New York in 1934, is an important figure in this lineage. In his discussion of existential dichotomies, Fromm observed that every human being is always simultaneously related and alone. Human beings live their lives amid others from womb to tomb, and we share a human nature. Happiness depends on the solidarity human beings feel with their fellows, including those of past and future generations (see Fromm, 1947, p. 43). Human beings detest isolation and loneliness (consider the fact that the way to frighten even a hardened criminal is to threaten them with solitary confinement). Nonetheless, every person is inevitably also alone by virtue of their uniqueness as an individual. Aloneness is also experienced in having to make judgments and decisions in life for oneself by the power of one's own reason (as opposed to mere conformity and obedience).

This paradoxical existential reality generates existential loneliness, which is part of the human condition. It is not identical to the many manifestations of loneliness human beings experience across cultures that are due to contingent circumstances (e.g., the COVID-19 lockdown, the sudden transition to telecommuting, etc.). Nonetheless, existential isolation and loneliness lie at the core of all contingent manifestations of loneliness. Cultures have generated myriad conditions that bring about unpleasant, sometimes crushing feelings of isolation and loneliness throughout history. Fromm, influenced in no small measure by Alfred Adler, underscored the various ways that contemporary human societies emphasize superficial, consumeristic *having* over *being* (and thus, over genuine being-with-others). Compounding the situation, these cultures are governed by power structures that disenfranchise masses of people. While these conditions may be temporary and remediable (at least theoretically), existential aloneness always remains a fact of life and must be faced courageously. Fromm suggested various means to accomplish this life task (e.g., relatedness, transcendence, rootedness, identity, and a frame of orientation, see DeRobertis, 2021b).

Several years later, Rollo May (1953) explored the historical, sociocultural, and psychological situation of loneliness, speaking of human beings as having been made over in the image of behaviorism.

May described human beings as hollow, self-alienated, and suffering from an anxiety of powerlessness and emptiness. Considering the inherently social nature of human existence (e.g., see his work on the inextricable, essential relationship between will and love; May, 1969), May observed that human beings have become outer-directed to a fault. Once the self is "emptied," all that is left is trying to be accepted by others at all costs, thereby precluding the possibility of genuine interpersonal experiences. This results in fundamentally lonely people who have no concrete, viable means for courageously confronting existential loneliness. Quite the contrary, human culture has come to pose formidable obstacles to finding such courage.

Yalom (1980) chose the term "existential isolation" to discuss this area of inquiry. He too distinguished between its contingent and existential manifestations, referring to the latter as "separation from the world" (p. 355). What he described in that text (without saying it explicitly) is what Paul Tillich (1980) called the fundamental estrangement of the human condition. Tillich considered estrangement to be the core contradiction underlying human life, experience, and thought: the fact of being simultaneously close to and separated from others, the world, and even oneself. We are not free to merely actualize the totality of our potentials and desires at will. Human becoming is a never-ending process, sometimes arduous, ambiguous, befuddling and forever proximal, incomplete, fallible, and marred by error and missteps (we will return to this below). Estrangement always leaves an opening for uncertainty and insecurity. There is no God's-eye view of anything (or anyone, even oneself). Husserl thus famously referred to phenomenology's infinite tasks to express the fact that in every aspect of life, the hard work of learning is never done.

Having said this, it is important to note that what is being discussed here is not the description of a mere cognitive limitation. Estrangement describes living-experience under the conditions of finite time and space. Stated more strongly, it describes the fundamental experience of human finitude itself. To be sure, Tillich's notion of estrangement is supported by the phenomenological description offered in this chapter. As Moustakas (1961) once observed, "Loneliness has a developmental history beginning in infancy, when the need for contact is temporarily unresolved" (p. 35).

It is no less important to note that to acknowledge the reality of estrangement does not necessitate a turn to sheer relativism, skepticism, or nihilism. Moustakas (1961), for example, observed that there is a terror in loneliness that nonetheless opens new vistas of experience and new possibilities for meaning-making. Everything depends on how we orient ourselves toward our estrangement and the horizons it reveals. As Fromm (1947) has shown, one might shrink before them or frustratedly resort to self-defeating and/or destructive behaviors. But one might also seize the opportunity to adopt a creative posture toward one's existential situation. What Moustakas discovered was that existential loneliness could become a conduit for establishing more meaningful relationships with oneself, others, and the world, bringing the specialness of everything and every moment into view.

Suffering

Existential isolation and loneliness speak to the inevitability of suffering in human existence. Again, however, it is important not to succumb to stereotypes of existentialism. Suffering is a fact of life. But, as Levinas (1969) has observed, to live is first and foremost to enjoy life. As he put it, to despair of life makes sense only because, originally, life is happiness. It is not correct to say that happiness is an absence of suffering. Suffering is a failing of happiness.

In psychology, Viktor Frankl's work echoes Levinas's philosophy (see DeRobertis & Iuculano, 2005). According to Frankl, suffering is a medium for the realization of attitudinal values. Attitudinal values are one of three classes of values, the other two being creative values and experiential values. The realization of these three kinds of values are the ways in which human life is made meaningful. They are the ways in which the human need for a meaningful life—the will-to-meaning—is fulfilled (Frankl, 1986). Creative values are active and actional in nature, and experiential values are passive and receptive. Attitudinal values lie in between, neither primarily active nor totally passive. A change of attitude is an act, but an act of a more restricted nature than those that actualize a creative value, which can result in manifold forms of doing. Attitudinal values make their special contribution to life's meaning by altering the way one experiences the inevitable, the unalterable. Another way of saying this is that attitudinal values are uniquely suited as a response to human limitation (we will return to this below).

Because suffering is inevitable, a basic life task involves learning how to suffer and make it worthwhile, how to make suffering grist for the mill rather than an excuse to languish or otherwise become a detriment or hindrance to becoming. Frankl further observed that suffering has an inherent meaning beyond its inevitability as a task of human living. Suffering (especially when it is self-conscious and courageously accepted as a fact of life) establishes a definitive experiential tension between a person's real and ideal self. It brings to light what one does not want, who they do not want to be. This, by implication, raises the question of what and who one does want to be. Grief, boredom, and "trouble" in life all precipitate this tension. They each represent a call to a higher state of development and fulfillment, the need to realize potentials, to actualize possibilities.

Thus, despite the discomfort of human suffering, despite it being an unwelcome and inevitable fact of life, human beings mature in suffering and grow because of it. Frankl noted that the more people try to ignore or flee from facing pain, death, and disquieting emotions like guilt, the more they entangle themselves in complicated, prolonged suffering. The hasty impulse to eliminate suffering rather than attending closely to what it is telling us about our lives truncates the meaning-making process and the overall process of human becoming. Frankl noted that one can be sick without being able to "suffer" in the most human, dignified, sense of that term: as a conduit to meaningful living. Conversely, one can suffer without being sick. The actualization of attitudinal values results in the ennoblement of human suffering. On this view, suffering is simply human before it is pathological. That is, it is existential and should be recognized as such before it is reduced to psychodynamics.

Meaninglessness

Taking his argument a step further, Frankl (1986) held that the "narcotization" of suffering (along with other factors, as we will see) was actually contributing to a mass sense of contemporary meaninglessness (p. 110). But here, too, meaninglessness has an existential significance beyond its historical, sociocultural emergence in the psychology of modern life. Its existentiality has a threefold foundation. First, the need for a sense of meaning in life and meaninglessness as its inevitable dark side are essential features of human existence and cannot be reduced to the sum of their empirical contingencies. Second (and already implied), along with the inevitability of suffering comes moments of radical discouragement in life, resulting in a global sense of life's futility. Meaninglessness lingers in the background of human living, at times rising up to capture focal attention. When it does erupt, it is a distinctly human form of consciousness, an existential form of suffering. Just as it is uniquely human to question the meaning of existence, so too is the confrontation with its possible meaninglessness. Third, life's moments of meaningfulness and meaninglessness always belong to someone, a unique person participating in the co-constitution of a world. Life cannot take on structural meaning or appear meaningless on its own. The formation and loss of meaning are dimensions of personal existence. Frankl consistently admonished that it is not we who ought to be asking "life" what its meaning is. Rather, life is "asking" the question of *us*, "What will you do with what you have been dealt?"

Again, however, one must take care not to succumb to superficial stereotypes. Frankl was careful to speak of the "apparent" meaninglessness of life (Frankl, 1978, p. 98). Just as suffering was noted to be a failing of happiness, forming a permanent paradox of life, the same holds true for the relationship between meaning and meaninglessness. As Tillich (1980) has shown, phenomenologically speaking, the act of accepting a futile, perhaps even largely wasted or "meaningless" life is a meaningful act. This reveals the dependence of the experience of meaninglessness on the experience of meaning. In a situation of utter despair, the threat of nonbeing is felt to be victorious over one's faith in existence (that is, the possibility of finding meaning and happiness in life). But feeling presupposes being. Phenomenologically, from the vantagepoint of living-experience, nonbeing is always dependent on the being it negates despite its ultimate unknowability and mystery (see Tillich, p. 55).

Of course, this does not change the profound effect that meaninglessness can have on human life. Frankl and other existential psychologists, especially the aforementioned Rollo May, spent much of their careers studying meaninglessness and its relationship to contemporary social problems. Frankl (1978) observed that political and technological advances have generated societies that allow human beings on a mass scale to turn their focal attention to what lies beyond the satisfaction of basic needs, to have the time to sit and think about the life they are leading. In other words, contemporary life has allowed existential concerns, like the need for a meaningful life, to shift from ground to figure in human living. But as this transformation occurred, the threat of meaninglessness became an increasing problem. Frankl referred to it as the *existential vacuum*. It is an existential problem of meaninglessness, exacerbated by empirical conditions, which sometimes gives rise to pathological manifestations (he sometimes spoke of a "mass neurosis" to refer to the latter; Frankl, 1978, p. 26).

Experiences of meaninglessness, though painful, are not necessarily pathological. But they can exacerbate pathology as conventionally understood. They are an inherent feature of human existence, and as a form of suffering can even lead to growth when faced courageously and productively. Frankl spoke of existential anxiety over the apparent meaninglessness of human existence as a spiritual, noölogical sort of crisis (think of Abraham Maslow's notion of meta-pathology). When it results in the development of psychopathological manifestations, it unleashes lust and aggression (he referred to these as the will-to-pleasure and will-to-power, and Rollo May similarly observed that spiritual emptiness reduces love to lust and will to aggression; see May, 1969).

Frankl described the existential vacuum of contemporary life as a lived form of nihilism, and he differentiated it from the academic nihilism that is sometimes associated with existential literature and philosophy. He spoke of the latter as a mere "theoretical" nihilism (Frankl, 1967, p. 121). It is less a disciplined description of the existential vacuum and more a symptom of a broader contemporary cultural crisis of meaning. Certain strands of existentialism, forgetful of their phenomenological foundations, unwittingly align themselves with naturalism when they embrace nihilism. They portray human beings as asking about the meaning of life as if they were looking through a window on the world interpreted as but a heap of matter. But theoretical nihilism when put to the test and lived out results in actual despair. Frankl considered academic nihilism to be another contributor to the existential vacuum. In addition to narcotization and academic nihilism, he cited numerous other sources of contemporary meaninglessness:

- A fatalistic attitude toward life that reflects the reductionism of naturalistic social science (e.g., seeing human beings as an anonymous reflection of "nature" and "nurture"; e.g., see Frankl, 1986, p. xxvii)
- An ephemeral attitude toward life, living in the shadow of the disillusionment instantiated by the second world war
- Conformist, collectivist thinking (or herd mentality), and fanaticism embraced as false solutions to the existential problem of meaninglessness
- The boredom that resulted from the forces of automation, which both alienated human beings from production and generated unprecedented free time
- The mass adoption of machine metaphors, as contemporary life is repeatedly made over again in the image of technologies (e.g., "I was multitasking")

- Retirement/unemployment "neurosis" (one might also add empty nest syndrome)
- "Executive's disease" (Frankl, 1967, p. 125), which consists of chronic boredom and compensatory prestige consumption

Limitation

Popular caricatures of existential philosophy and psychology tend to assign an exaggerated importance to human freedom. They conveniently gloss over the fact that existential thought conscientiously recognizes the ever-present reality of human limitation. Freedom is not arbitrariness. Freedom of the will is always thrown into a world not of its own choosing. It is contingent freedom, tied to factical conditions. Human freedom is always situated and always operates within a limited scope of openness to self, other, and world. The concept of limited freedom distinguishes the existential perspective from anthropological reductionism and idealism alike (Knowles, 1986).

Stated in more concrete terms, the concept of limited freedom implies that human beings can imaginatively call forth or envision more than they can make happen (i.e., actualize) at any given time in life. What is imaginable is not always realizable at a moment's notice or at all depending on the nature of one's circumstances. Situations are always only more or less under our command and control. Herein lies the existential background of the Serenity prayer: "God, grant me the serenity to accept the things I cannot change, the courage to change the things I can, and the wisdom to know the difference." Frankl's distinction between the realization of creative and attitudinal values is rooted in this perceived difference.

That freedom is always constrained by conditions is only half the story of human limitation. As Fromm (1947) observed, human freedom implicates a "freedom for" this or that possibility for being-and-becoming (i.e., not just a "freedom from" an otherwise limiting circumstance). This presents another layer of complexity and potential adversity in this area. When turning attention toward what possibilities one is free to actualize, one is suddenly confronted with the expanse of human possibility alongside the realities of responsibility. Situated agents are responsible for their decisions. This can be an exhilarating realization when the outcomes of responsibility result in enhanced feelings of empowerment, especially where one can feel proud of one's accomplishments. Further, as May (1969) has shown, responsibility that is actualized in the form of devotion and commitment unlocks the creative potentials of the imagination. But decision-making in life is prone to the experience of "groundlessness" in the sense of having no predetermined plan for a person's life, at least none that are set in stone.

We must participate in the establishment of the ground of our existence by the positive use of freedom in making the decisions that establish our life's trajectories. But our cultural embeddedness notwithstanding, there is ultimately no one to determine our destiny and identity but ourselves. It is we who give our lives the final stamp of approval. We bequeath it its definitive form (unless we allow for conformity and obedience to determine who we become, thus sacrificing the very process of existence itself). Decision-making also involves moments of indecision. When life's decisions become difficult or have tremendous consequences, the person of conscience (admittedly, not everyone is) suddenly discovers a tremendous weight of responsibility, especially given the time-limited nature of existence. Responsible decision-making can feel daunting, even paralyzing. The "dizzying" anxiety of groundlessness (see Kierkegaard, 1980) results from the simultaneous experience of the expanse of possibilities, personal responsibility, and the time-limited nature of life. Here, I am reminded of the desperation that my students sometimes feel when they cannot settle on a major. They feel like the goal of finishing school is getting away from them, that their friends are moving on without them, that they are missing out on life (calling forth echoes of death). But groundlessness is not wholly negative. As Kirk Schneider (2015) has observed, "most of our joys, breakthroughs, and liberations are . . . traceable to our suspension in the groundlessness of existence!" (p. 408). He went on:

> And this is where presence and the sense of awe, or the humility and wonder, sense of adventure toward living become so central to human vitality. I believe what Kierkegaard is saying, and Tillich, Rank, Becker, Laing, and others have elaborated, is that by staying present to our sense of groundlessness (the "truth" or "angst" of the human situation), grappling with it, learning how to coexist with and even revel in its many dimensions, we can become paradoxical selves; fluidly centered, many dimensional yet (ironically) grounded individuals—individuals who find "ground within the groundless." (p. 5)

Incompletion

That human life is lived through the exercise of limited freedom means that existence is not furnished to us in advance by the combined forces of so-called "nature" and "nurture." Life must be lived out in a participatory manner, as a series of ongoing relationships and projects. Human life is a perpetual unfolding, a process of becoming. Potentials must be realized; possibilities must be actualized. What and who we are must be enacted and brought into being. Just as contemporary cultures have afforded many human beings the luxury of contemplating the meaning of their lives, so too have they furnished them the opportunity to forge personal identities by the ongoing process of fulfilling individual destinies (Erikson, 1968; May, 1981).

As Maslow (1943, 1954, 1971) observed, human beings, when afforded the resources needed to rise above basic need gratification, will desire more advanced states of "perfection" or "completion" (to use Alfred Adler's (1979) terminology) for which many terms have been used over the years (e.g., self-realization, self-actualization, self-transcendence, self-fulfillment, happiness, eudaimonia, self-cultivation, and so forth). Of course, how human beings handle the desire for completion can vary greatly. And even under the best of circumstances, the process of becoming presents one with an everchanging set of challenges throughout the lifespan. Some approach these challenges head-on with great courage, striving, and success, while others do not. In either case, the fact is that we often figure out what we wish to do and who we wish to be by a sometimes arduous process of elimination (i.e., trying out alternatives and ruling them out until we finally settle on a committed lifestyle that feels satisfying). This can seem like a waste of time, but we cannot simply forgo process. We must live life on life's terms.

Assuming we have a vision of who we wish to become (or at least feel efficacious in the process of developing such a vision), our desire and our ability to envision possibilities will always exceed what we can realistically actualize and achieve in the time that we have been given. Here, we are confronted with the hard reality of human incompletion. This is especially pronounced in the experience of persons of conscience and those who are really striving to thrive in life. The striving to nurture the relationships and projects that we hold dear is worth it because it is how we sustain and enrich the meaning of our lives. Still, we will never be able to see many of our most prized creative endeavors to fruition. This is a tragic dimension of existence and another source of human suffering.

Another of the ways that incompletion gives rise to human suffering is existential guilt. The struggle for completion has it fair share of ambiguity, confusion, setbacks, failures, and regrets. This brings into view the anguish of mistakes made in the time-limited unfolding of life (ringing out still more echoes of death underlying the decision-making process). Existential guilt is one of the names given to this anguish. Existential guilt is rooted in the nature of human existence itself. It is not reducible to the violation of cultural-bound prohibitions; nor is it synonymous with neurotic guilt, which is growth-stifling, counter-productive, and held in place by defense mechanisms. Existential guilt emanates from the awareness of being a responsible agent in a time-limited situation where there are "always more" possibilities for being-and-becoming to realize. It transitions to the forefront of awareness with considerable force when a person can see clearly that they have been forgetful of the time-limited nature of existence (implying one's finitude and inevitable death) and become complacent by acts of omission or commission perceived as a "waste" of time. Existential guilt has thus been described as an ontological call to conscience (Heidegger, 1962), a beckoning for the person to reverse course and responsibly take ownership of their possibilities for being-and-becoming. It has also been described as the awareness of our fundamental indebtedness or being "in arrears" to the life we have been given (e.g., Boss, 1963, p. 48).

Having said this, it is important to note that existential guilt is not exclusive to those who are consciously trying to live life to the fullest. Neither is existential guilt the result of "perfectionism," which would give it a pathological (sometimes dubbed "neurotic") character, again limiting its emergence to certain segments of the population at large. Existential guilt is human. Finally, existential guilt is not limited to being a response to mere thoughtlessness, laziness, complacency, or oversight. Existential guilt is no less rooted in the inescapable reality of human evil. Thus, Tillich (1980), referring to what he called the anxiety of guilt and condemnation, described existential guilt as follows:

> A profound ambiguity between good and evil permeates everything [one] does, because it permeates personal being as such. Nonbeing is mixed with being in . . . moral self-affirmation . . . . The awareness of this ambiguity is the feeling of guilt. (p. 52)

Final Remarks

Before bringing this chapter to a close, it should be noted that what has been presented here focused on the tragic themes that have allowed existential psychology to make its distinctive mark on psychology. In the middle of the 20th century, existential psychology brought these themes to the humanistic tradition of psychology, ensuring that the darker side of human psychological life was properly represented. It resulted in the perspective that we now know as existential–humanistic psychology. But the scope of existential psychology extends beyond the tragic as well. Existential psychology has always had significant overlap with various forms of humanistic psychology and is not restricted to the tragic. As part of their comprehensive views of personality, Erich Fromm, Rollo May, and Viktor Frankl also wrote about love, fulfillment, meaning-in-life, willing, freedom, the creative potential inherent in responsibility, identity, destiny, and other topics (see DeRobertis, 2021b). This trend continues today. As we saw earlier, Kirk Schneider, one of the more renowned representatives of the existential school of thought in psychology, has been writing on the topics of life-enhancing anxiety and awe (see Schneider, 2004, 2009, 2023).

Existential psychology has an enduring relevance given the prominent challenges of our time. These include (but are not limited to) the following:

- Corporatizing, consumeristic cultures of planned obsolescence
- Our reliance on rapidly changing technologies
- The climate crisis
- The disruptive effects of globalization
- Pandemic disease
- Global violence
- The dislocation of peoples
- The exploitation and trafficking of vulnerable populations
- Children living in poverty
- Increasing needs for a growing population of the elderly (including centenarians)
- Political distrust and a looming sense of chaos
- Political polarization
- The spread of hate groups
- An unprecedented mass media misinformation machine

Considering these challenges, one cannot help but notice that virtually all of them involve high, potentially overwhelming levels of change, unfolding at a speed unprecedented in history. This will test and embattle our personal and interpersonal capacities for consolidating productive strategies for dealing with those challenges related to the human condition. These issues evoke the primal fear of nonbeing by threatening the dissolution of familiar, predictable ways of living. Change, the confrontation with the unknown and uncertain, and the feeling of real or impending chaos, all tend to make people panic. They are, in fact, generating a growing number of people who are increasingly uneasy and vulnerable to the spread of fear- and hate-evoking rhetoric that promotes false solutions to their discomfort. It disposes them to compensatory mechanisms to simulate the feeling of control. It is no wonder that Tillich (1980) noted that existential anxieties (and those dysfunctional attempts to compensate for them) tend to peak as cultures begin to disintegrate.

Ideally, contemporary existential psychology would be able to help instill a new sense of meaning and courageous resolve that resists the tendency toward authoritarian collectivism. I am wagering that the only way that this could come to pass is if we were somehow or other able to generate a conduit for the most rational and imaginative of those left and right of center to see clearly that we are all facing the same core existential dilemmas—an "existential reconnect," if you will. But we need this on a grand scale. In other words, we need an applied existential sociocultural–political psychology (marketed correctly and backed by a formidable database). Even more problematic, this cannot be accomplished solely at an academic level. It must be experiential, as Kirk Schneider (2020) has rightly observed. The problem is, how would we be able to see to its efficacy given what we are up against: the seemingly normal human distain for cognitive dissonance, compounded by the 24/7 influence of a mass media machine that throws fuel on the fires of our contemporary situation by the deliberate spread of misinformation and attitude inoculation.

Key Terms, Concepts, and Themes

- The animate, burgeoning spatial dimensionality of intrauterine life
- The inherent sociality of death anxiety
- Death and the human voice
- The multidimensional, ambiguous meaning of death in human development

- Death-in-the-light-of-life
- *Lieb* and *Körper* in a child's understanding of death
- Life-in-the-light-of-death
- Existential dichotomies
- Isolation and loneliness
- Having and being
- The fundamental estrangement of the human condition
- Inevitable human suffering
- Attitudinal values
- Creative values
- Experiential values
- The will-to-meaning
- Meaninglessness
- The existential vacuum
- Spiritual/noölogical crises (meta-pathology)
- Spiritual emptiness
- Lived nihilism
- Academic/theoretical nihilism
- A fatalistic attitude toward life
- An ephemeral attitude toward life
- Conformist, collectivist thinking (herd mentality)
- Fanaticism
- Contemporary boredom
- Machine metaphors and self-alienation
- Retirement/unemployment "neurosis"
- Empty nest syndrome
- "Executive's disease"
- Human limitation
- Groundless existence
- Responsibility
- Fundamental incompletion
- Existential guilt

Chapter 7

The Phenomenology of Anxiety: Anxiety as Existential, Psychological, and Pathological

The phenomenological reflection presented early in Chapter 6 began with the observation that death makes its presence felt, directly or indirectly, in the sense of vulnerability. Feeling vulnerable to danger is an experience of threat, which can manifest itself in different forms. At the highest level of generality, one can distinguish between two of its forms: anxiety and fear. Chapter 6 dealt with the most fundamental (existential) manifestations of vulnerability, which relate more to anxiety than fear. This distinction calls for further discussion. Thus, as a follow-up, this chapter will expand upon the nature of anxiety from an existential–phenomenological perspective.

Anxiety is a highly significant, if not central theme in existential–phenomenological psychology, especially in broader domains of study (i.e., personality, social psychology) and in applied psychology. Any capable professional working in the field of applied psychology is aware, to a greater or lesser degree, of the pervasiveness of anxiety in psychopathology. Anxiety is a problematic feature of conditions ranging from mild nicotine withdrawal to schizophrenia. The fact that anxiety disorders are the most common form of psychological disorder in the world forces one to agree, in some measure, with Erik Craig's (1988) statement that "Anxiety is very important for psychotherapists, at least for those who are open to acknowledging and understanding its presence in their own lives, for it provides them with a genuine basis for understanding, to some degree, the suffering of persons who solicit their care" (p. 10).

We have all experienced anxiety at one time or another. In this respect, the phenomenon is familiar to us. Yet, the meanings of anxiety and its unique role in human existence have proved to be elusive and difficult issues for natural science psychology to deal with. Researchers and clinicians alike have long debated the psychology of anxiety

(Fischer, 1991). In 1955, Gordon W. Allport spoke insightfully to some of the inadequacies he saw at the root of the difficulties encountered in the psychology of anxiety:

> It is true that psychology, thanks to Freud, has not neglected the problem of anxiety—at least not the type of anxiety aroused by feelings of guilt and fear of punishment. But psychology has had little to say about the dread of nonbeing (death) and still less about the anxiety over the apparent meaninglessness of existence . . . . Because current psychology is one-sided in its treatment of anxiety it falls short also in its view of striving and courage. (p. 80)

To be sure, striving and courage were not the only anxiety-related phenomena affected by this one-sided treatment. Phenomena such as joy and fear were also affected by this same one-sidedness, as Paul Tillich demonstrated so well in his *The Courage To Be* (1980). According to Tillich, the difficulties encountered in investigating and illuminating anxiety in psychology can be understood, in part, as a breakdown in the dialogue between the various disciplines in which the human way of being is an "object" of study. Tillich noted that psychology, in attempting to escape from any reliance on philosophy for its theoretical foundations, took its presuppositions about human existence unreflectively from medicine and lost touch with "that world which precedes [formalized] knowledge" (Merleau-Ponty, 1962, p. ix). That world is the lifeworld, the world of direct experience upon which "the whole universe of science is built" (p. viii). The existential foundations needed to guide psychological investigation and observation were covered over. As Tillich (1980) put it:

> Medicine, above all psychotherapy and psychoanalysis, often claims that healing anxiety is its task because all anxiety is pathological. Healing consists in removing anxiety altogether, for anxiety is sickness, mostly in a psychosomatic, sometimes only in a psychological sense. All forms of anxiety can be healed and since there is no ontological root of anxiety there is no existential anxiety. (pp. 70–77)

Medicine and psychology need a philosophical–anthropological doctrine of humanity to fulfill their theoretical tasks, says Tillich, and this cannot be developed without the permanent cooperation of all those disciplines whose central concern is the study of human life. Thanks to existential phenomenology, psychology has a conceptual avenue to reconnect with its philosophical foundations and thus make the contributions needed to achieve a more diversified, well-rounded understanding of the phenomenon of anxiety. The phenomenological method of systematically and rigorously describing (rather than explaining away) phenomena under the auspices of the epoché has provided an approach to anxiety that undercuts the subject–object dichotomy. It is this kind of approach to anxiety that has made it possible for phenomenological philosophers and psychologists to acquaint us with anxiety in its various living forms.

Philosophical–Anthropological Meanings of Anxiety: Anxiety's Existential Foundations

An insight that is basic to a phenomenological approach to anxiety is that anxiety is *not* fear. "Fear . . . can be objectivated, and the person can stand outside and look at it" (May, 1958a, p. 51). Anxiety, on the other hand, cannot be objectified. Anxiety has no object as such. Yet, fear and anxiety cannot be separated. Fear has its root in anxiety. Fear is anxiety that has been given an object. As Heidegger (1962) once put it, fear is anxiety that has "fallen into the world" (p. 234). Anxiety and fear "are immanent within each other. The sting of fear is anxiety, and anxiety strives toward fear" (Tillich, 1980, p. 37). This, of course, is question-begging. What is the nature of this "sting"? What gives rise to it?

Anxiety has "nothing" (literally no-thing) as its "object." When one is anxious, the inherent no-thing-ness of our existence is implicated (Heidegger, 1962, p. 231). That is one of two meanings of the word "nothingness" as it is used in existential phenomenology. This first meaning pertains to a threat to that which simultaneously *is* and is *non-objectifiable* (i.e., the illuminating world-openness of human presence). Here, nothingness denotes the characteristically human subjective potential to distantiate itself from all that is encountered and related to in life. It is the ability to differentiate oneself from the "hard" reality that is present to one's consciousness at any given time. As Wren (1965) noted, this meaning of nothingness is not a synonym for annihilation. Quite the contrary, human no-thing-ness does not do away with beings at all but rather gives them "room to breathe," so to speak (p. 46).

This insight was not completely novel in Heidegger's work. One can find its basis in the philosophies of Aristotle and St. Thomas Aquinas, who held that human subjectivity is radically different from everything else in creation due to its ability to separate an object's form from its matter and "take in" or intellectually appropriate the former without the latter. After Heidegger, the distancing characteristic of human world-openness reappeared in Sartre's (2018) writings on nihilation, Erwin Straus's studies of upright posture (Straus, 1966), Helmuth Plessner's (1964) studies of imitation in human expression, and Paul Ricoeur's (1973) work on distanciation in hermeneutic phenomenology. All these works describe ways in which living no-thing-ness as a modicum of productive distancing allows human worlds of meaning and value to emerge. However, since our existence has a finite and fallible character, the ability to co-form and responsibly stand by these meanings and values is not immune to threat. It is here that the potential for anxiety presents itself. Several of anxiety's primordial typological forms were presented as broad (existential) themes of living-experience in Chapter 6. Existential–phenomenological psychologists refer to existential anxiety when the freedom to participate in and co-actualize the relationships and projects that we identify with our existence collide with universal conditions of finitude and estrangement. As we have seen, these include the awareness of death (implicit or explicit), isolation, meaninglessness, and any situation where the striving for fulfillment has come to the precipice of human limitation; this also includes the realization of inevitable human suffering and incompletion (the latter of which gives rise to the anxiety known as existential guilt).

These themes expose the other meaning of the word nothingness in existential phenomenology: "the absolutely unknown 'after death,' the nonbeing which remains nonbeing even if it is filled with images of our present experience" (Tillich, 1980, p. 38). The finite nature of existence, which poses an ultimate threat to one's being-in-the-world, cannot be objectified or made a thing either. But here nothingness does not refer primarily to that which *is* (i.e., one's being-and-becoming). Rather, the emphasis shifts to the more commonly known meaning of annihilation. In this light, anxiety can be described as the experience of a threat to a person's non-objectifiable existence by the possibility of nonbeing. It is an ontological characteristic of being human. This being the case, anxiety cannot simply be eliminated. It must be faced to be "overcome" (Tillich, 1980, p. 39). Non-existence poses an ultimate threat to existence, which thereby threatens to block one's openness to the future out of apprehension. Explicated in this way, anxiety can be said to be existential, not pathological. Nor is it the case that existential anxieties can be reduced to the status of psychological, and nothing but psychological, phenomena. Uncovering the psychological meanings of anxiety is a distinct, but not separate, endeavor (some of these meanings were explored in Chapter 6 in the sections on isolation and loneliness, meaninglessness, and also in the final remarks). To be sure, the psychology of anxiety presents its own set of complications, as human beings are not typically conscious or reflectively aware of death. This does not alter the ever-present reality of finitude, of course. Thus, an existential–phenomenological psychology of anxiety is of necessity a "depth" psychology, as it were. As Wren (1965) noted, Heidegger established the basis for this perspective with his notion of fallenness:

> The fact that many or even most [people] are largely ignorant of death, especially in its ontological significations, does not argue against the fact that Dasein is basically a being towards death, but rather illustrates this fact through the phenomenon of fallenness. Dasein seeks to evade this possibility of its own impossibility. Recognizing its possibility of no longer being-in-the-world, it evades or flees from this possibility by absorbing itself into the world . . . . Its fallenness, therefore, is one of the most powerful illustrations of the otherness of its destiny, i.e., that it is progressing towards absolute Nothingness. (pp. 20–21)

Psychological Meanings of Anxiety

Whereas in a philosophical–anthropological (i.e., existential) investigation of anxiety one is focused on the fundamental characteristics of human existence as such, a psychological investigation of the meaning of anxiety allows us to focus more on factually contingent (i.e., context relative) meanings of anxiety (Boss, 1963). We all experience everyday anxieties that are neither profound enough to be considered existential nor desperate enough to be considered pathological. Anxiety, at its core, is elicited by the threat of nonbeing, and this precipitates existential anxieties. But human beings are also threatened with the loss of particular values that they embrace as central to their existence throughout their lives that do not rise to the level of an existential concern (May, 1979). Nonetheless, the threat of non-existence remains implicit as anxiety's foundational backdrop. As Tillich (1980) put it:

> Anxiety, if not modified by the fear of an object, anxiety in its nakedness, is always the anxiety of ultimate nonbeing.

> Immediately seen, anxiety is the painful feeling of not being able to deal with the threat of a special situation. But a more exact analysis shows that in the anxiety about any special situation anxiety about the human situation as such is implied. It is the anxiety of not being able to preserve one's own being which underlies every fear and is the frightening element in it. (p. 38)

Developmental Foundations

That anxiety is originally and primordially a life-and-death issue in the fullest sense can be observed at the outset of human development in infancy. To quote Knowles (1986):

> . . . We . . . identify the issue of hope or openness as being the central issue of the first stage of development. We also pointed to the fundamental nature of this issue; it is an issue of life and death. If the infant is not cared for or is cared for in an inadequate manner, the consequence is death. (p. 25)

With birth, the infant is no longer "sheltered within the world of the womb from any direct contact with the larger world" (Schachtel, 1959, p. 49). The infant is no longer attached to and embedded within the mother and must deal with the psychological and physiological demands of its new state of being. A new and heightened awareness of the world arises along with a new and heightened awareness of oneself as vulnerable and dependent upon others for survival. The infant becomes aware of the "closeness" of death as a possibility inherent in human existence (Knowles, 1986, p. 25). This can readily be seen in grossly neglected infants who in perceiving the world as uninviting lack "an invitation to live," become lethargic, and die (p. 29). Thus, it is not surprising to note that except for old age, the period between birth and the first two weeks of life has the highest mortality rate than any other period in the lifespan.

Ernest G. Schachtel (1959), thus, described anxiety as "originally and often also later on connected with leaving embeddedness or the threat of separation from embeddedness . . ." (p. 49). While the basic situation of what Schachtel called embeddedness is the intrauterine situation, the term is also used to refer to any state characterized by habit, predictability, routine, or "automatic" behavior (p. 52). Anxiety occurs at the point where some emerging potentiality or possibility faces the individual, but this very possibility involves the destruction of a present security. Still another way in which leaving the state of embeddedness may evoke anxiety becomes possible after early childhood. This is the anxiety over the possibility of not being able to emerge from one's embeddedness. This situation usually arises when a child has a guardian who does not want the child to become independent. The guardian's own need to stay embedded in the relationship with the child instills anxiety in the child over the possibility of leaving embeddedness. This situation gives rise to the child's becoming anxious in the face of the possibility of not being able to strive and grow (Schachtel, 1959, p. 49). While the original or basic anxiety associated with leaving embeddedness remains present for the child, it has transformed, and a new, different anxious situation has emerged.

In either case, anxiety is the experience of a threat to personal being-and-becoming, the organization and development of the situated self (May, 1953). An existential precondition for the psychological experience of anxiety is the fact human beings constitute and signify who they are as persons in the concrete and contingent day-to-day relationships and projects through which they attempt to achieve a greater sense of completion in life (Fischer, 1991). Anxiety ensues when one senses the emergence of a threat to this process and, thus, puts one's sense of "value as a self" in peril (May, 1958a, p. 51). Where anxiety is evoked by the possibility of leaving embeddedness, the self-understanding one has developed thus far is threatened. Who one is invested in being or not being is now in jeopardy. In other words, the kind of person one wants to continue to be or continue not being has been rendered uncertain. Where anxiety is evoked by the possibility of not being able to leave embeddedness, the capacity to fulfill new meanings in the actualization of one's unfolding self-understanding is threatened. Who one is invested in becoming is now in jeopardy (i.e., the kind of person one wants to become has been rendered uncertain).

Threat Response: Two Typological Variations

According to Fischer (1989), the psychological meaning of anxiety revolves around a newfound inability to move forward with one's life undividedly. This experience, this threat of coming undone, announces itself in an anxious body (e.g., muscle tension, butterflies in the stomach, weakness in the knees, strained breathing, etc.). However, these indicators do not guarantee that the person will seek out the source of the problem at hand. In fact, usually, one will try to turn away from what one's body is announcing, as it is uncomfortable. The person will flee from the discomfort by focusing on the particulars of the situation they are in with a flurry of action (often aggressive), sometimes attacking others or disparaging themselves. In other words, the person may or may not allow the body to communicate the meaning of the anxious situation, giving rise to two typological variants. In the first, the person will avoid anxiety, preferring instead to deal with objects of fear (see also, May, 1953). In the second variant, the anxious person will face the anxiety, explore its conflicting meanings, responsibly appropriate the ambiguity, and work toward a resolution that lends itself to a personal transformation. Stated differently, the anxious situation becomes the occasion for an event of *existential learning* (see DeRobertis, 2017).

Rollo May (1977) has written extensively on the divergence that characterizes these typological variations. As he described it, by preferring to preoccupy themselves with objects of fear (real or fantasized), a person may construct walls around themselves as a protection from anxiety. The outcome, however, would be that they inadvertently "shrink up" (i.e., constrict) their being-and-becoming-in-the-world (p. 381). This strategy for lessening anxiety curtails the development of self, truncates self-realization, and depletes and weakens the structure of the personality. Anxiety is evaded, but the price paid is the surrender of personal autonomy, the impoverishment of one's thinking and feeling capacities, and the curtailing of one's capacity to relate to other people. Attempts to blot out and avoid anxiety destroy the originality of the person. That is, they erode the creative power that stands at the heart of personality. Anxiety avoidance diminishes the person's ability to productively utilize their cognitive and affective resources for being with others. It lessens the person's capacity to evaluate experience realistically, even to the point of obfuscating what emanates from the world-pole of self-world interaction and what is projected on to the world by the self. May described this typological variation as tending toward a general dissolution of the self, which embattles the self-realization process (see p. 383).

The constriction of the personality as a means for avoiding conflict and anxiety-creating situations is contrasted with those instances in which individuals actively seek to realize their creative potentials for being-and-becoming by accepting (if not welcoming) a modicum of anxiety (May, 1977). In everyday discourse, this is sometimes referred to as leaving one's "comfort zone." May cited the developmental research of Torrance (e.g., 1966), who observed that children who are more creative seek out rather than avoid anxiety-creating situations.

They explore more, learn more, and have more potential for growth as a result. Of course, many factors are involved here, including the intensity of the anxiety, its duration, and the personal and social resources of the person. Whereas social-learning/social-cognitive theorists speak of resourcefulness in terms of self-efficacy, May (1977) focused on the Adlerian notion of the creative power of the person to productively transform the anxious situation (as he put it, human beings are "mammals with imagination"; see p. 389).

For May, the person who can face their anxiety in a transformative manner possesses the ability to both fully experience gaps between their expectations and reality and effectively integrate their expectations into reality without distortion. This, he held, is the hallmark of the productive–creative typology, as it might be called. Susceptibility to anxiety and creative ability emerge as two sides of the same capacity. Thus, May concluded, "*The positive aspects of selfhood develop as the individual confronts, moves through, and overcomes anxiety-creating experiences*" (May, 1977, p. 393; emphasis in original). In stark contrast, where the avoidance of anxiety has become persistent and developed into "neurotic anxiety," the cleavage between one's expectations and reality has become a seemingly unresolvable conundrum and a contradiction (p. 390). Expectation and reality cannot be reconciled, which may escalate to the point of requiring reality distorting and/or denying defenses. Here we have reached the conceptual bridge that crosses over into the problem of pathological anxiety.

The Foundations of Pathological Anxiety

According to Tillich, pathological anxiety is the consequence of a failure on some level of awareness to face and "take upon oneself" (i.e., creatively and productively appropriate) an existential anxiety that has manifested itself in a person's life. Existential anxieties, as we saw previously, cannot be simply remedied or "cured." To disavow this fact is to condemn oneself to a life of running from reality, which can only result in failure and suffering. As Tillich (1980) put it, "Anxiety turns us toward courage, because the other alternative is despair (hopelessness)"; (p. 66). The persistent inability to face existential anxiety gives anxiety its pathological character and marks the beginning of the flight into what has traditionally been referred to as "neurosis" or psychosis (the former term is antiquated,[1] but will be used throughout this chapter to avoid diverging into a terminological discussion).

The flight from existential anxiety is thus the precondition for the emergence of pathological anxiety. This does not, of course, mean that all pathology is the result of one's having contemplated the possibility of dying. Human beings are sensitive to nonbeing in varying degrees through the finite, limited aspects of their lives for a variety of reasons (e.g., inherent disposition, trauma, learning, and even the striving to achieve higher states of development). The person suffering from pathological anxiety has a "greater sensitivity to nonbeing" and consequently to the experience of threat when compared to the average person (Tillich, 1980, p. 68). As Tillich put it:

> The average person keeps . . . away from . . . extreme situations by dealing courageously with concrete objects of fear. Usually not aware of nonbeing and anxiety in the depth of [their] personality, [their] fragmentary self-affirmation is not fixed and defended against an overwhelming threat of anxiety. [They are] adjusted to reality in many more directions than the neurotic . . . superior in extensity, but . . . lacking in the intensity which can make the neurotic creative. Anxiety does not drive [the average person] to the construction of imaginary worlds. The neurotic is sick and needs healing because of the conflict . . . with reality. In this conflict [the neurotic person] is hurt by reality which permanently penetrates the castle of . . . defense and the imaginary world behind it. (pp. 68–69)

In neurosis, a limited, fixed self-affirmation saves one from the intolerable impact of anxiety but simultaneously constrains and more or less hobbles the personality by putting it at loggerheads with reality. This, in turn, inevitably sets the person up for another intolerable attack of anxiety and the need to reengage or bolster their defenses. In this sense, one can be said to be "self-estranged," at odds with one's essential nature and with the reality that harbors what the individual can't face. "Some or many . . . potentialities are not admitted to actualization, because [the] actualization of [one's] being implies the acceptance of nonbeing and

---

[1] The term neurosis is rooted in the assumptions of neurological reductionism. For more on this, see van den Berg (1961), who suggested the term *sociosis* as a superior alternative.

its anxiety" (p. 66). The neurotic "surrenders a part of [their] potentialities in order to save what is left" (p. 66). Thus, we see an idealized and unrealistic security, perfection, or certitude in the neurotic personality that is defended and guarded in a compulsory way with great tenacity (see Horney, 1950). But the neurotic person's defensive posture only serves to perpetuate their anxiety. They are now always guarding against the danger of having their defenses destroyed, which would make them less able to avoid the threat of nonbeing that is sensed throughout the depths of their personality.

Psychosis is the most aberrant form of despair. One's self-affirmation and sense of self as such are weakened to the point where they have been called into question in toto (rather than on a merely restricted basis). R. D. Laing (1990) described this situation as follows:

> Tillich . . . writes: 'Neurosis is the way of avoiding non-being by avoiding being.' The trouble is that the individual may find that the pretence has been in the pretending and that, in a more real way than [they] had bargained for, actually lapsed into that very state of non-being [they] so much dreaded, in which [they have] become stripped of [their] sense of autonomy, reality, life, identity, and from which [they] may not find it possible to regain [a] foothold 'in' life again by the simple repetition of [their] name. (p. 111)

As all of one's neurotic defenses against realty fail, "Anxiety creeps back more intensely than ever" (Laing, 1990, p. 138). One now falls into a state of psycho-spiritual death-in-life. The psychotic sacrifices self-development wholesale for the sake of remaining alive in the most narrowed, constricted way possible to avoid nonbeing. Laing, thus, paradoxically defined psychosis as "the denial of being, as a means of preserving being" (p. 150).

According to Laing, the anxiety experienced by the psychotic person takes on three major forms: engulfment, implosion, and petrification (Laing 1990). Due to the psychotic person's radically weakened sense of self, the possibility of relating to another human being (of being understood, grasped, comprehended, loved, or even simply seen) "threatens the individual with loss of identity" (engulfment; p. 44). Thus, the only safe alternative is to isolate from others. In addition, the psychotic person feels empty, like a vacuum. They experience the world as that which "crashes in" upon oneself, such that reality is foreboding (p. 46). To engage reality directly means to risk implosion. The psychotic person also feels highly depersonalized and experiences anxiety over the possibility of being "petrified," dehumanized, of being an "it" rather than a person (p. 46).

Faced with this situation, the psychotic person seeks safety by attempting to become a being that is basically detached from their body, observing the world from afar and relating to others only via *imagos* or "false selves" so that nothing and no one is engaged directly (Laing, 1990, p. 69). In this way, the individual attempts to guard what little subjectivity remains (p. 77). "But the tragic paradox is that the more the self is defended in this way, the more it is destroyed" (p. 77). No one can be treated as a lovable, autonomous individual or feel that way unless they enter some kind of genuine participatory relationship with the world and others.

Thus, in psychosis as well as neurosis (though in a much more far-reaching manner), the individual's anxiety drives them to use their imaginative capabilities for the creation of imaginary worlds as a substitute for creatively dealing with shared human reality. This reveals the central role of the imagination not only in the development of pathology but in human existence in general. As Murray (1986) put it:

> The imaginative horizon projected by the human sets the stage, as it were, for what it will effect, and such a stage is always being set, for [human beings are] ever at work in some manner. Even the highly depressed person—contrary to common opinion—who seemingly has written life off and is caught in paralyzing depths is one who had effected a tremendous imaginative achievement, which unfortunately has darkened [them] to the other dimensions of the life . . . . Just consider for a moment: to imagine that everything is meaningless, that nothing good is to be found anywhere . . . this is a huge imaginative accomplishment. With one gigantic stroke such a person wipes away everything, and no amount of reasoning can convince him otherwise. Without doubt this represents a gigantic imaginative feat, but unfortunately it is one that suffers, despite its imaginative dimensions, from the fact it is not imaginative enough. Such a person is crippled, not principally because [they are] imaginative, but because [they have] come to imagine that there is no other way to imagine . . . life. [They end up] caught in [their] own petard. (pp. 64–65)

In this light, one may gain valuable insight into the process of psychotherapy by seeing it as a highly imaginative endeavor. The patient is assisted in the process of reimagining their life, activating and reorienting their creative power to productively confront life's anxiety-evoking moments, events, and situations. The task of therapy can be seen as an attempt to co-constitute an emboldening environment with a patient wherein they can overcome self-alienation and move toward greater unity and wholeness. As Murray (1986) noted, "imagination" is the "unity-building power" (*Einbildungskraft* in German) within the person (p. 62).

Final Remarks

To review, anxiety and fear are interconnected phenomena, but they are nonetheless distinct in their respective essences. Fear has a determinate object. Anxiety does not. Anxiety pertains to existence as such, directly or indirectly implicating its immaterial substrate. Anxiety emerges when the no-thing-ness of meaningful being-and-becoming-in-the-world is threatened on some level by the absolute nothingness of nonbeing.

Given its broad existential significance, anxiety cannot be adequately understood based on psychological dynamics alone. Psychology must stay grounded in a philosophical anthropology that does not divorce itself from the world of living-experience to grasp the deeper, ontological nature of anxiety as belonging to existence as such. Importantly, this grounding brings into relief the fact that not all anxiety is pathological and in need of "removal." Adopting an existential–phenomenological descriptive approach to anxiety allows one to identify typological variants of anxiety. There are existential anxieties, normal day-to-day anxieties, and pathological anxieties of varying levels of severity.

Anxiety can be growth enhancing when it is confronted by the human imagination and its creative, productive potentials are brought to bear on one's situation. In contrast, pathological anxiety drives a person to use their imagination for counterproductive purposes. One feels compelled to construct world-blocking and/or world-distorting defenses to avoid the awareness of finitude (the fact that nonbeing is an inescapable part of being). Here, the imagination serves to alienate the person from the world of shared reality to varying extents. Pathological anxiety thereby constricts world-openness and hinders personal growth. These observations reveal the central importance of the imagination in human being-and-becoming in general and in the development of pathology (see DeRobertis, 2008, Chapter 10 for a fuller explication of this connection). This makes these observations important existential–phenomenological insights for clinical psychologists in developing a perspective on the process of psychotherapy.

To illustrate, in a previous volume (DeRobertis, 2017), I reviewed the results of various phenomenological investigations of the process of successful psychotherapy and found their results to be indicative of existential learning. To summarize, in the context of psychotherapeutic intervention, existential learning was found to have several core constituents. As its existential precondition, something about a person's life circumstances must have changed such that they cannot go on as before. The flow of being-and-becoming must have met with an interruption formidable enough to prompt the person to seek out a knowledgeable other for assistance. For the phenomenon to get off the ground, the person must enter a relationship with someone perceived to be a knowledgeable other. This other must be capable of instilling existential trust (otherwise known as *hope*) in the learner. This begins the process of relieving anxieties and forms a foundation for the establishment of a client–therapist relationship. From here, the perceived knowledgeable other collaborates with the existential learner in the imaginative recreation of meaning, which inevitably involves the recruitment of their will in the motivated, determined pursuit of a more competence-laden future.

Key Terms, Concepts, and Themes

- Anxiety
- Fear
- Medical model of anxiety
- Existential foundations of anxiety
- Nothingness as no-thing-ness/non-objectifiable existence
- Finitude and estrangement
- Death (implicit or explicit awareness)
- Isolation
- Meaninglessness
- Human limitation
- Inevitable human suffering
- Incompletion

- Existential guilt
- Nothingness as nonbeing
- Existential psychology as a "depth" psychology
- The unawareness of death as a characteristic of human fallenness
- Death anxiety in human development
- Anxiety over leaving embeddedness
- Anxiety over not leaving embeddedness
- The threat to one's sense of value as a self
- The anxious body
- Existential learning
- Constrictive and expansive responses to anxiety
- Pathological anxiety
- "Neurosis"/neurotic anxiety
- Fragmentary self-affirmation
- Psychosis
- Sociosis
- The anxiety of engulfment
- The anxiety of implosion
- The anxiety of petrification
- Imagos or false selves
- Imagination as unity-building power (Einbildungskraft)

Chapter 8

Existential–Phenomenological Psychology and the Unconscious

Talk of "the unconscious" has made its way into diverse areas of psychology, from neuroscience and perception to personality and social psychology. It is a common and often very important part of psychotherapeutic dialogue as well. However, the student of phenomenological psychology will soon come to realize that phenomenologists have found this to be a troublesome concept. When phenomenologists are critical of the concept of the unconscious, they are not willing to simply discount it. Rather, it is the traditional conceptualization of what has been termed "repression," the phenomenal status of something unconscious, and the strategies employed to explain the unconscious that the phenomenologist finds problematic. Briefly, the traditional account of how something becomes unconscious is as follows. An individual has an emotion, motive, desire, impulse, or memory that appears threatening to the conscious mind. To keep that which threatens the person and the ideas that represent it away from the conscious mind, the ego intercedes before the information makes it to consciousness. Much like a motion sensor, the ego snaps into action automatically, redirecting the material "downward" (i.e., represses it) into some separate, lower psychic locality known as "the unconscious" before it can be consciously apprehended. The repressed material then later returns in the form of inexplicable symptoms, possibly somatic symptoms.

This explanation is problematic when considered from a phenomenological perspective, which would seek its verifications by an appeal to living experience. The traditional explanation takes its lead from the ambiguous, confused, depersonalized feel of repression to the unconscious, then leaves the living-experience of the person behind in toto. It subsequently portrays the process in the mechanistic–theoretical terms of natural science. Not only are the repressed material and the process of repression conceptualized in a physicalistic–mechanistic fashion, but so is the "place" where this material has been repressed to as well. This falls in line with what has become our commonsense conceptualization of consciousness and unconsciousness. Consciousness and unconsciousness, as they have come to be understood, tend to imply reified psychic localities or the idea that "the conscious mind" and "the unconscious mind" refer to different localities in the mind and brain. This conception of human awareness as internal and bifurcated represents a twofold dualism that the phenomenologist finds unacceptable.

Phenomenologists are also uncomfortable with the dualistic overtones that come along with the concept of the *id* as the primary energy system of the unconscious. The unconscious (that is, the reification) is understood as being the seat of a self-contained repository of instincts or drives set against the rational ego and the conscious mind. Phenomenological description, however, doesn't support the idea of a repository of raw "animality" that is merely juxtaposed to and set against some force of pragmatic rationality in a human being. Moreover, the phenomenologist sees no reason why what is deemed unconscious must be interpreted as being exclusively sexual or aggressive in nature. While phenomenologists grant that aggression and sexuality are very important and powerful aspects of existence, they refuse deny, downgrade, and/or demean the possibility of other forms of unconsciousness in advance of study. Their idea is not without precedent. Carl Jung believed that what was unconscious could be "positive" or even spiritual (Lahey, 1989, p. 422).

Moving on to the nature of things repressed, the traditional Freudian theoretical framework makes it difficult to explain how someone could both have and simultaneously keep something like a troubling, painful memory or idea from oneself. Past life events are not "automatically" memories. Memories are not purely objective entities. A memory is an actual or potential "remembrance," a putting back together of past information. If one is blocked from being able to remember a past life event, then how exactly is it that one can be said to have a memory of it? Even more perplexing, how can someone have an unacceptable or anxiety-provoking idea but have no idea what it is? The traditional psychoanalytic perspective is forced to rely on physicalistic–theoretical contrivances to account for these apparent contradictions. They act as alternatives to steadfastly describing the world of the experiencing person struggling with anxieties. In this chapter, we will explore phenomenological alternatives to the "orthodox" Freudian model of the unconscious following a chronological manner of presentation.

On the Fringes and Gradations of the Experiential Field: Notable Forerunners

Phenomenological approaches to the unconscious were anticipated in different ways by two thinkers outside the mainstream of the phenomenological tradition: William James and William Stern. William James (1890) refuted the idea of an unconscious mind as had been proposed in psychology at the time of his *Principles of Psychology*. Specifically, he spoke of the "unintelligibility of the notion that a mental fact can be two things at once" (p. 76). Having said that, it is equally important to note that James was quite cognizant of the fact that the psychology of consciousness was too often disposed to intellectualism, overlooking the flowing, streaming life of human experience in which conscious awareness always finds itself and from which it always emerges. He dubbed this more original form of experiencing *sciousness*. In contrast to *con*-sciousness, sciousness refers to experience that has not yet been neatly partitioned into subject and object. The famed *Dasein* ("being there") as already engaged "being-in-the-world" of Heideggerian existential phenomenology is an expression of the same idea. Consciousness forever cycles in and out of what phenomenologists would later call a prereflective, pre-thematic, non-thetic flow of experience, which is not "conscious" in the narrow sense of the term. As James put it:

> Instead, then, of the stream of thought being one of *con*-sciousness, "thinking its own existence along with whatever else it thinks" . . . it might better be called a stream of *Sciousness* pure and simple, thinking objects of some of which it makes what it calls a Me,' and only aware of its 'pure' Self in an abstract, hypothetic or conceptual way. Each 'section' of the stream would then be a bit of sciousness or knowledge of this sort, including and contemplating its 'me' and its 'not-me' as objects which work out their drama together, but not yet including or contemplating its own subjective being. (p. 127)

The importance of James's perspective to phenomenological psychology was highlighted in Aron Gurwitsch's (1964) *The Field of Consciousness*. In this text, Gurwitsch articulated a rapprochement between James's work, phenomenology, and Gestalt psychology. From James, Gurwitsch took the idea that consciousness always has its "fringe" areas or margins, which have not yet become explicit in consciousness (i.e., consciousness is embedded in a field of sciousness). Using Gestalt terminology, Gurwitsch described how what is perceptually or conceptually figural at any given time always appears against the ground of a horizon. The latter highlights the importance of context in the psychology of consciousness, the fact that what is conscious is always ultimately given against a more or less indeterminate thematic field. Consciousness is a fluid, dynamic, developing Gestalt. In Husserlian phenomenology, one would speak of the genesis of consciousness as always occurring amid infinite horizons displaying varying degrees of determinateness and clarity of understanding. In Heideggerian phenomenology, one would speak of human world-openness as displaying a perpetual interplay of presence and absence.

William Stern (1924) is no less important to this line of thinking. For Stern, human knowledge bears the characteristic of experiential gradation, always appears along a dynamic, dialectical continuum of concretion and salience. Human awareness and knowledge are graded, ranging from concrete-leaning (i.e., more "embedded") to abstract-leaning (i.e., more "salient") in nature (Allport, 1968, p. 281). Perceptions and conceptions can be highly embedded or highly salient, relatively embedded or relatively salient. Accordingly, one may approach and cognitively appropriate events, objects, others, one's own body, and so forth in a manner of "embedding" or "withdrawing" from one's own unique situatedness-in-the-world. As Strasser (1977) described it:

> The process of withdrawal is simultaneously positive and negative. Positively, it signifies the progressive differentiation, stricter articulation, and greater objectivating power of experience; negatively, it signifies the estrangement and splitting of the natural unity of the person. An ever increasing withdrawal would endanger the unity of the person. From living experience [*Erleben*] "living-asunder" ["*Zer-leben*"] would develop. The various "withdrawals" must be reincorporated into the wholeness of personal life. (p. 93)

Rollo May: The Unconscious as an Awareness of Unactualizable Potentials and Possibilities

With the release of his co-edited volume *Existence*, Rollo May and colleagues (1958) observed that many psychologists who described themselves as existential rejected the notion of the unconscious. For example, Medard Boss (1963) was largely dismissive of Freud's notion of the unconscious. For Boss, what Freud referred to as unconscious could be accounted for by recognizing the inherently limited nature of human world-openness and the typically inauthentic, fallen character of self-understanding (see p. 96). The concept of "the unconscious" was superfluous for Boss. Ludwig Binswanger was perhaps more generous than Boss in his views of Freud's unconscious. As Needleman (1967) noted, Binswanger's use of Husserl's notion of the perceptual horizon left the door open for a phenomenological unconscious. Moreover, Binswanger approached Freud's unconscious as a dimension of existential thrownness, with human beings born into a set of thrown conditions in which they find themselves and which they must struggle to understand and appropriate as their own. But Binswanger also ultimately rejected the Freudian unconscious as a matter of principle based on what Needleman described as essentially Sartrean grounds.

Sartre (2018) argued that for a person to be able to censor their consciousness, they must already have some kind of preexisting knowledge (and thus recognition) of what will be rejected to prevent it from becoming conscious. This makes repression a matter of bad faith. Rollo May sympathized with the objections of his colleagues, noting that the reified "cellar" or "basement" view of the unconscious had provided a blank check for social scientists to conveniently insert the theoretical explanation of their choice at will. But he refused to accept an approach to psychology that too quickly jettisoned the depth notion of the unconscious and the insights about psychodynamics that Freud and others formulated in connection with it. For May (1969), any psychology that habitually uses a preconceived theoretical notion of unconscious functioning to explain away the phenomena of human consciousness is complacent on the grounds of reductionism. He referred to this explanatory impulse as the attempt at a complete determinism and rejected it as a logical contradiction (see Chapter 1). At the same time, however, he held that a purely academic phenomenology that refuses to explore what applied, clinical phenomenologists see as living manifestations of what have traditionally been called "unconscious phenomena" is in danger of becoming a superficial idealism.

May and other existential psychologists like Erich Fromm (1962) and Viktor Frankl (1975) embraced the phenomenological critique of the unconscious, but they retained the notion of unconscious functioning in modified form to import the richness of a "depth" dimension into existential psychology. For May, Fromm, and Frankl alike, the unconscious represents an excess of meaning and potential that extends beyond what has been actualized at any given time in a person's life. Historically speaking, May was more dedicated than his contemporaries to the task of working toward a phenomenologically and logically defendable reinterpretation of the unconscious. He was emphatic about the need to rehabilitate the notion of the unconscious because it vastly expanded one's scope of vision in confronting the complexity of human psychological life. His version of the unconscious was inspired by the more expansive analytic psychology of Carl Jung, but he also maintained that it was "compatible with" Husserlian phenomenology (May, 1979, p. 126). For May, "unconsciousness" is a concept that orients the psychologist to the infinite and protean (metamorphosizing, multifaceted, sometimes ambiguous) forms of human consciousness. As Kozyreva (2018) observed:

> For Husserl, consciousness encompasses both the sphere of explicit wakeful awareness and the obscure background of conscious life. In this spirit, in the *Ideas II*, he points out that the sphere of self-consciousness cannot be restricted only to the narrow scope of attentive or alert awareness, but must include in itself equally all "background," obscure conscious experiences. (p. 202)

Rollo May's conception of the unconscious is based on an understanding of human existence as a limited openness to potentialities and possibilities for living in-the-world-with-others. Part of what it means for a human being to have limited openness to potentialities and possibilities is that certain possibilities for reflective awareness may appear to be too threatening for an individual to actualize (May, 1979). These possibilities threaten one's sense of value as a self existing in the world amid valued others (May, 1969, 1979). Consequently, steps are taken to deny those possibilities. There may be possibilities for behaving that a person avoids actualizing to place restrictions on conscious awareness. There may be ways of thinking about self, other, and/or world that appear threatening. There may be motives, desires, feelings, or impulses that a person cannot let themselves recognize as their own and thereby fully express (Malan, 1992). For example, recognizing that one has been hateful toward another person may threaten one's self-image as "a very conscientious and gentle person." This person would experience anxiety in the face of the possibility of not being completely as they think they are for whatever set of reasons.

This avoidance, refusal, or denial of potentialities and possibilities can and often does prove to be a source of clinically significant psychological distress. As beings who *are* their relationships and projects, the inability to actualize important possibilities for action and/or understanding can lead to a painful narrowing or constriction of a person's freedom. Sometimes denied potentialities will nevertheless be symptomatically actualized by a person, perhaps bodily, as was alluded to earlier (May, 1979). For example, a woman who has been compliant all her life and who is married to an overbearing husband suddenly begins to have her body become numb every time he orders her around. Too afraid to entertain the possibility of standing up for herself, too threatened by the possibility of having her husband angry with her or openly expressing anger with him, the woman's desire to stand up for herself manifests itself as her paralysis. The meaning of her painful situation is felt and lived even though it has yet to be "cognized."

This example highlights a very curious state of affairs. The occurrence of such an event implies that human beings participate in qualitatively different forms of awareness. While the aforementioned woman has no idea as to the meaning of her paralysis, she is nevertheless participating in the meaningful psychological dynamics that are being lived out by her. As Sartre noted, anytime a person avoids being aware of an actuality or possibility they must have some kind of presence to it in their selective avoidance. A person may avoid realizing any number of things. But this does not have to lead to the positing of some psychic limbo. The traditional, mechanistic theory would have us believe that the defenses against the repressed occur outside all awareness and that the repressed material is thereby dualistically split off from consciousness. The phenomenologist, therefore, is compelled to approach these psychological dynamics differently.

To understand the nature of this situation, Rollo May insisted that we make an important distinction that remains largely unrecognized by social scientists. This is the distinction between awareness and consciousness. While the word "consciousness" is often used to speak of awareness or human awareness in general, consciousness has a more precise meaning. May (1979) articulated this distinction as follows:

> Awareness is a capacity we share with animals and much of nature. Indeed Whitehead and Tillich in their respective

> ontologies hold that awareness is characteristic of all things in nature, down to the attraction and repulsion between the molecular particles. Awareness without consciousness is highly depersonalizing. It is possible . . . to be aware without being conscious . . . . Consciousness is the distinctly human form of awareness—the particularly human capacity not only to know something but to know that I know it, that is, to experience myself as a subject in relation to an object or as an I in relation to a Thou . . . . When [one] rises on two legs, stands upright, and sees, [one] . . . is aware of a distance between [oneself] and the world. The same phenomenon is what makes "Man [*sic*], the Questioning Being." We could not question without being aware of the distance between us and the world. Questioning implies that I stand in some significant relationship to the world and thus is a distinguishing expression of consciousness. (pp. 124–125)

For May, consciousness and the capacity to refuse it exist in a dialectical relationship with a broader field of undifferentiated *awareness* (recall James's sciousness). It is possible for humans to have an awareness of something in their total lived experiential field without being consciously present to it as a subject attending to an "object" of interest. Consciousness involves a certain distance between a person and that which they are related to. This distance gives humans the ability to question their relations to the world (Straus, 1966). This kind of relationship to things is a prerequisite for the ability to bring something into focus and relate to it explicitly or linguistically. When a person denies themselves conscious awareness of something, that certain something remains embedded within a form of experiencing (recall Stern's embeddedness), an "awareness," that does not allow for its meaning and significance to be reflected upon. In contrast, languaging something grants things, whatever they may be, with an explicit presence or existence in the truest sense of the word ("existence" literally means "to stand out" or "emerge," May, 1958b, p. 12). Wording allows a thing to have a salience and an identity that it could not have prior to its admittance into discourse (Murray, 1986). Freud implicitly understood this when he engaged in his "talking cure." As Boss (1963) put it:

> Freud admonishes the patients to put all thoughts and emotions into words, in detail and without selecting. To do so is to assure

> that the process of becoming aware of myself does not stop at the halfway goal of a pseudo-honesty, confined to myself and therefore easily lost again. Instead, this process is to achieve an open, continuous adherence to being-whole, i.e., to accept and to take over all of one's own belongings—with responsibility. Freud emphasized verbalization again and again, because what is exists, in fact, only—and is undeniably preserved only—when it is verbally articulated. (p. 70)

J. H. van den Berg: The Unconscious Turned Inside Out

In 1972, J. H. van den Berg offered what was simultaneously an apologetic and a critical reading of Freud on the unconscious. Van den Berg's descriptive analysis began with the observation that human beings are capable of both lying and engaging in the more elaborate form of deceit that he referred to as self-concealment. Self-concealment is more than just a deception about this or that fact, more than a ruse to get something over on someone or hustle them. Self-concealment is a more thoroughgoing effort to put up a smoke screen or offer up a persona that hides who one is. It is to present an interpretation of one's body and world to the other that is fundamentally at odds with who one really is.

From here, van den Berg further noted that if a person were to truly believe their own fabrication, and if this belief were so strong that one could not "call the person back" (while being certain that they were not merely lying to create a ruse), then the person's comportment could legitimately be described as displaying "unconscious" experience or unconscious mental functioning. For van den Berg, the psychological category of what is "unconscious" is reserved for those instances where a person truly believes their own lie (see van den Berg, 1972, pp. 114–115). Unconsciousness thus implies a twofold genuine not-knowing: not-knowing self-concealment's status as a lie and not-knowing the meaning behind it. It is a kind of self-blindness, a self-imposed hole or disconnect in one's own consciousness. It is, in other words, a *self-deluded self-concealment.* This is the essential thrust of van den Berg's sympathetic, descriptive reading of Freud.

Van den Berg's critical reading of the Freudian unconscious focused on the reification of its "locality." According to van den Berg, what psychologists call the unconscious is misleading because it postulates that the content of the unconscious should be found inside the person or patient in therapy, within the mind and brain of the individual believing their own self-concealment. For van den Berg, the content of the self-concealment is exactly what the patient *lacks* until they get better. The content, meaning, associated insight, and so forth all reside in the other (e.g., the therapist) so long as the self-concealment is truly believed (see van den Berg, 1972, p. 123). The unconscious comprises self-knowledge that has been disavowed, banished, externalized, handed over to the consciousness of the other, and that is where its content resides. It does not reside in a deep layer of the personality for van den Berg, at least not a literal geological layer or locality in the mind and/or brain. To begin looking at the problem of unconsciousness phenomenologically, one must start by leaving the artificial construction that is the world inside one's head and begin to recognize that human beings live their lives out in the world. As van den Berg (1972) put it, "For the phenomenologist, there are no layers, there is just one layer (which we must not call a layer at all) of life as such" (p. 123). It is important to emphasize, however, that the terminology of "layers" is problematic specifically when it is reified and employed as a theoretically imposed alternative to the systematic description of experience. Other phenomenologists see no problem in working with the metaphorical terminology of layering so long as one has not succumbed to naturalistic reification. Husserl, for example, spoke of "sedimented" layers of unreflective belief, and Moran (2017) more recently described Husserl's concept of the human person as "layered," containing "analyses comparable to psychoanalytic explorations of the unconscious" (p. 3).

Henri Ey: The Unconscious as Part of the Always-Ambiguous Autoconstruction of the Self

Like Rollo May, Henri Ey adamantly advocated for the idea that the psychoanalytic unconscious ought to be rehabilitated on phenomenological grounds rather than discarded. Along with May (see May, 1979), Ey (1978) argued that Freud made a fundamental error in granting conceptual priority to a theorized unconscious before seeking to properly understand the nature of conscious being. As Moran (2017) noted of Husserl's phenomenology, "Only when 'wakeful' consciousness as such is clarified can a proper discussion of the unconscious as such be undertaken" (p. 8).

For Ey, to acquire a proper understanding of consciousness, one must take a genetic, developmental perspective on the life of the mind. The development of a person's consciousness does not occur in a vacuum. To state the matter figuratively, consciousness does not pick itself up from its own bootstraps. Consciousness emerges within a bodily, affective, and social field of interaction, which it never completely outstrips, even in its reflective, abstract, and speculative activity. Nonetheless, consciousness is an irreducible domain of human becoming and cannot be explained away based on any other aspect of existence. From this holistic perspective, a bifurcation of the mind into a free and rational conscious mind set against a completely irrational, animal unconscious has no foundation. This traditional, conventional notion of the unconscious cannot be defended by an analysis of pre-theoretical, living-experience. Ey maintained it is a theoretical contrivance descended from Cartesianism. As such, it is attractive in its seeming conceptual clarity, but its artificiality forces the psychologist into manifold blind alleys in attempting to account for those living-experiences that one might characterize as "unconscious" (which Ey demonstrated at length using Freud's constantly changing views as an example).

The pseudo-clarity of the neo-Cartesian unconscious prevents the psychologist from attaining a genuine appreciation of the inherent ambiguities of human psychological life. Appeals to a rationalistic/intellectualistic/idealistic alternative fare no better than reductionistic accounts. As Ey (1978) put it, "An idealism which will not admit any obscurity into being, or a realism which will admit no light, must be condemned [as] a 'plane psychology'" (p. 305;"plane" meaning an oversimplified, one-sided emphasis on mind or behavior). Both approaches exclude the possibility of a (holistic) perspective that sees consciousness as simultaneously situationally embedded (in a body, in space and time, in a family and a culture, entangled with language, etc.) and capable of reflective awareness exhibiting varying magnitudes of salience. Accordingly, both approaches remain forever limited in their ability to access the full spectrum of non-thetic consciousness (i.e., "consciousness" that is object-aware but not reflectively aware of itself as a subject taking up a position with respect to an object; see Sartre, 2018). To approach human consciousness holistically takes courage, because one will inevitably be forced to dwell with ambiguity in times when one would otherwise employ theoretical constructs to give the impression that a phenomenon has been disambiguated.

Ey's holistic approach to consciousness thus includes unconscious states as part of its standard manner of functioning. Conscious being unfolds as a continuous back and forth, a mutual interplay of "the imaginary and the real, of the automatic and the voluntary, of the unreflective and the reflective, of the given and the 'taken' . . ." (p. 296.). As Ey (1978) put it, "To be conscious and to be unconscious are two complementary modes of the ontological structure of . . . every human being" (p. xix). The unconscious is not "under" but rather "in" the organization of experience (p. 300). On this view, the unconscious encompasses more than the repressed content that is traditionally associated with the Freudian unconscious. Ey observed that the word "unconscious" had long been used in psychology both within and outside of psychoanalytic circles to describe diverse phenomena, encompassing everything from a distant memory and things on the fringes of consciousness to the symbolic content of hallucinations and delusions (p. 297). Thus, though it is not precluded as a possibility, the notion of the unconscious bears no immediate assumption of pathology. Again, Ey:

> In our thought and action, the origin of the motivation and the meaning of our lived-experience always escape us, only partially, but necessarily. And this "partially" is the very facticity of unconscious intentionality, which is constantly interwoven with the conscious direction of what I cause to appear to myself. All. . . lived-experience . . . involves some aspect of unintelligibility, something which resists the noematic legislative power of experience. The task of consciousness is precisely always to will to take possession of that which can never be entirely grasped or justified. (pp. 298–299)

For Ey (1978), human language is a critical and inherent part of this always-partial unintelligibility. Language is a constant dialectic of presence and absence. Words are not experiences, and so "language fills experience with its ambiguities" even as it allows human beings to articulate their life's predicaments and develop relevant insights (p. 299). Moreover, language is employed selectively in human development, which complexifies the dynamical shaping of presence and absence over time. "Consciousness is essentially selective and thematic in and through its actualization. Its 'topic' or the 'Gestaltization' of its lived-experience involves fringe areas, implications, and exclusions" (pp. 296–297). The basis of this selectivity is the fact that the complementary pair of consciousness–unconsciousness is enveloped within the development of the entire personality and the psychogenesis of the self as a domain of personality. Conscious being emerges from within the ongoing process of personality development, which involves the autoconstruction of the self.[1]

Here, Ey's work converged with the works of seminal humanistic psychologists like Gordon Allport, Carl Rogers, and Charlotte Bühler (see DeRobertis, 2008, 2021b). While Bühler also used the term *self*, Allport spoke of the *proprium* and Rogers spoke of the *self-concept*. For Ey (along with Allport, Rogers, Bühler, and many other humanistic psychologists), selfhood is not coextensive with the totality of the personality. The self is a specific portion of the personality, albeit the "core" portion composed of the person's strongest identifications and sense of agency. The development of self and personality is dynamic, changing, and laden with tensions and conflicts of varying magnitudes. The boundary areas between self and personality are fluid and not always crystal clear. In Ey's view, Freud saw clearly that human development is not free of oversights or ambivalent intra- and interpersonal relations. But Freud was so dazzled by what he saw that he placed too much power in the hands of the unconscious in its relation to consciousness. He then spent a career trying in vain to carve out the conceptual boundaries of a sovereign unconscious mind split off from consciousness. For Ey, this project was doomed to failure because the autonomy of consciousness is what gives meaning and structure to repression (no matter how it might be conceived) and, thus, the unconscious. It is necessary to grasp the structuration and ongoing structural transformations of consciousness to understand what would be "left out" or "kept away" and why. Thus, there must be a much closer interrelationship between consciousness and unconsciousness than what conventional Freudian metapsychology would allow, and Freud himself began speaking of a non-repressed form of unconscious later in his career. In the end, Ey (1978) noted, Freud considered all the systems of the mind (id, ego, and superego) to be more or less unconscious (and thus, more or less conscious). This brought the mature Freud closer to what phenomenological psychology would espouse (p. 324).

Unconsciousness, for Ey, reveals itself as the "other side" or inverse dimension (coming in many varieties and many extents) of consciousness in the total formation or Gestalt that is the self. Of course, the unintelligible dimensions of living-experience result not only from

[1] This refers to self-development that originates from spontaneous, creative interactions with one's body, other people, and the world, which makes it genuinely generative rather than the mere byproduct of anonymous forces.

the incidental limitations of factical existence. They are sometimes the result of an emotionally charged situation that causes anxiety, thus implicating a pointedly *affective unconscious* (Ey, 1978, p. 298). The affective unconscious implicates the more common meanings associated with the Freudian unconscious: the tension-filled, conflict-prone world of drives, feelings, emotions, and motivations. When conflict emerges with considerable force, the affective unconscious "shuffles the cards of perception and, more generally, of the organization of the field of consciousness" (p. 298). Language is now used to selectively cover over realities that would affectively upset and perturb or unravel the organization of the personality. Spontaneous saying is displaced by motivated not-saying and/or saying in a distorted manner. As a result, the scope of unconscious experience is expanded.

What is the phenomenal ground of this conflict? The answer brings us back to the autoconstruction of selfhood. Human beings are at issue for themselves. They care about who they have been, who they are being, and who they are becoming. The autoconstruction of self is a value-laden (axiological) and affectively charged process. It demands that one embrace certain kinds of knowledge of self and world while overlooking or all-out rejecting others (see p. 322). This relates back to the insights of May (1979) noted above. In the autoconstruction of selfhood, there is a continual process of taking or not taking proprietorship and responsibility for aspects of one's own becoming. The self is not always aware of its taboo motivations and bad faith rationalizations. It denies certain things access to consciousness by generating purposeful, motivated, but unrecognized blindnesses in the process of distinguishing what belongs to the self and what does not (i.e., what is non-self or "other" in a broad sense). The psychogenesis of self sometimes exhibits manifestations of consciousness that are non-reflective and unthematized for its own protection. Aspects of oneself are thus forcibly and unreflectively jettisoned to the "thither" side of consciousness, as it were, which is in no way intracranial. Like van den Berg (1972), Ey (1978) asserted, "The very nature of conscious being allows the unconscious to appear only furtively or only to the 'objective' gaze of another" (p. 302).

William F. Fischer: The Unconscious as a Function of Self-Deception

By the mid-1980s, existential–phenomenological psychology had made considerable headway in the study of the unconscious, but there was more work to be done. What had yet to be provided to the wider community of psychologists was a systematic and rigorous study of the self-deceptive process. In general, existential-phenomenology's research base needed to demonstrate that it was founded on a clearly articulated methodology that utilized research participants. William F. Fischer (1985) responded, studying self-deception in a sample of participants using the Giorgi method. Analyzing his findings, Fischer found that three existential preconditions were necessary for the possibility of self-deception to arise:

> The possibility of deceiving oneself arises when three interrelated conditions are co-present: (1) when one is already committed to a particular understanding of some phenomenon of one's world; (2) when certain emerging significations of that phenomenon render that understanding ambiguously uncertain, and (3) when one anxiously lives this ambiguous uncertainty as threatening not only one's commitment to that particular understanding, but also, albeit horizonally, one's commitment to related understandings of other phenomena. (p. 152)

Fischer (1985) further asked, "How it is that in the course of one's disavowing/refusing/avoiding [meanings and understandings] one does not explicitly discover that which is being disavowed/refused/avoided" (p. 137)?" He went on, "In other words, if one is . . . present, either tacitly or unreflectively, to that which is to be disavowed/refused/avoided, then how does it show itself as such and still fail to be explicitly discovered" (p. 137)? Stated differently, how is it exactly that we can have an awareness of what we are avoiding and yet keep it away from consciousness? How does such a process unfold? Fischer's findings (recapitulating themes noted in the sections on Rollo May and Henri Ey) were as follows:

> . . . The possibility of deceiving oneself arises when one is already committed to a particular understanding of some phenomenon of one's world. That is to say, one has posited what

> it meant, means, and/or could mean and one is disinclined, if not adamantly unwilling, to consider alternatives to this. Stated positively, one is oriented toward verifying/elaborating/actualizing one's understanding rather than discovering new profiles or significations that might call for its reformulation. Now, in rendering one's already posited understanding ambiguously uncertain, the emerging significations, although present, are hidden by that which they threaten. In other words, one is thematically present to the threatened, that is, to the already posited understanding to which one is committed, rather than to that which threatens it. Further, in being present to this threatened understanding, one is anxious, and the intrusive phenomenal manifestations distract one's attention as well as one's ease . . . The emerging of one's anxiousness . . . intervenes and overrides one's presence to the emerging [other possible] significations. (pp. 146–147)

As implicated in the above-noted existential preconditions, Fischer observed that the sense of threat experienced by his participants implicated their commitments to both direct self-interpretations (i.e., who they have been, who they are, who they are becoming) as well as those horizonal meanings related to their sense of self that would fall under the category of one's general worldview (i.e., we identify with our ways of construing the world and life itself).

To summarize, Fischer's research demonstrated that self-deception arises in response to emerging anxieties (recall Chapter 7). These anxieties generate a dis-integrating emotional upset that perceptually muddies and clouds over contradictory emerging meanings. This is compounded by a panicked scramble to repair and reintegrate the preexisting structure of one's consciousness by an unproductive use of language. Articulation and thematization are apportioned prejudicially to the meanings and understandings that one has already committed to. Fischer observed that one can rigidly reaffirm already posited meanings and understandings by various means. One might preoccupy oneself with intellectual refuting or befogging emerging meanings and, thus, the ambiguously uncertain character of the anxious situation (Ey's shuffling the cards of perception). One might occupy oneself with attacking other people deemed responsible for having introduced new threatening meanings. Alternatively, the person may flee the anxious situation to immerse themselves elsewhere in situations that reconfirm preexisting meanings and understandings. Echoing Rollo May (1977,

1979), to engage in self-deception is to refuse to be informed productively by anxiety (thus preventing the possibility of learning from experience, see DeRobertis, 2017). By remaining explicitly or thematically present to the meanings and understandings one is committed to, those possibilities for awareness that threaten one's prior understandings are denied full realization. Insights, new possibilities for becoming consciously aware, are avoided and left only partially (i.e., pathologically or symptomologically) actualized at best.

Neo-Husserlian Contributions

In more recent times, there have been notable contributions to the phenomenology of the unconscious emanating from the ranks of philosophy. As Moran (2017) observed, these contributions draw on Husserl and the works of numerous interpreters of Husserl, including the likes of Eugen Fink, Maurice Merleau-Ponty, and Paul Ricoeur. These works have sought to "piece together" a schematic of what Husserl would have developed as a perspective on the unconscious had he lived long enough to see it through to fruition (Moran, 2017, p. 9). This literature has been developing slowly but surely for some time, especially since the 1990s, and it has gained more momentum in the 2000s. Thus, the current overview cannot be comprehensive, but it can nonetheless provide a sense of the themes that are prominent in this still-unfolding current of thought.

As Rollo May (1979) noted, Husserl's philosophy is often mischaracterized as a highly restrictive philosophy of reflective, conscious awareness. But his work is pregnant with possibilities for conceptualizing and studying unconscious awareness. For Husserl, the irreducible transcendental ego is inseparable from the empirical ego, meaning that the "I" is not bifurcated or doubled. What is transcendental and empirical in a subject is only distinguishable by the adoption of contrasting attitudes. The empirical and transcendental are researched using different styles of inquiry, but even at the highest levels of analysis, employing the highest levels of conceptual abstraction, subjectivity always bears a relationship to world-embeddedness. The transcendental ego is always also a transcendental person (i.e., "the transcendental ego in its fullest 'concretion'"; Luft, 2005, p. 141). The active, reflective, cognitive dynamics of consciousness take place within the broader context of embedded human becoming. Subjectivity is always already caught up in the intersubjective field (composed of the "I" and the "not-I"). It always participates in the life of instinct (see Allen, 1976). Subjectivity is always embedded within a typically unarticulated complex field of motivation, habituality, memory, "passive" experiential synthesis, associations of meaning, historically sedimented knowledge, and fantasy (Biceaga, 2010). Indeed, consciousness has much to contend with, and only a select "portion" of it could possibly be made explicit at any given time (Moran, 2017).

Neo-Husserlian contributions to the study of the unconscious have approached it as a function of the unfolding temporal co-constitution of subjectivity and of various processes involved in passive synthesis. The following section explores Moran (2017) and Bernet's (2002) introduction of the temporal co-constitution of unconscious consciousness, with an emphasis on the role of the imagination; Thomas Fuchs's (2012) example of how one may expand the horizonal or "horizontal" aspect of the unconscious by using the phenomenology of embodied spatiality as one's departure; and Anastasia Kozyreva's (2018) example of how one may expand the "vertical," affective dimensions of the unconscious (recall Ey's designation of an affective unconscious above).

Imagination and the Temporal Co-Constitution of Unconscious Consciousness

For the mature Husserl (i.e., in his later period, he developed genetic phenomenology), consciousness of the present is surrounded by the horizons of a past and a projected, imagined future. The experiential world of a person is always an amalgam of past, present, and future. Thus, the "hard" reality of the current moment is never as hard as it seems prima facia. It is mutable due its always being appropriated in tandem with the personally meaningful processes of remembering and anticipating. The present is buttressed by good and bad memories and as-yet unfulfilled wishes and apprehensions. The experiential life of the present is interpenetrated with perspectives on the past and future that are formed within the context of the bodily, affective, and social life of the person. As Moran (2017) noted:

> Husserl's phenomenology of experiential, conscious life recognises its extremely complex textured unity. Even perceptions of objects can be interwoven with dreams, memories, fantasies, recalled fantasies and fantasized memories. These memories/fantasies wrap around the present

> object and the present act of experiencing. Someone looking at her lover does not see just the bare person in front of her – but the person as disclosed in emotion, love, memory, expectation, fantasy, hope. (p. 23)

Moreover, Husserl's analyses of imagination and reproductive consciousness can be used to describe how a person can generate and maintain more than one relatively discrete experiential profile of self-and-world, as in a mind at odds with itself. The conscious "egoic centre" lives amid an expanse of overlapping horizons, including "fantasized selves and modifications of selves (dream personae and so on)"; (Moran, 2017, p. 16). As is obvious, these considerations already extend beyond a philosophy of sheer conscious presence. Bernet (2002) has discussed imagination and reproductive consciousness at some length. In doing so, he spoke of "unconscious consciousness" as part of an effort to establish a rapprochement between Husserl and Freud (p. 327). Though it is largely unknown to psychoanalysts and other psychologists, Husserl conceived of consciousness as participating in the life of instinct. For Husserl, instinctually driven affectivity undergirds the life of consciousness not as a univocally foreign, diametrically opposed force (i.e., a univocally anonymous and oppressive "id"), but as a potential partner to the life of reason. The life of instinct in Husserl's works involves not only adaptation, survival, and what usually goes for the "dark side" of humanity, but also the striving for general life satisfaction through the progressive spatiotemporal unification of the total experiential field (see Moran & Cohen, 2012).

According to Bernet, since consciousness in the everyday life of the person exhibits instinctive and affective needs, there will be times when consciousness must protect itself when those needs are threatened. A need for self-protection would be pronounced where consciousness is haunted by difficult or traumatic memory traces. Consciousness is given the means to protect itself due in part to its reproductive potentials, its perpetual involvement in appropriating and representing what comes before it from the positionality of its concrete situation. Perception typically gets top billing in Husserl's writings and those of his interpreters (e.g., Merleau-Ponty's "primacy" perception). But Bernet argues for the overlooked centrality of "phantasy" and the imaginative potentials of consciousness. Phantasy maximizes the productive aspects of the mind's synthetic, reproductive world engagement. Says Bernet (2002), phantasy is a modified form of perception that indicates the possibility of an experience that does not strictly presuppose something's "factual givenness" (p. 340). This less appreciated aspect of Husserl's works can be seen as foundational for the works of his most famous successors: Heidegger, Merleau-Ponty, and Sartre (see, for example, Sartre's works on the imagination; Sartre, 2010, 2012). The productive potential of consciousness inherent in phantasy allows the possibility of distanced, symbolic forms of self-consciousness that contrast with the impressional (meaning more immediate and less creative) consciousness of perception. Thus, Bernet (2002) asserted:

> Perceptual consciousness, in which the subject immediately gives itself over to its drive to see, appears to be a type of loss of self (*Selbstverlust*) or, more precisely, a loss of the *distanced* self-representation (*Selbstdarstellung*) of drive. Regarded from this point of view, phantasy enjoys a privilege over perception and there are therefore good grounds to doubt Husserl's prioritizing of perception over phantasy. (p. 340)

What Bernet demonstrated with this analysis is that there is a way in which Husserl's phenomenology casts the productive power of the imagination as more foundational to the determination of the subject as an agentic, authenticating self than perception. But, of course, this description would not hold under all circumstances. The imaginative power at the heart of human existence can either open one to the expanse of infinite and protean forms of consciousness or it can become the secret agent in the establishment of a consciousness divided against itself. The power of phantasy can be productive or counterproductive. The distance that one achieves from the embedded world of perceptual consciousness need not lead to self-transparency. It may lead to self-protective obfuscation. Phantasy, in dealing with a reality that has come to be characterized by emotional difficulties and traumatic experiences, makes for a higher likelihood of slippages in perception, divergences in the experiential exchanges that occur between self and other, anomalies and distortions in the sense of identity inherent in consciousness. Thus, Bernet (2002) concluded:

> A new determination of consciousness on the lines of Freud's concept of the Unconscious must make comprehensible how consciousness can appear to itself as something alien . . . . The phenomenological determination of *phantasy* as a process in which something alien or non-present presently appears as

> such and in which one's own self achieves a distanced and alienated self-awareness and self-representation proved to be a fruitful point of departure for the still incomplete fulfilment of this task. (p. 349)

The "Horizontal" Expansion of the Unconscious: Restricted Bodying Forth

According to Moran (2017), the living body is an important element in any Husserlian interpretation of the unconscious, and he cited the work of Thomas Fuchs (2012) to illustrate. Fuchs used Merleau-Ponty's Husserl-inspired analyses of bodily-sedimented memory traces to render a phenomenological interpretation of the unconscious. Merleau-Ponty's phenomenological philosophy of embodied subjectivity made creative use of Husserl's concepts of sedimented lived-meaning and functioning intentionality (renamed operative intentionality) and Heidegger's related concept of ready-to-hand world engagement. Fuchs demonstrated that this philosophical framework could be used to reinterpret the unconscious as a conspicuously sedimented, embodied schema of practical engagement or ready-to-hand being-in-the-world. This sedimented (already functioning or operative) intentional predisposition colors the way we "interpret reality, fill in the gaps of uncertainty, and invest our social interactions with meaning" on a prereflective, implicit basis (Kozyreva, 2018, p. 199).

Fuchs argued that phenomenology can contribute a horizontal unconscious of the living body in intercorporeal space to complement the individual vertical unconscious of depth psychology. Without realizing it, Fuchs brought together the basic insights of van den Berg, May, and Ey, using the living body as an explicit organizing principle. According to Fuchs, unconscious fixations are like restrictions in the spatial possibilities of the acting person, instantiated by a past that is implicit in the present and resistant to the forward-moving process of human becoming. Traces of the past live on through a perpetual figure–ground dynamic, sometimes touching consciousness, and sometimes breaking through only to be quickly reinterpreted and shifted away from perceptual salience into the background of the experiential field. The blind spots and mistakes of everyday life normally associated with the vertical unconscious are seen as manifestations of the horizontal unconscious in the sense that a bodily memory has persisted in a non-thematized way in present behavior. In other words, we are not dealing with a series of discrete memories subject to censure. Memory traces live on in an ambiguous way, residing in the twilight zone between the embodied adjustment to one's surroundings and "cognitive processes," as conventionally understood.

In its defense, psychoanalysis did study body language, but Freud established the body of anatomy and physiology as its focus. Ricoeur (1970) referred to this as Freud's reductionistic hermeneutics of suspicion. Against this depersonalized cellar view of the unconscious, Fuchs (2012) asked how a subject could be in a position to make an alien meaning their own again in the process of therapy unless it was their own all along in both its origin and its latency. To this incomprehensible "vertical" account, Fuchs proposed (in harmony with van den Berg's perspective) the alternative of a horizontal unconscious that has no layers. Body memory consists of implicit, non-declarative memories that are active in one's present situation on a lived, bodily level. These memories are neither explicit nor strictly individualistic. They always emerge in and through an intersubjective field of concrete interaction. According to Fuchs, the other may see more about the individual's psychological life in their expressive world engagement than the individual themselves, especially in the case of the unconscious (just as van den Berg and Ey maintained years earlier).

Following the tradition established by Sartre (2018), Fuchs used Kurt Lewin's (1935) concept of life space (see Chapter 5) to articulate the field of conscious and unconscious bodily engagement. The living body accrues memory traces that contribute to the co-constitution of a meaningful life space fit with values and valences. This brings up the issues of attraction, repulsion, and the dynamics of proprietorship as discussed by Ey above. The living body operating in its life space displays a continuum ranging from embraced (even strongly claimed) domains of interaction to disavowed and repugnant domains of possible interaction. These domains are typically active without clear conceptual boundaries. They are fluid, full of ambiguities and indeterminate zones of operation (Fuchs, 2012). Thus, behavior can manifest in a manner that seems senseless, alien, and "other" to the person, but does not come from a source truly exterior to subjectivity (i.e., a reified psychic locality) as Henri Ey had observed. This otherness is, paradoxically, simultaneously alien and one's own. The horizontal unconscious of the living body in lived space makes its presence felt as the hidden reverse side of the lifestyle that typifies one's day-to-day world engagement (see Fuchs, 2012, p. 100). Unconscious fixations are restrictions in a person's space of potential behavior produced by an implicit but still present past that resists participating in the continuing progress of life (which confirms Rollo May's assertion that his work was a continuation of Husserlian thought).

The "Vertical" Expansion of the Unconscious: Affectively Modified Sedimented Meanings

Anastasia Kozyreva (2018) took up Husserl's phenomenology to contribute to the expansion of the vertical unconscious as a complement to Fuchs's horizontal unconscious. She did this by explicating (as Henri Ey did) an affective unconscious from the works of Husserl, which first appeared in his lectures on active and passive synthesis. This work deals with the realm of pre-predicative experience (i.e., experience before it becomes "packaged" for explicit consciousness, as it were; see Moran & Cohen, 2012, p. 259). According to Kozyreva (2018), "Husserl, approaches the unconscious in terms of affective 'non-vivacity,' as a sphere of sedimentation and the horizon of the distant past which stays affectively connected to the living present" (p. 199). However, this affective connection can become conflictual, which would alter its manner of appearance in the present looking out toward future horizons.

According to Kozyreva, the Husserlian affective unconscious is a region of darkness and obscurity in the life of consciousness where knowledge resides in the background of psychological life. For something to be truly unconscious (as opposed to merely pre-affective, prereflective, and pre-conscious), the knowledge must recede so far into the background of one's experiential world that it no longer has the "aliveness" characteristic of that which appears in the foreground of consciousness. This furthest region of background functioning (which is not the mere opposite of consciousness, not a complete and total nothing) is a null point of vitality or "affective zero-horizon" (Kozyreva, 2018, p. 211). The affective null point is not a flattening of affect as conventionally understood in psychology. Rather, in the language of perceptual psychology, the knowledge no longer has any "attentional capture," as it were. Meanings at the null point of vitality are no longer accessible to intuitive insight in the unfolding of personal becoming. In the spirit of William Stern, we may talk about knowledge that escapes salience altogether (see also, Fuchs, 2012, p. 91, on the "fused," undifferentiated, indiscernible nature of body memories). Like Fuchs, Kozyreva maintained, "The difference between conscious and unconscious is grasped in terms of foreground/background differentiations," but she approached the matter from the viewpoint of "affective power and powerlessness" (p. 211).

Between retention (which bears a conspicuous connection to the present) and the completely forgotten lies a continuum of events from one's past, ranging from the not-so-distant past to the distant past or remote horizon. As events transition from present to an ever more remote past, they can lose their vivaciousness and accessibility to varying extents. Their "affective gradations" can progressively lessen as their meanings become increasingly sedimented (Kozyreva, 2018, p. 213). There can be knowledge that is still operative in the functioning of the personality that has become part of a sedimented unconscious of the distant past lacking affective vivacity. What is forgotten does not disappear altogether but instead becomes part of an implicit background of subjective experience without taking the form of "intuitive recollections" (p. 221). As is, this rendering of the unconscious would still not satisfy the psychologists dealing with the affectively charged propensity for human self-deception and the world of defenses against anxiety. There must be a way to account for that which has been swept away into background consciousness but then intrudes upon the present with all the affective overdetermination that psychoanalytic psychology has described.

To accomplish this task, the matter of conflict must be handled. Sedimentation can take on different qualitative forms, non-conflicted or conflicted. Husserl held that the latter consisted of an "affective relation between opposite or antagonistic tendencies," "rivalry," and "the dissension of opposite things" (Kozyreva, 2018, p. 216). In instances of conflictual sedimentation, an incongruence generates negative, potentially unmanageable affective force emanating from the past horizon of consciousness, the effects of which could spill over into living presence. This can then lead to the need to suppress concurrent, clashing affections, which would only serve to further increase tension and affect. Rivalry and suppression thus result in a paradoxical increase of the affective vivacity of sedimented background knowledge. Here, we would have a suppression into background non-intuitiveness but *not* into non-vivacity. "On the contrary," says Kozyreva, "the vivacity gets augmented in the conflict" (p. 216). Kozyreva concluded, "In this sense, it is plausible to accept the zero-affectivity of the past-horizon and repressed affectivity as *two main types of affective modification*, both of which contribute to the phenomenological understanding of the unconscious" (p. 218).

Final Remarks

Existential–phenomenological psychology is better known for its criticisms of the concept of the unconscious than for its attempts to explicate its experiential origins and describe its structural dynamics. As this chapter shows, there have always been voices within existential–phenomenological psychology opting for the latter. Far from rejecting the concept of the unconscious, existential–phenomenological psychology has embraced an expanded view of the unconscious. Its philosophical foundations in no way limit inquiry to the narrow range of reflective knowledge and conscious self-awareness. Rather, phenomenological description is conceived as taking place within overlapping experiential fields, exhibiting manifold horizons. Within these fields, subjects display gradations of "consciousness," sciousness, or awareness.

In the broad view of existential–phenomenological psychology, unconsciousness refers to an excess of meaning and potential beyond what is currently actualizable. Meaning in the life of persons extends far beyond what one can reflect upon at any given moment in our becoming. It extends beyond presence. Thus, Henri Ey spoke of a dialectical system of conscious–unconscious operating within the broader autoconstruction of selfhood. From the perspective of the broad view, the unconscious represents what Rollo May referred to as infinite and protean forms of consciousness. The "geography" of consciousness (von Eckartsberg, 2010) is multileveled in the sense that it is comprised of everything from highly depersonalized, undifferentiated (ambiguous) forms of awareness to acts of reflection displaying high degrees of experiential differentiation and integration.

In addition to the broad view, existential–phenomenological psychology also describes the dynamics of how meanings and potentials are denied actualization and the full light of consciousness. This is a more specialized discourse concerning what would be deemed unconscious, where meanings and potentials can appear too threatening to actualize, so they are denied the full array of cognitive and behavioral resources that would facilitate their realization. Pathways to perceptual salience that would otherwise be available must be closed. This defines the subdomain of the affectively charged, motivationally colored unconscious. Here, a distinction is made between what can be appropriated with responsibility and what must be kept at an arm's length from the proprium or self. The former is thematizable by the subject, the latter is not because it arouses anxieties. Meanings and understandings are kept at varying distances from conscious awareness, ranging from absolute darkness to awareness that eludes experiential differentiation and/or integration to such an extent that it persistently prevents salience. At this level of analysis, for something to qualify as unconscious, the elusiveness would have to be genuine to distinguish it from a commonplace ruse. In other words, this manifestation of the unconscious denotes genuinely self-deluded self-concealment. Self-deluded self-concealment is carried out by the process of self-deception, as described by Fischer (1985). Articulation and thematization are apportioned prejudicially to the meanings and understandings that one has already committed to. The process is quite social. It implicates how one views oneself and one's extended array of personally meaningful viewpoints within the larger theater of social existence. Moreover, strategies of self-deception often entail social isolation from or aggression toward those others deemed the bearers of self-discordant information. Thus, in cases of self-deluded self-concealment, the subject jettisons knowledge from the ego center out toward the body–world–other nexus (van den Berg, 1972). Consequently, the person's unconscious is more discernable and "locatable" in the consciousness of the other. This perspective reflects existential–phenomenological psychology's view of subjectivity as existing intentionally in the world, participating in qualitatively different forms of awareness rather than spread out between two opposing localities residing within the cranium.

Existential–phenomenological psychology anticipated the more recent Husserlian-inspired philosophical contributions to the phenomenology of the unconscious (though this is generally unacknowledged). Contemporary neo-Husserlian literature is in the process of offering a more a robust philosophical framework and a rigorously detailed language to existential–phenomenological psychology that confirms and bolsters its various descriptive explications. Time is an all-important theme in this literature, drawing on Husserl's studies of protention and retention; the overlapping horizons of past, present, and future; the intermingling of memory, imagination, phantasy, and the reproductive potentials of consciousness. These concepts cast the movement back and forth between focal consciousness and background unconsciousness as a dynamical interplay of presence and absence.

The neo-Husserlian philosophical literature has also cast the phenomenological expansion of the unconscious as having horizontal and vertical dimensionality. The horizontal dimension articulated by

Fuchs (2012) revives talking points inherent in the views of Rollo May and Henri Ey using the concepts of functioning intentionality, sedimentation, and embodiment. The horizontal unconscious is comprised of sedimented, implicitly functioning body memories that truncate the process of becoming. There is an "unrecognized reverse side of our experience and conduct, "its other, hidden meaning" (Fuchs, 2012, p. 94). This reverse side can be merely background (thus representing what was referred to as the broad view of unconsciousness above) or bound up in conflict. Concerning the latter, Fuchs observed:

> One does not know something *and* does not want to know it; one does not see something *and* does not want to see it—in other words, one looks past it intentionally-unintentionally. Consciousness is not fully transparent to itself because it hides itself from itself. (p. 101)

The horizontal unconscious operates in the space of action, of possibilities *not* to be actualized (as contrasted with the conventional notion of repression to a psychic domain inside the individual).

The expansion of the vertical dimension plunges into the affective dynamics involved in the constitution of the unconscious. As Kozyreva (2018) showed, as the events of one's past approach the null point of affective vivacity, they can be said to be fading into unconsciousness. This is her Husserlian contribution to the broad view of the unconscious. But, as she also noted, when the events of one's past become embroiled in conflict, they can break through into the present as a mass of disorganizing affect. The increase in affect does not activate a clearly discernable memory trace that can serve some productive purpose. Rather, it generates turbulence in the experiential field, which poses obstacles to rational agency.

Key Terms, Concepts, and Themes

- "The" unconscious (unconsciousness as traditionally conceived)
- Repression
- Reified psychic localities
- Twofold dualism in the theory of the unconscious
- Blank check theory of the unconscious
- Sciousness

- "Fringe" areas or margins in consciousness
- Horizons of consciousness
- Gradations of concretion and salience in consciousness (embedding and withdrawing)
- The unconscious as an awareness of unactualizable potentials and possibilities
- Unconsciousness and bad faith
- "Depth" existential psychology
- Infinite and protean forms of human consciousness
- Consciousness and Awareness
- Languaging as facilitating consciousness (and unconsciousness)
- The unconscious as consciousness handed over to the body and the other
- The unconscious as genuinely self-deluded self-concealment
- The unconscious as part of the always ambiguous autoconstruction of the self
- Plane psychology
- Self, proprium, self-concept
- Freud's mature view of the unconscious
- Unconsciousness as the inverse dimension of consciousness
- The affective unconscious
- The unconscious as a function of self-deception
- Imagination and the temporal co-constitution of unconscious consciousness
- The impressional consciousness of perception
- Fantasized selves and modifications of selves
- Phantasy/fantasy and symbolic forms of self-consciousness
- The horizonal or "horizontal" expansion of the unconscious
- The unconscious as restricted bodying forth
- Sedimented, bodily lived-meaning
- Functioning/operative intentionality
- Ready-to-hand world engagement
- Life space
- Indeterminate zones of operation
- The "vertical" expansion of the unconscious
- Affectively modified sedimented meanings
- Affective non-vivacity
- A paradoxical increase in the affective vivacity of sedimented knowledge

Chapter 9

Assessing the Road Ahead: Existential–Phenomenological Psychology's Footholds, Challenges, and Opportunities

To conclude this text, I would like to make some broad observations concerning the future of existential–phenomenological psychology. I will not digress into issues specific to existential psychology as a standalone current of thought, nor will I expand my focus to address issues related to the whole of existential–humanistic psychology. I have written on these topics, especially the latter, at length elsewhere (e.g., DeRobertis, 2012b, 2015a, 2013, 2016a, 2021b).

This chapter will revolve around three foci: existential–phenomenological psychology's footholds, challenges, and opportunities in the field of psychology. These discussions are not intended to be comprehensive, as that would be impossible due to space constraints. At times, they may be speculative, but I think they are necessary, nonetheless. Existential–phenomenological psychologists would do well to think and talk more about their collective future. With any luck, this ending may serve to stimulate a new beginning, a renewed spirit of discourse among a community of researchers. As noted in the Preface, phenomenologists are perpetual beginners. In this light, what could be more phenomenological than an ending that beckons a beginning?

Footholds

Existential–phenomenological psychology continues to have peer-reviewed journals wherein its research can be published and disseminated, including the *Journal of Phenomenological Psychology*, the *Indo-Pacific Journal of Phenomenology*, *The Humanistic Psychologist*, the *Journal of Humanistic Psychology*, *Phenomenology and the Cognitive*

Sciences, *The Journal of Theoretical and Philosophical Psychology*, *Phenomenology & Practice*, *Theory & Psychology*, and *Janus Head*. Phenomenological research also sometimes appears in journals that typically feature more conventional natural scientific psychological content (e.g., Young, 1992). The internet offers still more opportunities for existential–phenomenological psychologists to promote their perspective and their work, including Academia.edu and ResearchGate, for example.

It is no less important to note that principles of existential–phenomenological psychology are still taught, to varying extents and with varied aims, in graduate programs such as those at Duquesne University, Seattle University, the University of Dallas, the University of West Georgia, Saybrook University, Sonoma State University, the Michigan School of Professional Psychology, Point Park University, the California Institute of Integral Studies, and the Pacifica Graduate Institute. Moreover, there are existential–phenomenological psychologists who are working quite hard to bring their perspective to students in otherwise "mainstream" psychology departments (I am one of them).

Existential–phenomenological psychologists can also engage in professional development that is specific to phenomenology by participating in the activities of numerous professional societies. The Society for Phenomenology and the Human Sciences (SPHS) held its first official meetings in 1981 jointly with the Society for Phenomenology and Existential Philosophy (SPEP) at Northwestern University. They continue to hold an annual conference. Its emphasis is the application of phenomenological methods for concrete investigations in diverse fields that include anthropology, communication studies, counseling, education, ethnography, ethnomethodology, geography, history, linguistics, nursing, pedagogy, philosophy, political theory, psychology, social theory, and sociology. Similarly, the International Human Science Research Conference (IHSRC), founded by Giorgi and colleagues in 1982, has been holding annual meetings for over 40 years. They welcome interdisciplinary contributions, and their conferences are followed by the release of the *International Human Science Research Conference Newsletter*, which is published by the Department of Psychology at Seattle University.

Finally, there have also been some recent developments that are positive signposts for existential–phenomenological psychology's future. The Interdisciplinary Coalition of North American Phenomenologists (ICNAP) formed in 2008 and has been hosting conferences since 2009. This organization is committed to fostering interdisciplinary connections among phenomenologists from areas as diverse as architecture, communicology, philosophy, political science, psychology, and sociology, literature, nursing and health care, psychiatry, social work, education, musicology, and ecology. Their stated goal is to recruit scholars and practitioners into applying phenomenology, going beyond textual exegesis. In 2011, the Society for Qualitative Inquiry in Psychology (SQIP) became an official section of the American Psychological Association's Division 5. SQIP is an organization that seeks to develop and disseminate research based on qualitative methods that analyze experience holistically, as it is lived, including phenomenology. To this end, SQIP has launched a journal called *Qualitative Psychology.*

Challenges

These facts notwithstanding, existential–phenomenological psychology is facing some challenges worth mentioning. Pillars of the existential–phenomenological psychological community are retiring. At institutions where existential phenomenology is taught, it is increasingly giving way to various currents of postmodernism. As Amedeo Giorgi noted in his last public speaking engagement (the 2017 ICNAP conference, May 27, Ramapo College of New Jersey), phenomenology is thriving in philosophy. But, historically, in those places where it has developed a head of steam in psychology, it has receded and "died" (Giorgi's words, not my own). How are we to make sense of this pattern of repeated withdrawal? Surely, there are many reasons, and I cannot pretend to have all the answers. But there are certain facts that cannot be denied.

Proliferating Methodological Diversity

A strong, sustained departmental commitment to existential phenomenology involves a sustained departmental commitment to a methodology, or at least a definite cluster of methodologies deemed phenomenological, rigorous, and thus capable of producing results that are worthy of peer-reviewed publication. But, in the early days of phenomenological psychology's development in Europe, there was very little articulation of what the phenomenological method involved; nor was there any attempt at a theoretical integration, still less unanimity, among its adherents (see Strasser, 1957a). This methodological non-specificity (or worse, ambiguity), if embraced and/or celebrated, can invite an "anything goes" perspective on phenomenological psychological research. This does not lend itself to sustainability. Amedeo Giorgi, seeing this as a problem that would have to be dealt with moving forward, spent a career working out the phenomenological method for psychological application. He and the members of the Duquesne school were able to give phenomenology a new life in the United States.

But Giorgi was never alone, and there has never been a time when someone has not offered an alternative phenomenological method for social scientific application (e.g., Colaizzi, 1973; Moustakas, 1994; van Kaam, 1966; van Manen, 1990). While there has always been diversity in phenomenological methods, there has been a virtual explosion of research methods calling themselves phenomenological in recent years. It seems that new articles and texts presenting their own versions of "phenomenological" procedures (or hardly any procedures at all) appear annually. These works are coming out so fast it is hard to keep track of them. Thus far, from what I have seen, the perspectives and quality of these writings varies quite a bit. To see just a small sampling of these methods, the reader is referred to Giorgi's (2006) and Wertz's (2023) reviews, but they are not exhaustive.

To give the reader some idea of how the current state of methods might confuse trainees, consider how the current text has discussed the epoché as an important methodological feature of phenomenological research. The epoché, it was noted, founds an approach that does not operate based on the presuppositions of naturalistic research. Among other things, it gives the phenomenological researcher an alternative to testing preconceived hypotheses derived from theories. Zahavi (2021) has recently proclaimed the epoché unnecessary, while Larsen and Adu (2022) have advocated an approach to phenomenological psychological research that involves developing a theoretical framework to be applied in data analysis. Alternatively, consider how Chapter 2 of the current text set the tone for the methodological considerations that followed with a detailed outline of procedures capable of achieving nomothetic results. Interpretive Phenomenological Analysis or "IPA" (Smith et al., 2009) was designed as a phenomenologically inspired, ideographically-oriented exploration of what experiences are like for research participants that resist fixed methods (see Giorgi, 2011). Still other authors advocate that aspiring phenomenological researchers create their own phenomenological methods, one that suits their personal experience (e.g., Peoples, 2021).

Such diversity is bound to be confusing and overwhelming to future generations of would-be phenomenological psychological researchers. Further, psychology's broader community of research psychologists is likely to view this proliferation as evidence that phenomenological research is a disorganized, unsystematic dead-end that allows researchers to engage in all sorts of activities that feel satisfying but lack rigor. Without minimizing the potential value of diverse viewpoints, it seems to me that the advancement of phenomenological research will depend on the possibility of a sustained, respectful, and critical dialogue among phenomenological psychologists that establishes some degree of theoretical integration. We need to hear more from members of our research community on issues of rigor, research context, and the aims of their respective research projects. Crucially, we need to discuss the processes involved in disseminating criteria for the process of student mentorship. Theses, dissertations, research articles, and books are being written all over the world using "phenomenology," but the rationale for their chosen methods and the understanding of the methods are not always altogether clear.

Some kind of meta-narrative discourse must be embraced by phenomenological psychologists to help students identify and avoid problematic or false paths to phenomenological research and make informed selections from among those methods that have been properly vetted through peer review. I hope to have contributed to such a discourse with this text, specifically the material in the methodology section, especially as expressed in the outline from Chapter 2. Interestingly, Finlay (2013) has brought up overlapping issues in her efforts to contribute this kind of discourse, asserting the following:

> The essence of the phenomenological research approach encompasses five mutually dependent and dynamically iterative processes: (a) embracing the phenomenological attitude, (b) entering the lifeworld (through descriptions of experiences), (c) dwelling with horizons of implicit meanings, (d) explicating the phenomenon holistically, and (e) integrating frames of reference. The author argues that studies that focus on experience are not necessarily phenomenological. The line being contested is the extent a study goes beyond subjectivity and into the broader realm of lifeworld experience. (p. 172)

Finlay's five processes correspond to points outlined in this text. Embracing the phenomenological attitude corresponds to what I called returning to the things themselves as given in experience. Entering the lifeworld through descriptions of experiences corresponds to what I referred to as returning to the participants themselves and the methodical, rigorous description of living-experience. Dwelling with horizons of implicit meanings relates to attending to the "how" of the phenomenon and its temporal horizons, as well as the extended narrative presented in Chapter 3 on interpretation. Explicating the phenomenon holistically corresponds to what I called attending to the complex, multifaceted whole.

Integrating frames of reference is perhaps the place in which my viewpoint differs from Finlay's (2013), though I am not certain. I have not spoken to her about the issues involved. Finlay described integrating frames of reference as follows:

> At various points in the explication of a phenomenon there will be an opportunity to engage scholarly contemplation of the wider contexts and literature. In particular, phenomenological philosophy can become a lens through which to deepen the analysis of lived worlds. (p. 192)

In my outline, I made no provision for engaging extant literature because that work should, in my opinion, be done in the discussion section after the data analysis is complete. Finlay goes on to mention drawing on phenomenological philosophies for methodological guidance (which can differ, as noted in Chapter 3), but in the same paragraph switches over to speaking about drawing on theories to explicate findings (see p. 192). These are two different things. Researchers generally make decisions about their methodological procedures before analysis, whereas the notion of drawing on theories to explicate findings is a hermeneutic procedure that pertains to the content of the analysis, not the methodological approach per se. While I have no objection to this kind of research activity, I maintain that one needs to proceed with caution when engaging in it. As I have noted several times in this text, the originality of the phenomenological method can be put in peril if one explicates findings by importing the findings of phenomenological philosophers with implicit faith. The work of the researcher must be done under the auspices of the epoché (as noted in Chapter 5) to safeguard the originality of one's description. One must be guided first and foremost by the data and be willing to differ from the philosophical phenomenological heritage that one is tapping into.

The most important historical precedent for the establishment of a phenomenological methodological "core," as it were, comes from Frederick J. Wertz. Wertz's focus on the core of the phenomenological method in psychological research goes back over 40 years. He has argued that all movements in the history of psychology, including even Skinner's radical behaviorism, have relied on the core of the phenomenological method in some way.[1] Wertz's radical thesis is that the core of the method is required in any competent psychology and must therefore be acknowledged as central and essential in its research operations because the entire point of the method is to elucidate the very essence of psychological life. Here, "essence" means (as it has throughout this text) "what it is," in this case what psychological life or the psychological phenomenon under investigation, is—for example, perception, operant conditioning, self-efficacy expectation, and problem solving. Of course, the core of the method can be carried out with self-consciousness or without any explicit or articulated understanding (recall Chapter 4). It can be used with other methods that may or may not be fittingly integrated with the phenomenological core (e.g., hypothesizing, mathematical modeling, cognitive mapping). It can be practiced better, worse, or even erroneously. The primary thrust of Wertz's viewpoint has not changed significantly since the beginning of his career. What has changed is the parsimony with which he has presented the core of the phenomenological method. To illustrate, an early breakdown of the method's primary constituents (Wertz, 1983) follows:

- Empathic presence to the described situation
- Slowing down and patiently dwelling
- Magnification, amplification of the situation
- Suspending belief and employing intense interest
- Turning from objects to meanings
- Recognition and utilization of an "existential baseline"

[1] As noted in Chapter 4, this would be even more obvious in the case of qualitative methods. In *Five Ways of Doing Qualitative Analysis* (Wertz et al., 2011), the concluding chapter focuses on the commonalities of five methods (phenomenological psychology, grounded theory, discourse analysis, narrative research, and intuitive inquiry) and delineates what is practiced by all five ways of analyzing, including those that are not formally acknowledged by the originator or its practitioners. Among those are the phenomenological epochés as well as those commonalities that Wertz had previously found to be operative in psychoanalysis (Wertz, 1983). All in all, the five methods were found to have more in common than is different among them.

- Distinguishing constituents
- Reflection on judgment
- Grasping implicit meaning
- Thinking through relations among constituents
- Thematization of recurrence
- Interrogation of opacity
- Imaginative variation and seeing the essence of the case
- Conceptually guided reflection
- Languaging
- Verification, modification, and reformation
- Finding general validity of insights in the analysis of a single case
- Comparison of insights about different individual cases
- Imaginative variation and generation of individual cases to see essential generality
- Explicit formulation of generality

With each subsequent rendering, the overview of the core of the research process was streamlined. Three years later, Wertz (1986) presented the core of the method with these descriptors:

- Empathic immersion in the described world
- Dwelling and magnifying
- Turning from objects to meaning
- Suspending belief and investigating psychological origins
- Distinguishing constituents
- Explication of the relational whole
- Identification of recurrent meanings
- Comparison of various real cases
- Comparison involving imaginative variations and examples
- Psychological speaking
- Verification

More recently (Wertz, 2023), the core was distilled to the following areas:

- The *phenomenological attitude* (technically the epoché and reduction), a wondering thrall, faithfully discloses lived experience in concrete examples of the phenomena under investigation.

- *Intentional, existential analysis* reflects on lived experience in all its details, including implicit and hidden dimensions, and explicates its processes and meaningful presentations of objects and situations.
- *Eidetic analysis* methodically moves from individual examples of the phenomena under investigation to grasp and conceptualize their *essential* (common, general) structures by imaginatively varying their features and distinguishing invariance from the incidental facts of examples.
- *Description* in natural language faithfully elucidates insights into experiential phenomena, including those that are non-, pre-, and extralinguistic. Knowledge claims are supported and illustrated with *evidence* in concrete examples.

In its current form, Wertz (personal communication, June 20, 2024) summarizes the core of the phenomenological method as follows:

- Studying concrete examples
- Phenomenological epoché/phenomenological reduction
- Eidetic intuition and analysis
- Description of findings

(Intentional, existential, and hermeneutic analyses pervade all four constituents.)

All aspects of the phenomenological method as presented in the current text have been touched upon by Wertz across these presentations, with the greatest linguistic similarity occurring in the second and third articulations noted here (Wertz, 1986, 2023). Moreover, in contrast to Finlay (at least potentially), Wertz and I share a similar view on the use of theory, which he referred to as conceptually guided reflection (1983). Conceptually guided reflection describes how theories may be used in the phenomenological research process, and of this Wertz notes that if guiding concepts are taken from others, they must be considered part of a secondary sort of operation. This kind of work poses the danger of imposing presuppositions on to the data, so any such work would have to take its lead from the case at hand. The emerging structure must be the guide, not the concepts that have been imported.

Psychology's Movement in the Direction of Becoming a STEM Discipline

A major challenge to the advancement of existential-phenomenology in the discipline of psychology concerns the direction that contemporary psychology is heading, meaning the paradigm that it is envisioning as its ideal. Departments are changing. There is pressure for them to become more STEM oriented and, thus, more naturalistic. This trend does not look like it is going to let up any time soon. Were psychology to decisively transform into a STEM discipline, it would put existential–phenomenological psychology at quite a disadvantage. To secure a place for itself, existential–phenomenological psychologists would have to make the argument that the "S" in STEM could refer to human science (not just natural science). But to make that argument, technology, engineering, and mathematics would all have to be articulated in a consonant manner. Technology, engineering, and mathematics would have to be envisioned in ways that are not only non-reductionistic, but also do not relegate phenomenology to the second-class status of being merely propaedeutic. Technology and engineering would have to be taken up by extending the work of thinkers like Emmanuel Levinas and Don Idhe (see Bergen & Verbeek, 2021; Idhe, 2012; Miller & Mitcham, 2020; Peperzak, 1992). Mathematics would likewise have to be taken up phenomenologically, extending the work of Husserl himself (see Hartimo, 2010, 2021). But even if a community of existential–phenomenological psychologists committed to working on such a project, the powers that be in the field of psychology would hardly want to hear about it. STEM status comes with funding, after all. A phenomenological reinterpretation of STEM would likely be seen as a threat to that funding and a liability.

A different way of addressing the problem of philosophical and theoretical divergence is the proposal that phenomenology ought to be naturalized. The issue of phenomenology's naturalization has emerged with considerable force in the area of neurophenomenology. Ever since the famed decade of the brain, neuroscience has come on strong as one of psychology's most dominant perspectives. It has become one of the two most high-profile approaches to psychology, tarrying alongside cognitive psychology. They have joined forces to create various forms of cognitive neuroscience, which has been embraced as a means through which psychology can be refounded in the image of a STEM discipline. Fortunately, phenomenology has made its way into cognitive neuroscience in the form of neurophenomenology, spearheaded by Francisco Varela (see Rudrauf et al., 2003). Neurophenomenological researchers and commentators have opened a space for phenomenologists to contribute to a highly influential current of thought. But, their fine work notwithstanding, there are questions concerning what phenomenology is to this new generation of scholars (see Giorgi, 2018; Lopes, 2024). It is, after all, neurophenomenology, not phenomenological neurology. The proposal that phenomenology ought to be naturalized is part of their ongoing dialogue, but it is a controversial proposition (e.g., see Albertazzi, 2018; Moran 2013). There is controversy as to how to go about it and, depending how it is done and what one means by a "naturalized phenomenology," a thoroughgoing naturalization of phenomenology would likely guarantee that it will go on to be embraced as merely propaedeutic to natural science research. If the past is any gauge of the future, the rhetoric of natural science will likely, as it always has, overtake and suppress the originality and profundity of human science (Rennie, 1995).

The originality and profundity of the phenomenological method emerges from its ability to produce insightful results that do not dissolve into naturalistic interpretations. Naturalizing phenomenology could merely amount to an "if you can't beat 'em, join 'em" philosophy. Erwin Straus (e.g., 1966, 1967) gave phenomenologists a non-naturalistic neurological foundation to work from (recently revived by McGilchrist, 2009). But how phenomenology will engage neuroscience in the future remains to be seen. Will it give way to a permanent relegation of the world as viewed from the perspective of living-experience to the world as viewed naturalistically, as a neurologism? Or will it sow the seeds of change in psychology in a positive direction for phenomenology?

Problems Related to Representation and Scientific Presence

Another challenge to the future of existential–phenomenological psychology is the fact that there is too little of it taught at lower levels of education. It tends to be cast as an advanced topic area, something more suitable for graduate school. But how would students find their way to it? Less presence at the undergraduate level means that every other school of thought, along with their respective approaches to research, have ample time to germinate. Existential–phenomenological psychology thus stands at a pedagogical disadvantage. "Phenomenology" appears less and less in college texts, and when it has appeared, it has often been mischaracterized, if not disparaged (e.g., see Churchill, 1988; Henry, 2017; Wertz, 1992). Introductions to existential–phenomenological psychology written by someone more knowledgeable would be a valuable tool in attempting to ameliorate this problem, but these texts have been a problem in their own right. Obviously, this text is an attempt to address this problem, and it is something I have been struggling with since 1996 (as discussed in the Preface).

Yet another challenge that existential–phenomenological psychology must face pertains to the development of its database. Whereas conventional natural scientific psychology values replication, phenomenological research seeks the repetition of findings for the purpose of fine tuning its general structural descriptions and expanding its typological roadmap. But to accomplish this task, more researchers are needed. In addition to sheer numbers, there is an issue that needs to be addressed (nowise specific to existential–phenomenological psychology) related to what seems to me to be a pervasive trend of neglect when it comes to the literature review portion of research. I have been reviewing articles for several journals for many years now. Over the years, I have been sent numerous research articles in need of review where the authors make no mention of prior works that have yielded the same or similar results (including studies that have confirmed results from my own research). In defense of those doing phenomenological research, this may be related to the additional problem of dissemination. More of the fine phenomenological research that has been done in theses, dissertations, articles, and books needs to be more efficiently and effectively disseminated so that existential–phenomenological programs of research can build upon what has been done.

Interestingly, Carl Rogers (1985) once spoke out disappointedly that not enough progress was being made with respect to getting human science research published. As he phrased it at the time:

> I am puzzled by this lack of publication, because a number of these [publications] seem worthy of presentation to the professional public. Is it that we still doubt the worth of such studies, feeling that they are somehow inferior to research based on statistical analysis? I feel it is most unfortunate that these investigations simply sit in their institutional files without being known to our profession. Instead of "Publish or perish," our slogan should be, "Don't hide your light under a bushel!" (p. 19)

Rogers went on to note that much of this research is being done by aspiring clinicians who are content to leave their hard work behind as they transitioned into practice. This is likely still relevant. Many students who are attracted to existential-phenomenology are headed for clinical careers. Among those who wish to continue to do research, many (probably most) are focused on research projects that will help them with their clinical work. This is laudable, of course. But this may or may not translate into an abiding concern for the kind of rigor that would resonate with the wider community of non-clinical psychological researchers. The priority of many a research practitioner may just as likely be whatever method opens creative avenues to work with clients. This is not a putdown, but it does present another layer of complexity to the problem of developing a strong existential–phenomenological psychology database (not to mention methodological integration).

Areas of Opportunity

There are many ways to assess areas of opportunity for existential–phenomenological psychology. One could, for example, consider how lines of established research by groundbreaking phenomenologically oriented social scientists (e.g., Erwin Straus, Eugene Minkowski, Viktor Emil von Gebsattel, Alfred Schutz, Aron Gurwitsch) might be extended using contemporary, formalized phenomenological procedures. One could also consider how new lines of psychological research might be developed from phenomenological philosophical research (one such line will be mentioned at the end of this chapter). But rather than undertake such an ambitious task, which would likely require an entire chapter for even the most general of overviews, the current discussion will instead piggyback on emerging trends in psychology.

To be clear, I am not suggesting that existential–phenomenological psychology ought to become more "trendy." Having examined a list of 11 emerging trends in psychology for 2023 in the *Monitor on Psychology* (American Psychological Association, 2023), I have noted that much of what is presented there as "emerging trends" are actually manifestations of changes that have been taking place in psychology for quite some time. As I see it, dominant themes are evident across these trends and are revelatory of these changes. The themes are embedded in the following eight of the eleven emerging areas:

- Worker well-being is in demand.
- Efforts to improve children's mental health are increasing.

- New funding from venture capitalists is focusing on mental health apps for children and teens, as well as platforms that incorporate coaching.
- Suicide prevention is getting renewed attention and is less often being viewed as a symptom of mental illness. Recent efforts to lessen suicide rates have yielded some positive results, but the benefits have not been shared equally. White men and women were the primary beneficiaries. Moreover, young people are increasingly considering suicide. It has become the second most common cause of death in young people, and attempted suicide rates are disproportionately higher for girls than for boys.
- Psychologists are joining forces with other professions to tackle big societal problems, from childhood mental health to police violence in communities.
- Psychologists are expanding the one-to-one therapy approach to strengthen psychological health across populations.
- Psychological research is becoming more inclusive.
- "EDI" (i.e., equity, diversity, and inclusion) roles are expanding in psychology.

Two overlapping themes dominate this list: an emphasis on health and well-being (with a special developmental concern for the health and well-being of children and adolescents) and a broader focus on diversity (including an interest in the health of entire communities). While the specifics of these foci may have new dimensions to them (e.g., the integration of apps), the overarching themes are familiar. The focus on health and well-being was reawakened by positive psychology's humanistic revival around the turn of the millennium. The developmental concern for children's mental health extends back to the works of humanistic pioneer Alfred Adler (1904) and has always been a central theme in existential–humanistic developmental psychology (see DeRobertis, 2023). The focus on diverse populations has been steadily increasing since the middle of last century, especially since the turn of the millennium when psychology saw a spike in interest in multiculturalism (see DeRobertis, 2015b).

Existential–phenomenological psychology has an opportunity to grow, and also to demonstrate its scientific utility and insightfulness, by furthering its contributions to the contemporary literature on human health (Messas et al., 2018; Murray, 2001; Picton et al., 2017). Positive psychology has left a door open for phenomenological contributions to its database since its advancement in the work of Mihaly Csikszentmihalyi (see Csikszentmihalyi, 1990; Murray, 2001). But the wider movement of positive psychology largely turned its back on phenomenology in favor of a strict reliance on quantitative methods. Fortunately, a new generation of positive psychology's adherents are listening to criticisms from various quarters of psychology (e.g., existential–humanistic, theoretical, multicultural) and are striving to grow beyond the strictures of Martin Seligman's initial vision (see DeRobertis & Bland, 2021). But there is work to be done. Many positive psychologists have yet to get phenomenology right (e.g., see Churchill, 2014; Morley 2014; Waterman 2013). Self-determination theory has affiliated itself with positive psychology, humanistic psychology, and phenomenology, and the prospects for future dialogue are promising. But they have not yet had enough of their phenomenological foundations exposed for critical examination. Further, they have not integrated a specifically phenomenological psychological line of research into their database, so phenomenology remains propaedeutic to their work (see DeRobertis & Bland, 2018).

Existential–phenomenological psychologists ought to make their voices heard amid the slow disintegration of positive psychology's initial myopia. They ought to make their presence felt so that positive psychology's next generation of researchers features quality phenomenological research. After all, being-and-becoming, transcendence, self-transcendence, fulfillment, self-realization/self-actualization, maturity, the good life, happiness, and the like are all important topics within existential phenomenology. My own work on happiness (DeRobertis, 2016b) and Prasetya and colleagues' (2023) more recent study of grit are select examples of how phenomenological research can get involved in this increasing focus on health and well-being. There have also been special issues of journals, such as the *Indo-Pacific Journal of Phenomenology* (see Guse, 2017) and *Metodo* (see Guccinelli & Iocco, 2020) dedicated to phenomenology and positive psychology. But existential–phenomenological psychology's response to positive psychology has not been terribly organized. The special issue of *Metodo* is quite good, but it is almost completely philosophical. Only one article includes a study that employs a psychological method in the form of IPA (Motta & Bortolotti, 2020). The special issue of the *Indo-Pacific Journal of Phenomenology* contains several studies, but the methods, when they are used, are quite different from each other: case studies, IPA, Grounded Theory, and Dahlberg and colleagues' (2008) reflective lifeworld research or "RLR." In the *Journal of Positive Psychology*, "phenomenology" almost always refers to some vague notion of subjective experience with an emphasis on "feelings." The journal contains one study using van Manen's method (Chauhan et al., 2020), and the founder of IPA contributed an article commentary (Smith, 2017) arguing that his experiential approach ought to be utilized in positive psychology.

Existential-phenomenological psychology is similarly poised to expand its specialized contributions to the literature on mental health in childhood, youth, and adolescence. There is a long tradition of phenomenological research in philosophy, psychology, and pedagogy of studying childhood, youth, and adolescence. Some of this work is explicitly focused on health and optimal development (e.g., see DeRobertis, 2008, 2012b, 2017), while many other works deal with myriad issues and themes that are related to health without stating it as such. There is much to consider here, far too much than can be covered in the current chapter. For an overview of these contributions, see DeRobertis (2023) and DeRobertis (2026). Meanwhile, more will be said of the possibilities of a phenomenologically driven developmental psychology in the discussion of culture, to which we now turn.

Existential-phenomenological psychology should ramp up its efforts to actualize its cultural dimensions so that it may go on to become a key player in psychology's ongoing multicultural awakening. Existential-phenomenological philosophy has always offered more than existential-phenomenological psychology has taken and applied in this area. One very simple example is the work of Frantz Omar Fanon who, drawing on thinkers like Jean-Paul Sartre, wrote extensively about the experience of living as a person of color in a world dominated by whiteness (e.g., Fanon, 2004, 2008; Laubscher et al., 2022). More recently, Ngo (2017) made a fine contribution to racial phenomenology in her, *The Habits of Racism: A Phenomenology of Racism and Racialized Embodiment*. There is a long tradition of phenomenological studies in feminine experience going back at least to the work of *de Beauvoir* (2009). A notable work in this area is Dolezal's (2015) *The Body and Shame: Phenomenology, Feminism, and the Socially Shaped Body*. But we need to hear more from both phenomenological philosophy and psychology on the varieties of racial and ethnic experience (e.g., Hoyos, 2012; Køster & Kofod, 2022; Lau, 2016; Oliver et al., 2023), including the diverse experiential worlds of sexual and gender minorities. We need more existential phenomenology of the "other," all those others who have traditionally struggled to be seen and heard, especially those who have been alienated by forces of oppression.

Fortunately, culturally themed phenomenological work in psychology has increased in recent years. Hannush (2007) has brought up the importance of a multiculturally sensitive phenomenology with respect to counseling and phenomenologically based qualitative research. Hereford and colleagues (2023) have spoken to this in terms of case conceptualizations in psychotherapeutic intervention. And numerous studies of various cultural phenomena have been surfacing. Predictably, methodological diversity abounds. More importantly, the way this diversity is evolving reinforces the aforementioned need for a larger conversation about the development of a meta-narrative that emphasizes both rigor and selection criteria. Studies in this area regularly cherry-pick from among varied methods, sometimes methods representing different approaches to the application of phenomenology, leaving one to wonder if each study is applying a unique method designed by each and every researcher (e.g., see Alhazmi & Kaufmann, 2022; Chang & Berk, 2009; Choi & Luke, 2011; Hart, 2018; Leigh-Osroosh & Hutchinson, 2019; Peters et al., 2017). Such proliferation forces one to question whether a new generation of phenomenological psychological researchers are seeking to understand the deeper implications of the methods and procedures that they are borrowing from. This may turn out to be a problem that could truncate existential–phenomenological psychology's efficacy and relevance in this area.

This would be quite unfortunate. For existential–phenomenological psychology to actualize its cultural dimensions is tantamount to it becoming what it set out to be all along. As Strasser (1957a) noted, from the time of its emergence, phenomenological psychology's alternative to natural science psychology advocated for a view of human beings as "more . . . the creator of a world of culture than as a species in the world of organism" (p. 34). Many years later, von Eckartsberg (1989) eloquently described how the unfolding meaning of intentionality in the history of phenomenology (overwhelmingly in philosophy) has resulted in a magnification of the importance of culture creation, which he (in the language of Alfred Adler) dubbed "*cooperative-way-of-life-creation*"; p. 155).

For my own part, I have been working to found a culturally sensitive, phenomenologically driven perspective in the area of developmental psychology based on these principles for quite some time. After the release of my first developmental text, *Humanizing Child*

Developmental Theory: A Holistic Approach (DeRobertis, 2008), my attention increasingly turned toward the sociocultural and historical dimensions of human development. Several articles addressing these issues were brought together to seed the text, *The Whole Child: Selected Papers on Existential–Humanistic Child Psychology* (DeRobertis, 2012b). This then set the stage for a subsequent chapter in an edited volume that was explicitly dedicated to the possibility of a multicultural model of development informed by phenomenological thinkers and insights (DeRobertis, 2015b). The chapter spoke broadly to the intertwined relevance of culture, diversity, and narrative in development. Human development was conceptualized as a *self-cultivation* process.

According to this conceptualization, development is a dynamically unfolding story that emerges on an implicit basis from within a field of stories that permeate the culture in question. In each case, the ongoing story of one's development originates in rhythmic, highly tactile sensorimotor–affective exchanges with the primary caregiver and radiates outward, manifesting varying degrees and styles of world-openness. The world-openness of one's life story begins (but does not end) with this primordial intersubjective synchronization (or lack thereof).

Human development is seen as optimally facilitated when it occurs in a cultural context that is rich with narrative meanings that reflect the inherently transcendent, "transpersonal" potentials of unfolding human existence and maturing selfhood. On this view, human growth and development involves the intertwined bio-cultural situatedness of the developing person and the imaginative, autopoietic, autogenetic evolution of selfhood. Human growth and development are seen a process of *situated becoming oneself.* Conceptually, this is an effort to steer a path between depersonalizing forms of reductionism (e.g., biologism, sociologism, and historicism) and various forms of ethnocentric individualism. In terms of the experiential world of the developing person, the self-cultivation process unfolds through a dynamic, situationally responsive integration of one's potentials for learning and creating (DeRobertis, 2017). To achieve optimal levels of growth and health, self-cultivation entails creatively negotiating life's myriad existential dualities (e.g., essence–existence, differentiation–integration, stability–change, being–nonbeing, dependence–independence, being a body–having a body, participation–consumption, activity–passivity, completion–incompletion), which will inevitably manifest in different ways depending on one's cultural context and relative level of maturity (DeRobertis & Bland, 2020b). The research on cross-cultural learning presented in Chapter 2 illustrates the research trajectory of this work. It dovetails with Husserl's work on homeworlds and alienworlds (see DeRobertis & Bland, 2020a), of which more will be said momentarily.

Final Remarks: A Return to Beginnings

Early on in this text, the methods section (Chapter 3) discussed arriving at points of obscurity in one's data analysis, which can create opportunities for interdisciplinary collaboration. Along related lines, we just (last chapter) completed an exploration of phenomenological approaches to consciousness as itself exhibiting varied forms and gradations of obscurity (i.e., of *un*consciousness). The current discussion of culture extends this theme of relative obscurity, bringing the text full circle. Culture figures as an important horizonal consideration for existential–phenomenological psychology, permeating everything from the proximal, still-accessible margins of consciousness to the farther reaches of what was called the "horizontal" unconscious in Chapter 8 (Corrington, 1991; Moran, 2017). As van den Berg (1961, 1971) has shown, the Freudian unconscious erupted at a very specific affectively tumultuous time in Western history, thus implicating culture in the "vertical" (Kozyreva, 2018) formations of the unconscious as well. So much culturally embedded meaning functions silently in the background of every human being's experiential world. I see this regularly in my cross-cultural psychology classes. The most challenging aspect of that course is for students to account for their own cultural backgrounds in the formation of their attitudes and dispositions. Students struggle to realize that factors as varied as ethnicity, skin color, sexuality, religion, gender, language, and socioeconomic status are having a formative influence on their ways of perceiving and relating to themselves, other people, and the world at large. They are typically only vaguely aware at best of the extent to which their meaning-making activity is "othered."

The goal of the course is not to one-sidedly disparage one's inevitably multicultural embeddedness as mere "bias." Obviously, bias is always a possibility to be considered, but the broader aim is to increase one's awareness and understanding of oneself as a fundamentally relational, "othered" being. Students learn to see themselves in a more robust, lucid manner by learning about the broader field of meaning-making within which they have developed (and continue to develop). But learning about oneself also extends beyond the cultures to which one belongs. Each week the class involves readings on cultural diversity and discussions among students wherein they learn about one another's cultural embeddedness. In the process, they develop a better grasp of the presuppositions and boundaries of both their own and other people's worldviews. The process is inherently reciprocal. Self-sameness and difference co-modulate each other in a growth process (for a discussion of the extant psychological literature on this in the light of phenomenological research findings, see DeRobertis & Bland, 2020a).

This dynamical relationship makes it imperative that existential–phenomenological psychology revisit the philosophical origins of its concept of "world," extending all the way back to its formulation in Heidegger and especially Husserl. In Chapter 1 it was noted that in existential–phenomenological psychology "world" is not a mere sum of material beings existing independent of human subjectivity. Rather, world denotes a network of meanings intelligible in the light of a person's relatively organized relationships and projects, which emerge from thrown, factical conditions. To be-in-a-world is to co-constitute a meaningful situation. This involves being in a particular body (implicating gender, race, beauty, ability, disability, and so forth), being in a particular time and place in a family, society, culture, and history, speaking a specific language, and being oriented toward horizons of future possibility. Yet, within this text, there have also been references to being-in-*the*-world (e.g., see Chapter 1) and *the* world of living-experience (e.g., see Chapter 3). The fact is that in existential–phenomenological psychology, terms like being-in-the-world and "the lifeworld" are ways of naming a dynamic tension. To be in *the* world is to simultaneously, without contradiction, live in and amid diverse *worlds.* Again, we return to the existential–phenomenological paradox introduced in the Preface. Existential–phenomenological psychology approaches human psychological life as involving the typical and the unique, the universal and the particular (Natanson, 1970). What appears to be a conundrum is human participation in a pervasive metaphysical duality. In the face of it, phenomenology has always had to perform a delicate balancing act. It has always been a persistent effort to navigate between the extremes of an oppressive, alienating universalism and an equally oppressive, alienating relativism. It has had to steer away from the notion of a single, uniform, totalizing world without resorting to a perspective that would open the door for a paralyzing proliferation of essentially incommunicable worlds.

Human psychological life unfolds in that perpetual in-between that Husserl described as the liminal experiential structure homeworld/alienworld (Steinbock, 1995). It is in this line of analysis that the future and fulfillment of existential–phenomenological psychology lies. The conceptual backdrop has its origins in varied sources. From the ranks of phenomenological philosophy, Husserl guides us toward the process of encountering the alien (see Steinbock, 1995, 2017; Waldenfels, 1990). Gabriel Marcel, Martin Buber, Franz Rosenzweig, Emmanuel Levinas, and Remy Kwant sharpen our focus with their work on alterity (see DeRobertis & Iuculano, 2005; Strasser, 1978; Treanor, 2006). Strasser (1969) gave the name *dialogal phenomenology* to this focus of investigation. Paul Ricoeur (1992) offers it a multidimensional, integrative ontology in his aptly titled text *Oneself as Another*. From within the social sciences, we find that we have a partner in phenomenological sociology, which favors us with investigations of "the stranger" (e.g., McLemore, 1970; Schuetz, 1944; Simmel, 1908). More recently, phenomenologies of the stranger have reemerged in philosophy (Kearney, 2011). They need to erupt in existential–phenomenological psychology. This is a road that must be traveled as we all (as we always do) begin again.

Key Terms, Concepts, and Themes

- Publication outlets for phenomenological psychological literature
- Places to study phenomenological psychology
- Professional organizations for phenomenological psychology
- Proliferating methodological diversity
- Seeking a phenomenological methodological "core" (Wertz, Finlay, & DeRobertis)
- Conceptually guided reflection
- Psychology as a STEM Discipline
- Neurophenomenology
- Naturalized phenomenology
- Neurologism
- Dwindling presence of phenomenological psychology in textbooks and education
- Health and well-being as an area of opportunity for phenomenological psychology

- Health in childhood and adolescences as area of opportunity for phenomenological psychology
- Diversity an area of opportunity for phenomenological psychology
- Cooperative-way-of-life creation
- Self-cultivation
- Situated becoming oneself
- The problematic of "the world" in phenomenology
- Homeworlds
- Alienworlds

References

Aanstoos, C. M. (2003). The relevance of humanistic psychology. *Journal of Humanistic Psychology, 43*(3), 121–132. https://doi.org/10.1177/0022167803043003010

Adler, A. (1904). Der arzt als erzieher. *Ärztliche Standeszeitung, 15*(3), 4–5.

Adler, A. (1958). *What life should mean to you*. Capricorn Books.

Adler, A. (1979). *Superiority and social interest.* W. W. Norton & Company.

Adler, J. M. (2008). Two modes of thought: The narrative/paradigmatic disconnect in the Bailey book controversy. *Archives of Sexual Behavior,* 37(3), 422–425. https://doi.org/10.1007/s10508-008-9318-0

Albertazzi L. (2018). Naturalizing phenomenology: A must have? *Frontiers in Psychology, 9,* Article 1933. https://doi.org/10.3389/fpsyg.2018.01933

Alhazmi, A. A., & Kaufmann, A. (2022). Phenomenological qualitative methods applied to the analysis of cross-cultural experience in novel educational social contexts. *Frontiers in Psychology, 13,* Article 785134. https://doi.org/10.3389/fpsyg.2022.785134

Allen, J. (1976). A Husserlian phenomenology of the child. *Journal of Phenomenological Psychology, 6*, 164–179. http://dx.doi.org/10.1163/156916276X00052

Allport, G. W. (1955). *Becoming: Basic considerations for a psychology of personality*. Yale.

Allport, G. W. (1968). *The person in psychology: Selected essays.* Beacon Press.

American Psychological Association (n.d.-a). Mechanistic theory. In APA Dictionary of Psychology. https://dictionary.apa.org/mechanistic-theory

American Psychological Association (n.d.-b). Conation, conative. In APA Dictionary of Psychology. https://dictionary.apa.org/conation

American Psychological Association (2023, January/February). 11 emerging trends for 2023: What's ahead for psychologists and the field? *Monitor on Psychology*. https://www.apa.org/monitor/2023/01/trends-report

Apsler, R. (1975). Effects of embarrassment on behavior toward others. *Journal of Personality and Social Psychology, 32*(1), 145–153. https://doi.org/10.1037/h0076699

Aristotle (1985). *Nicomachean ethics*. Hackett Publishing Company.

Aristotle (2017). *De Anima*. Hackett Publishing Company.

Ashworth, P. D. (2009). William James's "psychologist's fallacy" and contemporary human science research. *International Journal of Qualitative Studies on Health and Well-being, 4*, 195–206. http://dx.doi.org/10.3109/17482620903223036

Aue, T., Lavelle, L. A., & Cacioppo, J. T. (2009). Great expectations: What can fMRI research tell us about psychological phenomena? *International Journal of Psychophysiology, 73*(1), 10–16. https://doi.org/10.1016/j.ijpsycho.2008.12.017

Babcock, M. K. (1988). Embarrassment: A window on the self. *Journal for the Theory of Social Behaviour, 18*(4), 459–483. https://doi.org/10.1111/j.1468-5914.1988.tb00510.x

Babcock, M. K., & Sabini, J. (1990). On differentiating embarrassment from shame. *European Journal of Social Psychology, 20*(2), 151–169. https://doi.org/10.1002/ejsp.2420200206

Bacon, F. (2011) *The works of Francis Bacon, Vol. 3, Philosophical Works.* Cambridge University Press.

Bandura, A. (2008). Reconstrual of "free will" from the agentic perspective of social cognitive theory. In J. Baer, J. C. Kaufman, & R. F. Baumeister (Eds.), *Are we free? Psychology and free will* (pp. 86–127). Oxford University Press.

Bell, D. (1990). *Husserl.* Routledge.

Bergen, D. (2008). *Human development: Traditional and contemporary theories.* Pearson.

Bergen, J.P., & Verbeek, P.-P. (2021) To-Do Is to Be: Foucault, Levinas, and Technologically Mediated Subjectivation. *Philosophy & Technology, 34*, 325–348. https://doi.org/10.1007/s13347-019-00390-7

Bernet, R. (2002). Unconscious consciousness in Husserl and Freud. *Phenomenology and the Cognitive Sciences, 1*(3), 327–351. https://doi.org/10.1023/A:1021316201873

Biceaga V. (2010). *The concept of passivity in Husserl's phenomenology.* Springer.

Binswanger, L. (1963). *Being-in-the-world: Selected papers of Ludwig Binswanger.* Harper Torch Books.

Bolton, N. (1982). The lived world: Imagination and the development of experience. *Journal of Phenomenological Psychology, 13*, 1–18. https://doi.org/10.1163/156916282X00082

Boss, M. (1963) *Psychoanalysis and daseinsanalysis.* DaCapo.

Bourgeois, W. (1976). Verstehen in the social sciences. *Journal for General Philosophy of Science, 7*(1), 26–38.

Brentano, F. (1995). *Descriptive psychology.* Routledge.

Brentano, F. (2015). *Psychology from an empirical standpoint.* Routledge

Bruner, J. (1986). *Actual minds, possible worlds.* Harvard University Press.

Bruner, J. (1990). *Acts of meaning.* Cambridge. Harvard University Press.

Buytendijk, F. J. J. (1974). *Prolegomena to an anthropological physiology.* Duquesne University Press.

Chang, D. F., & Berk, A. (2009). Making cross-racial therapy work: A phenomenological study of clients' experiences of cross-racial therapy. *Journal of Counseling Psychology, 56*(4), 521–536. https://doi.org/10.1037/a0016905

Chauhan, P. H., Leeming, D., & King, N. (2020). A hermeneutic phenomenological exploration of feeling joyful, *The Journal of Positive Psychology, 15*(1), 99–106. https://doi.org/10.1080/17439760.2019.1690670

Choi, K. M., & Luke, M. (2011). A phenomenological approach to understanding early adult friendships of third culture kids. *Journal of Asia Pacific Counseling, 1*(1), 47–60.

Churchill, S. D. (1988). Humanistic psychology and introductory textbooks. *The Humanistic Psychologist, 16*(2), 341–357. https://doi.org/10.1080/08873267.1988.9976830

Churchill, S. D. (2012). Teaching phenomenology by way of "second-person perspectivity" (from my thirty years at the University of Dallas), *Indo-Pacific Journal of Phenomenology, 12*(3), 1–14. https://doi/10.2989/IPJP.2012.12.3.6.1114

Churchill, S. D. (2014). At the crossroads of humanistic psychology and positive psychology, *The Humanistic Psychologist, 42*(1), 1–5, https://doi.org10.1080/08873267.2014.891902

Churchill, S. D. (2016). Les dimensions descriptives et interprétatives de la recherche phénoménologique. Complémentaires ou mutuellement exclusives? *Recherches Qualitatives, 35*(2), 45–63. http://www.recherche-qualitative.qc.ca/revue/

Churchill, S. D. (2018). On the empathic mode of intuition: A phenomenological foundation for social psychiatry. In M. Englander (Ed.), *Phenomenology and the social context of psychiatry* (pp. 65–94). Bloomsbury.

Churchill, S. D. (2022). *Essentials of existential phenomenological research*. American Psychological Association. https://doi.org/10.1037/0000257-000

Churchill, S. D., & Wertz, F. J. (2015). An introduction to phenomenological research in psychology: Historical, conceptual, and methodological foundations. In K. J. Schneider, J. F. Pierson, & J. F. T. Bugental (Eds.), *The handbook of humanistic psychology: Theory, research, and practice* (pp. 275–295). Sage.

Clegg, J. W. (2016). Reconsidering philosophy of science pedagogy in psychology: An evaluation of methods texts. *Journal of Theoretical and Philosophical Psychology, 36*(4), 199–213. http://dx.doi.org/10.1037/teo0000035

Colaizzi, P. F. (1973). *Reflection and research in psychology: A phenomenological study of learning*. Duquesne University Press.

Corballis, M. C. (2007, May–June) The uniqueness of human recursive thinking. *American Scientist,* 95(3), 240. https://doi.org/10.1511/2007.65.240

Corrington, R. S. (1991). Horizons and contours: Toward an ordinal phenomenology. *Metaphilosophy, 22*(3), 179–189.

Costa, R. E., & Shimp, C. P. (2011). Methods courses and texts in psychology: "Textbook science" and "tourist brochures." *Journal of Theoretical and Philosophical Psychology, 31*(1), 25–43. https://doi.org/10.1037/a0021575

Craig, E. (1988). Daseinsanalysis: A quest for essentials. *The Humanistic Psychologist, 16*(1), 1–21. https://doi.org/10.1080/08873267.1988.9976809

Csikszentmihalyi, M. (1990). *Flow: The psychology of optimal experience.* Harper & Row.

Dahlberg, K, Dahlberg, H., & Nyström, M. (2008). *Reflective lifeworld research.* Studentlitteratur.

Davidson, L. (2021). *Overcoming psychologism: Husserl and the transcendental reform of psychology*. Springer

de Beauvoir, S. (2009). *The second sex.* Vintage Books.

DeRobertis, E. M. (1996). *Phenomenological psychology: A text for beginners.* University Press of America

DeRobertis, E. M. (2008). *Humanizing child developmental theory: A holistic approach.* iUniverse.

DeRobertis, E. M. (2011). Deriving a third force approach to child development from the works of Alfred Adler. *Journal of Humanistic Psychology 51*(4), 492–515. https://doi.org/10.1177/0022167810386960

DeRobertis, E. M. (2012a). *Existential–phenomenological psychology: A brief introduction.* Kindle Direct Publishing.

DeRobertis, E. M. (2012b). *The whole child: Selected papers on existential–humanistic child psychology*. Kindle Direct Publishing.

DeRobertis, E. M. (2013). Humanistic psychology: Alive in the 21st century? *Journal of Humanistic Psychology, 53*(4), 419–437. https://doi.org/10.1177/0022167812473369

DeRobertis, E. M. (2015a). Philosophical–anthropological considerations for an existential–humanistic ecopsychology. *The Humanistic Psychologist, 43*(4), 323–337. https://doi.org/10.1080/08873267.2014.961637

DeRobertis, E. M. (2015b). Toward a humanistic–multicultural model of development. In K. J. Schneider, J. F. Pierson, & J. F. T. Bugental (Eds.), *The handbook of humanistic psychology: Theory, research, and practice* (pp. 227–242). Sage.

DeRobertis, E. M. (2016a). On framing the future of humanistic psychology. *The Humanistic Psychologist, 44*(1), 18–41. https://doi.org/10.1037/hum0000014

DeRobertis, E. M. (2016b). The phenomenology of happiness: Stephen Strasser's eidetic explication. *The Humanistic Psychologist, 44*(1), 72–88. https://doi.org/10.1037/hum0000012

DeRobertis, E. M. (2017). *The phenomenology of learning and becoming: Enthusiasm, creativity, and self-development.* Palgrave.

DeRobertis, E. M. (2021a). Piaget and Husserl: Comparisons, contrasts, and challenges for future research. *The Humanistic Psychologist, 49*(4), 496–518. https://doi.org/10.1037/hum0000183

DeRobertis, E. M. (2021b). *Profiles of personality: Integration, paradox, and the process of becoming* (2nd ed.). University Professors Press.

DeRobertis, E. M. (2021c). The humanistic revolution in psychology: Its inaugural vision. *Journal of Humanistic Psychology, 61*(1), 8–32. https://doi.org/10.1177/0022167820956785

DeRobertis, E. M. (2022). Epistemological foundations of humanistic psychology's approach to the empirical. *Journal of Theoretical and Philosophical Psychology, 42*(2), 61–77. https://doi.org/10.1037/teo0000181

DeRobertis, E. M. (2023). Historical foundations of existential–humanistic developmental psychology. *The Humanistic Psychologist.* Advance online publication. https://doi.org/10.1037/hum0000315

DeRobertis, E. M. (2026). Existential–humanistic developmental psychology. In L. Hoffman, L. X. Vallejos, D. Hocoy, & P. Tummala-Narra (Eds.), *APA handbook of humanistic and existential psychology* (Vol. 1, *History, research, philosophy, and theory*, pp. 521–543). American Psychological Association

DeRobertis, E. M., & Bland, A. M. (2018). Tapping the humanistic potential of self-determination theory: Awakening to paradox. *The Humanistic Psychologist, 46*(2), 105–128. https://doi.org/10.1037/hum0000087

DeRobertis, E. M., & Bland, A. M. (2020a). From personal threat to cross-cultural learning: An eidetic investigation. *Journal of Phenomenological Psychology, 51*(1), 1–15. https://doi.org/10.1163/15691624-12341368

DeRobertis, E. M., & Bland, A. M. (2020b). Lifespan human development and "the humanistic perspective": A contribution toward inclusion. *The Humanistic Psychologist, 48*(1), 3–27. https://doi.org/10.1037/hum0000141

DeRobertis, E. M., & Bland, A. M. (2021). Humanistic and positive psychologies: The continuing narrative after two decades. *Journal of Humanistic Psychology*, Advance Online Publication. https://doi.org/10.1177/00221678211008353

DeRobertis, E. M., & Iuculano, J. (2005). Metaphysics and psychology: A problem of the personal. *Journal of Theoretical and Philosophical Psychology, 25*(2), 238–256. https://doi.org/10.1037/h0091261

Descartes, R. (1993). *Discourse on method and meditations on first philosophy* (3rd ed.). Hackett Publishing Company.

Devine, S. (2020, March 25). The four horsemen of the crisis in psychological science. Blog: *Trial and Error.* https://doi.org/10.36850/kr5s-q873

Dilthey W. (1977). *Descriptive psychology and historical understanding.* Martinus Nijhoff.

Dilthey W. (1988). *Introduction to the human sciences: An attempt to lay a foundation for the study of sociality and history.* Wayne State University Press.

Dolezal, L. (2015). *The body and shame: Phenomenology, feminism, and the socially shaped body.* Lexington Books.

Donohoe, J. (2004). *Husserl on ethics and intersubjectivity: From static to genetic phenomenology.* Humanity.

Dreyfus, H. L. (1972). *What computers can't do: A Critique of artificial reason.* Harper & Row.

Drummond, J. J. (2020). Empathy, sympathy, compassion. Metodo, 8(2), 149–166. https://doi.org/10.19079/metodo.8.2.149

Edie, J. (1987). *William James and phenomenology.* Indiana University Press.

Ekman, P. (1992). An argument for basic emotions. *Cognition and Emotion, 6*(3–4), 169–200. https://doi.org/10.1080/02699939208411068

Ellis, H. C., & Hunt, R. R. (1989). *Fundamentals of human cognition.* Wm. C. Brown.

Embree, L. (2010). Interdisciplinarity within phenomenology. *The Indo-Pacific Journal of Phenomenology, 10,* 1–7.

Englander, M., & Morley, J. (2021). Phenomenological psychology and qualitative research. *Phenomenology and the Cognitive Sciences, 22*(1), 25–53. https://doi.org/10.1007/s11097-021-09781-8

Erikson, E. H. (1968). *Identity: Youth and crisis.* W. W. Norton & Company.

Erikson, E. H. (1961). The roots of virtue. In J. Huxley (Ed.), *The humanist frame* (pp. 147–165). Harper and Brothers.

Ey, H. (1978). *Consciousness: A phenomenological study of being conscious and becoming conscious.* Indiana University Press.

Fanon, F. (2004). *The wretched of the earth.* Grove Press.

Fanon, F. (2008). *Black skin, white masks.* Grove Press.

Feinberg, M., Willer, R., & Keltner, D. (2012). Flustered and faithful: Embarrassment as a signal of prosociality. *Journal of Personality and Social Psychology, 102*(1), 81–97. https://doi.org/10.1037/a0025403

Fink, E. (2016). *Play as symbol of the world and other essays.* Indiana University Press.

Finlay, L. (2009). Debating phenomenological research methods. *Phenomenology & Practice, 3*(1), 6–25.

Finlay, L. (2013). Unfolding the phenomenological research process: Iterative stages of "seeing afresh." *Journal of Humanistic Psychology, 53*(2), 172–201. https://doi.org/10.1177/0022167812453877

Fischer, C. T., & Wertz, F. J. (1979). Empirical phenomenological analyses of being criminalized. In A. Giorgi, R. Knowles, & D. L. Smith (Eds.), *Duquesne studies in phenomenological psychology* (Vol. 3, pp.135–158). Duquesne University Press.

Fischer, W. F. (1985). Self-deception: An empirical–phenomenological investigation. In A. Giorgi (Ed.), *Phenomenology and psychological research,* Duquesne University Press.

Fischer, W. F. (1989). An empirical-phenomenological investigation of being anxious: An example of the phenomenological approach to emotion. In R. S. Valle & S. Halling (Eds.), *Existential-phenomenological perspectives in psychology: Exploring the breadth of human experience* (pp. 127–136). Plenum Press.

Fischer, W. F. (1991) The psychology of anxiety: A phenomenological description. *The Humanistic Psychologist, 19*(3), 289–300. https://doi.org/10.1080/08873267.1991.9986769

Fisette, D. (2022). Emotions and moods in Husserl's phenomenology. In H. Jacobs (Ed.), *The Husserlian Mind* (pp. 220–231). Routledge.

Frankl, V. E. (1967). *Psychotherapy and existentialism: selected papers on logotherapy*. Simon and Schuster/Touchstone.

Frankl, V. E. (1969). *The will to meaning: Foundations and applications of logotherapy*. Nal.

Frankl, V. E. (1975). *The unconscious God*. Simon and Schuster.

Frankl, V. E. (1978). *The unheard cry for meaning*. Washington Square Press.

Frankl, V. E. (1986). *The doctor and the soul*. Vintage.

Frankl, V. E. (2006). *Man's search for meaning*. Beacon Press.

Friedman, M. (1991). *The worlds of existentialism*. Humanities Paperback Library.

Fromm, E. (1947). *Man for himself: An inquiry in the psychology of ethics*. Rinehart and Company.

Fromm, E. (1962). *Beyond the chains of illusion: My encounter with Marx and Freud*. Simon and Schuster.

Fuchs, T. (2012). Body memory and the unconscious. In D. Lohmar & J. Brudzínska (Eds.), *Founding psychoanalysis phenomenologically, Phaenomenologica 199* (pp. 69–82). Springer.

Fuller, A. R. (1990). *Insight into value*. State University of N.Y. Press.

Gallagher, S. (2019). Dilthey and empathy. In E. Nelson (Ed.), *Interpreting Dilthey: Critical essays* (pp. 145–158). Cambridge University Press. https://doi.org/10.1017/9781316459447.008

Gendlin, E. (2018). *Saying what we mean: Implicit precision and the responsive order*. Northwestern University Press.

Giorgi, A. (1967). A phenomenological approach to the problem of meaning and serial learning. *Review of Existential Psychology and Psychiatry, 7*, 106–118.

Giorgi, A. (1968). Learning as a function of meaning levels with American and German subjects. *Psychological Reports, 23*, 27–39.

Giorgi, A. (1970). *Psychology as a human science: A phenomenologically based approach*. Harper and Row.

Giorgi, A. (1975). An application of phenomenological method in psychology. In A. Giorgi, C. Fischer, & E. Murray (Eds.), *Duquesne studies in phenomenological psychology* (Vol. 2, pp. 82–103). Duquesne University Press. https://doi.org/10.5840/dspp197529

Giorgi, A. (1979). Phenomenology and psychological theory. In A. Giorgi, R. Knowles, & D. L. Smith, *Duquesne studies in phenomenological psychology* (Vol. 3, pp. 60–80). Duquesne University Press.

Giorgi, A. (1985). Sketch of a psychological phenomenological method. In A. Giorgi (Ed.), *Phenomenology and psychological research* (pp. 8–22). Duquesne University Press.

Giorgi, A. (1987). Phenomenology and experimental psychology: II. In A. Giorgi, W. F. Fischer, & R. Von Eckartsberg (Eds.), *Duquesne studies in phenomenological psychology* (Vol. 1, pp. 17–29). Duquesne University Press.

Giorgi, A. (1992). Whither humanistic psychology? *The Humanistic Psychologist, 20*(2–3), 422–438. https://doi.org/10.1080/08873267.1992.9986807

Giorgi, A. (1993). Psychology as the science of the paralogical. *Journal of Phenomenological Psychology, 24*(1), 63–77. https://doi.org/10.1163/156916293X00044

Giorgi, A. (2006). Concerning variations in the application of the phenomenological method. *The Humanistic Psychologist, 34*(4), 305–319. https://doi.org/10.1207/s15473333thp3404_2

Giorgi, A. (2009). *The descriptive phenomenological method in psychology: A modified Husserlian approach.* Pittsburgh: Duquesne University Press.

Giorgi, A. (2011). IPA and science: A response to Jonathan Smith. *Journal of Phenomenological Psychology, 42*(2), 195–216. https://doi.org/10.1163/156916211X599762

Giorgi, A. (2014). Phenomenological philosophy as the basis for a human scientific psychology. *The Humanistic Psychologist, 42*(3), 233–248. https://doi.org/10.1080/08873267.2014.933052

Giorgi, A. (2018) *Reflections on certain qualitative and phenomenological psychological methods.* University Professor's Press.

Giorgi, A. (2019). *Psychology as a human science: A phenomenologically based approach.* University Professors Press. (Original work published in 1970)

Goffman, E. (1953). *Communication conduct in an island community* [Doctoral dissertation, University of Chicago]. https://archive.org/details/GOFFMAN1953CommunicationConductInAnIslandCommunity

Goffman, E. (1956a). Embarrassment and social organization. *American Journal of Sociology, 62*(3) 264–271. https://doi.org/10.1086/222003

Goffman, E. (1956b). *The presentation of self in everyday life.* University of Edinburgh Social Sciences Research Centre.

Greenberg, J., Vail, K., & Pyszczynski, T. (2014). Terror management theory and research: How the desire for death transcendence drives our strivings for meaning and significance. In A. J. Elliot (Ed.), *Advances in motivation science* (Vol. 1, pp. 85–134). Elsevier Academic Press.

Guccinelli, R., & Iocco, G. (2020). Positive feelings on the border between phenomenology, psychology, and virtue ethics. *Metodo, 8*(2), 7–28. https://doi.org/10.19079/metodo.8.2.7

Guilford, J. P. (1950). Creativity. *American Psychologist, 5*(9), 444–454. https://doi.org/10.1037/h0063487

Gurwitsch, A. (1964). *The field of consciousness.* Duquesne University Press.

Gurwitsch, A. (1974). *Phenomenology and the theory of science.* Northwestern University Press.

Guse, T. (2017). Special edition on positive psychology and phenomenology. *Indo-Pacific Journal of Phenomenology, 17.*

Haggbloom, S. J., Warnick, R., Warnick, J. E., Jones, V. K., Yarbrough, G. L., Russell, T. M., Borecky, C. M., McGahhey, R., Powell, J. L. III, Beavers, J., & Monte, E. (2002). The 100 most eminent psychologists of the 20th century. *Review of General Psychology, 6*(2), 139–152. https://doi.org/10.1037/1089-2680.6.2.139

Halling, S. (2005). When intimacy and companionship are at the core of the phenomenological research process. *The Indo-Pacific Journal of Phenomenology, 5*(1), 1–11. https://doi.org/10.1080/20797222.2005.11433897

Halling, S., Kunz, G., & Rowe, J. O. (1994). The contributions of dialogal psychology to phenomenological research. *Journal of Humanistic Psychology, 34*(1), 109–131. https://doi.org/10.1177/00221678940341007

Hannush, M. J. (2007). An existential–dialectical–phenomenological approach to understanding cultural tilts: Implications for multicultural research and Practice. *Journal of Phenomenological Psychology, 38*(1), 7–23. https://doi.org/10.1163/156916207X190229

Hart, K. A. (2018). *Multicultural inclusion: A phenomenological study of men of color who are professional counselors* (4063). [Doctoral dissertation, Northern Illinois University]. https://huskiecommons.lib.niu.edu/allgraduate-thesesdissertations/4063

Hartimo, M. (2021). *Husserl and mathematics.* Cambridge University Press. https://doi.org/10.1017/9781108990905

Hartimo, M. (Ed.) (2010). *Phenomenology and mathematics* (*Phaenomenologica book 195*). Springer.

Heidegger, M. (1962). *Being and time.* Harper Collins.

Heidegger, M. (1966). *Discourse on thinking.* Harper Torchbooks.

Heidegger, M. (1971). *Poetry, language, thought.* Harper Colophon Books.

Heidegger, M. (1977). *Basic writings.* Harper San Francisco.

Henry, C. D. (2017). Humanistic psychology and introductory textbooks: A 21st-century reassessment. *The Humanistic Psychologist, 45*(3), 281–294. https://doi.org/10.1037/hum0000056

Hereford, M., Wilcox, M. M., & Pollard, E. (2023). A phenomenological exploration into therapists' multicultural case conceptualizations. *Journal of Psychotherapy Integration, 33*(3), 302–320. https://doi.org/10.1037/int0000299

Higuchi, M., & Fukada, H. (2002). A comparison of four causal factors of embarrassment in public and private situations. *The Journal of Psychology, 136,* 399–406.

Horney, K. (1950). *Neurosis and human growth: The struggle toward self-realization.* W. W. Norton & Company.

Hoyos G. (2012). Fenomenología del multiculturalismo y pluralismo intercultural. *Revista Peruana de Medicina Experimental y Salud Publica, 29*(4), 555–560. https://doi.org/10.1590/s1726-46342012000400022
Husserl, E. (1964). *The Phenomenology of internal time-consciousness.* Indiana University Press.
Husserl, E. (1965). *Phenomenology and the crisis of philosophy.* Harper Torchbooks.
Husserl, E. (1969). *Formal and transcendental logic.* Martinus Nijhoff.
Husserl, E. (1970). *The crisis of European sciences and transcendental phenomenology.* Northwestern University Press.
Husserl, E. (1971) "Phenomenology," Edmund Husserl's article for the Encyclopaedia Britannica (1927): New complete translation by Richard E. Palmer. *Journal of the British Society for Phenomenology, 2*(2), 77–90.
Husserl, E. (1973). *Experience and judgment: Investigations in a genealogy of logic.* Northwestern University Press.
Husserl, E. (1989). *Ideas pertaining to a pure phenomenology and to a phenomenological philosophy: Second book.* Kluwer Academic Press.
Husserl, E. (2001). *Logical investigations.* Routledge.
Husserl, E. (2009). *Philosophie als strenge wissenschaft.* Felix Meiner Verlag.
Husserl, E. (2014). *Ideas for a pure phenomenology and phenomenological philosophy: First book.* Hackett Publishing Company.
Idhe, D. (2012). *Experimental phenomenology: Multistabilities.* SUNY.
Ihde, D. (1971). *Hermeneutic phenomenology: The philosophy of Paul Ricoeur.* Northwestern University Press.
Jager, B. (1988). Theorizing as artful inscription. *The Humanistic Psychologist, 16*(2), 331–340. https://doi.org/10.1080/08873267.1988.9976829
James, J. L. (2007). *Transcendental phenomenological psychology: Introduction to Husserl's psychology of human consciousness.* Trafford.
James, W. (1890). *The principles of psychology.* Henry Holt & Company.
James, W. (1961). *Psychology: The briefer course.* Harper Torchbooks.
James, W. (1996). *Essays in radical empiricism.* University of Nebraska Press.
Kearney, R. (2011). *Phenomenologies of the stranger: Between hostility and hospitality.* Fordham University Press.
Keen, E. (1975). *A primer in phenomenological psychology.* Holt, Rinehart, and Winston.
Keltner, D. (1995). Signs of appeasement: Evidence for the distinct displays of embarrassment, amusement, and shame. *Journal of Personality and Social Psychology, 68*(3), 441–454. https://doi.org/10.1037/0022-3514.68.3.441
Keltner, D., & Buswell, B. (1996). Evidence for the distinctness of embarrassment, shame, and guilt: A study of recalled antecedents and facial expressions of emotion. *Cognition and Emotion, 10,*155–172. https://doi.org/10.1080/026999396380312
Keltner, D., & Buswell, B. (1997). Embarrassment: Its distinct form and appeasement functions. *Psychological Bulletin, 3*, 250–270.

Kierkegaard, S. (1980). *The concept of anxiety*. Princeton University Press.

Knowles, R. T. (1986). *Human development and human possibility: Erikson in the light of Heidegger*. University Press of America.

Kopcsó, K., & Láng, A. (2023). Adolescents' fear of the dark: Associations with fear of death and trait-anxiety. *European Journal of Developmental Psychology*. Advance online publication. https://doi.org/10.1080/17405629.2023.2186394

Køster, A., & Kofod, E. H. (2022). *Cultural, existential and phenomenological dimensions of grief experience*. Routledge.

Kozyreva, A. (2018). Non-representational approaches to the unconscious in the phenomenology of Husserl and Merleau-Ponty. *Phenomenology and the Cognitive Sciences, 17*(1), 199–224. https://doi.org/10.1007/s11097-016-9492-9

Krishna, A. Herd, K. B., & Aydınoglu, N. Z. (2018). A review of consumer embarrassment as a public and private emotion. *Journal of Consumer Psychology, 29*(3), 4–92-516. https://doi.org/10.1002/jcpy.1086

Krishna, A., Herd, K. B., & Aydinoglu, N. Z. (2015). Wetting the bed at twenty-one: Embarrassment as a private emotion. *Journal of Consumer Psychology, 25*, 476–486. https://doi.org/10.1016/j.jcps.2015.02.005

Kruger, D. (1979). *An introduction to phenomenological psychology*. Duquesne University Press.

Kuenzli, A. E. (Ed.) (1959). *The phenomenological problem*. Harper & Brothers.

Kwant, R. C. (1965). *Encounter*. Duquesne University Press.

Lahey, B. B. (1989). *Psychology: An introduction*. Wm. C. Brown.

Laing, R. D. (1990). *The divided self: An existential study in sanity and madness*. Penguin.

Langeveld, M. J. (1983). The "secret place" in the life of the child. *Phenomenology & Pedagogy, 1*(2), 181-1–94. Retrieved January 2, 2006, from http://www.phenomenologyonline.com/articles/langeveld2.html

Larsen, H.G., & Adu, P. (2022). *The theoretical framework in phenomenological research: Development and application*. Routledge. https://doi.org/10.4324/9781003084259

Lau, K-Y (2016). *Phenomenology and intercultural understanding: Toward a new cultural flesh*. Springer.

Laubscher, L., Hook, D., & Desai, M. U. (Eds.) (2022). *Fanon, phenomenology, and psychology*. Routledge.

Leigh-Osroosh, K., & Hutchinson, B. (2019). Cultural identity silencing of Native Americans in education. *Race and Pedagogy, 4*(1). https://soundideas.pugetsound.edu/rpj/vol4/iss1/3

Leone, D. R., Ray, S. L., & Evans, M. (2013). The lived experience of anxiety among late adolescents during high school: An interpretive phenomenological inquiry. *Journal of Holistic Nursing: Official Journal of the American Holistic Nurses' Association, 31*(3), 188–199. https://doi.org/10.1177

Levinas, E. (1969) *Totality and infinity: An essay on exteriority*. Duquesne University Press.

Lewin, K. (1935). *A dynamic theory of personality*. McGraw-Hill.

Lizardo, O., & Collett, J. L. (2013). Embarrassment and social organization: A multiple identities model. *Social Forces, 92*(1), 353–375. https://doi.org/10.1093/SF%2FSOT078

Locke, J. (1996). *An essay concerning human understanding*. Hackett Publishing Company.

Longbottom, S., & Slaughter, V. (2018). Sources of children's knowledge about death and dying. *Philosophical transactions of the Royal Society of London. Series B, Biological sciences, 373*(1754), 20170267. https://doi.org/10.1098/rstb.2017.0267

Lopes, J. (2024). On the psychologism of neurophenomenology. *Phenomenology and the Cognitive Sciences, 23(*1), 85–104. https://doi.org/10.1007/S11097-021-09773-8

Luft, S. (2005). Husserl's concept of the 'transcendental person': Another look at the Husserl–Heidegger relationship. *International Journal of Philosophical Studies, 13*(2), 141–177. https://doi.org/10.1080/09672550500080371

Luijpen, W, & Koren, H. J. (1969). *A first introduction to existential phenomenology*. Duquesne University Press.

MacDonald, P. S. (2006). Husserl against Heidegger against Husserl. In P. D. Ashworth & M. C. Chung (Eds), *Phenomenology and psychological science: History and philosophy of psychology* (pp.101–122). Springer. https://doi.org/10.1007/978-0-387-33762-3_6

Malan, D. (1992). *Individual psychotherapy and the science of psychodynamics*. Butterworth Heinemann.

Marcel, G (1965). *Being and having: An existentialist diary*. Harper Torchbooks.

Marcel, G. (1964). *Creative fidelity*. Noonday Press.

Marchel, C., & Owens, S. (2007). Qualitative research in psychology: Could William James get a job? *History of Psychology, 10*(4), 301–324. https://doi.org/10.1037/1093-4510.10.4.301

Marcus, D. K., & Miller, R. S. (1999). The perception of "live" embarrassment: A social relations analysis of class presentations. *Cognition and Emotion, 13*, 105–117. https://psycnet.apa.org/doi/10.1080/026999399379393

Maser, M. (2023). *Insight-out: A phenomenological exploration of the nature and appearance of learning.* [Doctoral dissertation, Simon Fraser University]. Knowledge Commons. https://hcommons.org/deposits/item/hc:60951

Maslow, A. H. (1943). A theory of human motivation. *Psychological Review, 50*(4), 370–396. https://doi.org/10.1037/h0054346

Maslow, A. H. (1946). Problem-centering vs. means-centering in science. *Philosophy of Science. 13 (4): 326–331.* https://doi.org/10.1086/286907

Maslow, A. H. (1954). *Motivation and personality*. Harper & Brothers.

Maslow, A. H. (1961). Health as transcendence of environment. *Journal of Humanistic Psychology, 1*(1), 1–7. https://doi.org/10.1177/002216786100100102
Maslow, A. H. (1966). *The psychology of science: A reconnaissance.* Harper Collins.
Maslow, A. H. (1969). Toward a humanistic biology. *American Psychologist, 24*(8), 724–735. https://doi.org/10.1037/h0027859
Maslow, A. H. (1971). *The farther reaches of human nature.* Esalen.
May, R. (1953). *Man's search for himself.* New American Library.
May, R. (1958a). Contributions of existential psychotherapy. In R. May, E. Angel, & H. Ellenberger (Eds.), *Existence: A new dimension in psychiatry and psychology* (pp. 37–91). Basic Books.
May, R. (1958b). The origins and significance of the existential movement in psychology. In R. May, E. Angel, & H. Ellenberger (Eds.), *Existence: A new dimension in psychiatry and psychology* (pp. 3–36). Basic Books.
May, R. (1969). *Love and will.* W. W. Norton & Company.
May, R. (1977). *The meaning of anxiety.* W. W. Norton & Company.
May, R. (1979). *Psychology and the human dilemma.* W. W. Norton & Company.
May, R. (1981). *Freedom and destiny.* W. W. Norton & Company.
May, R., Angel, E., & Ellenberger, H. (Eds.)(1958). *Existence: A new dimension in psychiatry and psychology.* Basic Books.
McCall, R. J. (1983). *Phenomenological psychology.* The University of Wisconsin Press.
McGilchrist, I. (2009). *The master and his emissary: The divided brain and the making of the Western world.* Yale University Press.
McLemore, S. D. (1970). Simmel's 'stranger': A critique of the concept. *The Pacific Sociological Review, 13*(2), 86–94.
Meacham, D. (2013). Biology, the empathic science: Husserl's addendum XXIII of the crisis of European sciences and transcendental phenomenology. *Journal of the British Society for Phenomenology, 44*(1), 10–24/ https://doi.org/10.1080/00071773.2013.11006785
Merleau-Ponty, M. (1962). *The phenomenology of perception.* Routledge.
Merleau-Ponty, M. (1963). *The structure of behavior.* Beacon Press.
Merleau-Ponty, M. (1964). *The primacy of perception.* Northwestern University Press.
Merleau-Ponty, M. (1968). *The visible and the invisible.* Northwestern University Press.
Merleau-Ponty, M. (2010). *Child psychology and pedagogy.* Northwestern University Press.
Merleau-Ponty, M. (2020). *The sensible world and the world of expression: Course notes from the Collège de France, 1953.* Northwestern University Press.
Messas G, Tamelini M, Mancini M, & Stanghellini G (2018). New Perspectives in phenomenological psychopathology: Its use in psychiatric treatment.

Frontiers in Psychiatry, 9, Article 466. https://doi.org/10.3389/fpsyt.2018.00466

Miller, G., & Mitcham, C. (2020). Designing and constructing the (life)world: Phenomenology and engineering. In G. Miller & A. Shew (Eds.), *Reimagining philosophy and technology, reinventing Ihde* (*Philosophy of engineering and technology series* (Vol. *33*, pp. 175–189). Springer. https://doi.org/10.1007/978-3-030-35967-6_11

Miller, R. S. (1992). The nature and severity of self-reported embarrassing circumstances. *Personality and Social Psychology Bulletin, 18*(2), 190–198. https://doi.org/10.1177/0146167292182010

Miller, R. S. (2001). On the primacy of embarrassment in social life. *Psychological Inquiry, 12*(1), 30–33.

Modigliani, A. (1968). Embarrassment and embarrassability. *Sociometry, 31*(3), 313–326.

Moran, D. (2004). The Problem of empathy: Lipps, Scheler, Husserl and Stein. In T. A. Kelly & P. W. Rosemann (Eds.), *Amor Amicitiae: On the Love That Is Friendship. Essays in Medieval Thought and Beyond in Honor of the Rev. Professor James McEvoy* (pp. 269–312). Peeters.

Moran, D. (2005). *Edmund Husserl: Founder of phenomenology*. Polity.

Moran, D. (2011). Revisiting Sartre's ontology of embodiment in *Being and Nothingness*. In B. V. Petrov (Ed.), *Ontological landscapes: Recent thought on conceptual interfaces between science and philosophy* (pp. 263–294). DeGruyter. https://doi.org/10.1515/9783110319811.263

Moran, D. (2013). 'Let's look at it objectively': Why phenomenology cannot be naturalized. *Royal Institute of Philosophy Supplement, 72*, 89–115. http://dx.doi.org/10.1017/S1358246113000064

Moran, D. (2017). Husserl's layered concept of the human person: Conscious and unconscious. In D. Legrand & D. Trigg (Eds.), *Unconsciousness between phenomenology and psychoanalysis* (pp. 3–24). Springer.

Moran, D., & Cohen, J. (2012). *The Husserl dictionary*. Continuum International Publishing Group.

Morley, J. (2010). It's always about the epoché: On phenomenological methodology. In T. Cloonan (Ed.), *The redirection of psychology: Essays in honor of Amedeo Giorgi* (pp. 223–232). University of Quebec Press.

Morley, J. (2014). A phenomenologist's response to Alan Waterman. *American Psychologist, 69*(1), 88–89. https://doi.org/10.1037/a0034866

Mosher, D. L., & White, B. R. (1981). On differentiating shame and shyness. *Motivation and Emotion, 5*, 61–74.

Motta, V., & Bortolotti, L. (2020). Solitude as a positive experience: Empowerment and agency. *Metodo, 8*(2), 119–147. https://doi.org/10.19079/metodo.8.2.119

Moustakas, C. E. (1961). *Loneliness*. Prentice-Hall.

Moustakas, C. E. (1994). *Phenomenological research methods*. Sage.

Mruk, C. J. (1985). Integrated description: A phenomenologically oriented technique for researching large scale, emerging human experience and trends. In E. C. Hirschman & M. B. Holbrook (Eds), *NA-Advances in Consumer Research* (Vol. 12, pp. 556–559). Association for Consumer Research.

Mulligan, K. & Smith, B. (1985). Franz Brentano on the ontology of mind. *Philosophy and Phenomenological Research, 45*(4), 627–644.

Murphy, K. (2016, August 27). Do you believe in God, or is that a software glitch? *New York Times, Sunday Review News Analysis.* http://www.nytimes.com/2016/08/28/opinion/sunday/do-you-believe-in-god-or-is-that-a-software-glitch.html?_r=1

Murray, E. L. (1986). *Imaginative thinking and human existence.* Duquesne University Press.

Murray, E. L. (2001). *The quest for personality integration: Reimaginizing our lives.* Simon Silverman Phenomenology Center.

Nameche, G. F. (1961). Two pictures of man. *Journal of Humanistic Psychology, 1*(1), 70–88. https://doi.org/10.1177/002216786100100108

Natanson, M. (1970). *The journeying self.* Addison Wesley.

Needleman, J. (1967). The dasein as constitutive: Binswanger, Heidegger, Sartre. In *Being-in-the-world: selected papers of Ludwig Binswanger* (pp. 101–138). Harper Torch Books.

Ngo, H. (2017). *The habits of racism: A phenomenology of racism and racialized embodiment.* Lexington Books.

Nicholson, G. (1984). The role of interpretation in phenomenological reflection. *Research in Phenomenology, 14*, 57–72.

Orgilés, M., Espada, J. P., & Méndez, X. (2008). Assessment instruments of darkness phobia in children and adolescents: A descriptive review. *International Journal of Clinical and Health Psychology, 8*(1), 315–333.

Osbeck, L. M., & Held, B. S. (Eds.). (2014). *Rational intuition: Philosophical roots, scientific investigations.* Cambridge University Press. https://doi.org/10.1017/CBO9781139136419

Oliver, A. Lamola, M. J., & Sands, J. (Eds.) (2023). *Phenomenology in an African context: Contributions and challenges.* SUNY.

Packer, M. J. (1992). Hermeneutic inquiry in the study of human conduct. In R.B. Miller (Ed.), *The restoration of dialogue, readings in the philosophy of clinical psychology* (pp. 271–289). American Psychological Association.

Packer, M. J. & Addison, R. B. (1989). *Entering the circle: Hermeneutic investigation in psychology*. State University of New York Press.

Park, Y. S., Konge, L., & Artino, A. R. (2020). The positivism paradigm of research. *Academic Medicine, 95*(5), 690–694. https://doi.org/10.1097/ACM.0000000000003093

John Paul II, Pope (1994). *Crossing the threshold of hope.* Knopf.

Peoples, K. (2021). *How to write a phenomenological dissertation: A step-by-step guide.* Sage.

Peperzak, A. (1992). Levinas on technology and nature. *Man and World, 25*, 469–482. https://doi.org/10.1007/BF01252430

Peperzak, A. (1993). *To the other: An introduction to the philosophy of Emmanuel Levinas.* Indiana: Purdue University Press.
Peters, A., Softas-Nall, B., & Martinez, M. (2017). Belonging to multiple nationalities: A phenomenological study. *Advances in Social Sciences Research Journal, 4(7)* 218–237. https://doi.org/10.14738/assrj.47.3068
Peters R. S. (1965). *Brett's history of psychology.* The MIT Press
Pezdek, K., & Roe, C. (1994). Memory for childhood events: How suggestible is it? *Consciousness and Cognition: An International Journal, 3*(3–4), 374–387. https://doi.org/10.1006/ccog.1994.1021
Pfänder, A. (1967). *Phenomenology of willing and motivation.* Northwestern University Press.
Piaget, J., & Inhelder, B. (1969). *The psychology of the child.* Basic Books.
Picton, C. J., Moxham, L., & Patterson, C. (2017). The use of phenomenology in mental health nursing research. *Nurse researcher, 25*(3), 14–18. https://doi.org/10.7748/nr.2017.e1513
Plessner, H. (1964). On human expression. In E. W. Straus (Ed.), *Phenomenology: Pure and applied* (pp. 63–74). Duquesne University Press.
Prasetya, A., Pasca Rina, A., & Sukiatni, D. S. (2023). A phenomenological study of grit among teachers in remote areas. *Proceedings of The 2nd International Seminar of Multicultural Psychology, Surabaya, Indonesia 2*(1), 341–349. https://jurnal.untag-sby.ac.id/index.php/ISMP/article/view/9470
Rennie, D. L. (1995). On the rhetorics of social science: Let's not conflate natural science and human science. *The Humanistic Psychologist, 23*(3), 321–332. https://doi.org/10.1080/08873267.1995.9986833
Ricoeur, P. (1970). *Freud & philosophy: An essay on interpretation.* Yale.
Ricoeur, P. (1973). The hermeneutical function of distanciation. *Philosophy Today, 17*(2), 129–141.
Ricoeur, P. (1992). *Oneself as another.* The University of Chicago Press.
Robbins, B. D., & Parlavecchio, H. (2006). The unwanted exposure of the self: A phenomenological study of embarrassment. *The Humanistic Psychologist, 34*(4), 321–345. https://doi.org/10.1207/s15473333thp3404_3
Rodgers, J. L. (2010). The epistemology of mathematical and statistical modeling: A quiet methodological revolution. *American Psychologist, 65*(1), 1–12. https://doi.org/10.1037/a0018326
Rogers, C. R. (1953). Persons or science? A philosophical question. *CrossCurrents, 3*(4), 289–306. https://www.jstor.org/stable/24456533
Rogers, C. R. (1985). Toward a more human science of the person. *Journal of Humanistic Psychology, 25*(4), 7–24. https://doi.org/10.1177/0022167885254002
Romania, V. (2019). Goffman in Dixon. Ethnographer or performer? *Italian Sociological Review, 9*(2), 235–249. http://dx.doi.org/10.13136/isr.v9i2

Rudrauf, D., Lutz, A., Cosmelli, D., Lachaux, J. P., & Le Van Quyen, M. (2003). From autopoiesis to neurophenomenology: Francisco Varela's exploration of the biophysics of being. *Biological research, 36*(1), 27–65. https://doi.org/10.4067/s0716-97602003000100005

Ryle, G. (1949). *The concept of mind.* Barnes & Noble.

Sánchez Guerrero, H. A. (2021). A phenomenologically grounded empirical approach to experiences of adolescent depression. *Phenomenology and the Cognitive Sciences, 22,* 81–105. https://doi.org/10.1007/s11097-021-09751-0

Sartre, J. P. (2010). *The Imaginary: A Phenomenological Psychology of the Imagination.* Routledge.

Sartre, J. P. (2012). *The imagination.* Routledge.

Sartre, J. P. (2018). *Being and nothingness: An essay in phenomenological ontology.* Washington Square Press.

Schachtel, E. G. (1959). *Metamorphosis: On the development of affect, perception, attention, and memory.* Basic Books. http://dx.doi.org/10.1037/14419-000

Schachter, D. L. Guerin, S. A., & St. Jacques, P. L. (2011). Memory distortion: An adaptive perspective. *Trends in Cognitive Science, 15*(10), 467–474. https://dx.doi.org/10.1016%2Fj.tics.2011.08.004

Schneider, K. (2009). *Awakening to awe: Personal stories of profound transformation.* Jason Aronson.

Schneider, K. J. (2004). *Rediscovery of awe: Splendor, mystery, and the fluid center of life.* Paragon House.

Schneider, K. J. (2015). My journey with Kierkegaard: From the paradoxical self to the polarized mind. *Journal of Humanistic Psychology, 55,* 1–8. https://doi.org/10.1177/0022167814537889

Schneider, K. J. (2020). *The depolarizing of America: A guidebook for social healing.* University Professors Press.

Schneider, K. J. (2023). *Life enhancing anxiety: Key to a sane world.* University Professors Press.

Schudson, M. (1984). Embarrassment and Erving Goffman's idea of human nature. *Theory and Society, 13*(5), 633–648. https://doi.org/10.1007/BF00160911

Schuetz, A. (1944). The stranger: An essay in social psychology. *American Journal of Sociology, 49*(6), 499–507.

Scribner, S. (1979). Modes of thinking and ways of speaking: Culture and logic reconsidered. In I. O. Freedle (Ed.), *New directions in discourse processing* (pp. 223–243). Ablex.

Shadish, W. R. (1995). Philosophy of science and the quantitative-qualitative debates: Thirteen common errors. *Evolution and Program Planning, 18*(1), 63–75. https://doi.org/10.1016/0149-7189(94)00050-8

Sheehan, T. (1997). Husserl and Heidegger: The making and unmaking of a relationship. In T. Sheehan & R. E. Palmer (Eds.), *Edmund Husserl: Psychological and transcendental phenomenology and the confrontation with Heidegger (1927–1931)* (pp. 1–34). Springer-Science & Business Media, B. V.

Sheets-Johnstone, M. (2020). The lived body. *The Humanistic Psychologist, 48*(1), 28–53. https://doi.org/10.1037/hum0000150

Sheets-Johnstone, M. (2022). *The primacy of movement.* John Benjamins.

Sigelman, C. K., & Rider, E. A. (2018). *Life-span human development, 9th edition*. Thomson Cengage Learning.

Silver, M., Sabini, J., & Parrott, W. G. (1987). Embarrassment: A dramaturgic account. *Journal for the Theory of Social Behaviour, 17*(1), 47–61. https://doi.org/10.1111/j.1468-5914.1987.tb00087.x

Simmel, G. (1908). *Soziologie: Unt chungen über die formen der vergesellschaftung*. Duncker & Humblot.

Smith, J. A. (2017). Interpretative phenomenological analysis: Getting at lived experience. *The Journal of Positive Psychology, 12*(3), 303–304. https://doi.org/10.1080/17439760.2016.1262622

Smith, J. A., Flowers, P., & Larkin, M. (2009). *Interpretive phenomenological analysis: Theory, method and research*. Sage.

Solomon, R. C. (1988). *Continental philosophy since 1750: The rise and fall of the self.* Oxford.

Solomon, R. C. (1989). *Introducing philosophy*. Harcourt Brace Jovanovich.

Spencer, M. K. (2012). *Thomistic hylomorphism and the phenomenology of self-sensing*. [Doctoral dissertation, University at Buffalo, State University of New York].

Spiegelberg, H. (1972). *Phenomenology in psychology and psychiatry*. Northwestern University Press.

Spinelli, E. (1989). *The interpreted world: An introduction to phenomenological psychology*. Sage.

Stein, E. (1989). *On the problem of empathy.* ICS Publications.

Steinbock, A. J. (1995). *Home and beyond: Generative phenomenology after Husserl*. Northwestern University Press.

Steinbock, A. J. (2017). *Limit-phenomena and phenomenology in Husserl*. Roman & Littlefield.

Stern, W. (1924). *Psychology of early childhood up to the sixth year of age*. Henry Holt and Company.

Storms, M. D. (1973). Videotape and the attribution process: Reversing actors' and observers' points of view. *Journal of Personality and Social Psychology, 27*(2), 165–175. https://doi.org/10.1037/h0034782

Strasser, S. (1957a). Phenomenological Trends in European Psychology. *Philosophy and Phenomenological Research, 18*(1), 18–34.

Strasser, S. (1957b). *The soul in metaphysical and empirical psychology*. Duquesne University Press.

Strasser, S. (1963). *Phenomenology and the human sciences: A contribution to a new scientific ideal*. Duquesne University Press.

Strasser, S. (1969). *The idea of dialogal phenomenology*. Duquesne University Press.

Strasser, S. (1977). *Phenomenology of feeling*. Duquesne University Press.
Strasser, S. (1978). Buber und Levinas: Philosophische besinnung auf einen gegensatz. *Revue Internationale de Philosophie, 32*(126–4), 512–525.
Strasser, S. (1985). *Understanding and explanation*. Duquesne University Press.
Strasser, S. (1986). *Clefts in the world and other essays on Levinas, Merleau-Ponty, & Buytendijk*. Simon Silverman Phenomenology Center.
Straus, E. W. (1958). Aesthesiology and hallucinations. In R. May, E. Angel, and H. F. Ellenberger (Eds.), *Existence: A new dimension in psychiatry and psychology* (pp. 139–169). Basic Books.
Straus, E. W. (1966). *Phenomenological psychology*. Basic Books.
Straus, E. W. (1967). On anosognosia. In E. W. Straus & R. M. Griffith (Eds.), *The second Lexington conference on pure and applied phenomenology: Phenomenology of will and action* (pp. 103–126). Duquesne University Press.
Tangney, J. P., Miller, R. S., Flicker, L., & Barlow, D. H. (1996). Are shame, guilt, and embarrassment distinct emotions? *Journal of Personality and Social Psychology, 70*(6), 1256–1269. https://doi.org/10.1037/0022-3514.70.6.1256
Tillich, P. (1980). *The courage to be*. Yale University Press.
Torrance, E. P. (1966). Stress-seeking as a factor in high achievement. *Gifted Child Quarterly, 10*(4), 169–173. https://doi.org/10.1177/001698626601000401
Treanor, B. (2006). *Aspects of alterity*. Fordham University Press.
Urmson, J. O., & Rée, J. (Eds.) (1991). *The concise encyclopedia of western philosophy and philosophers.* Routledge.
Vallelonga, D. (1986). *The lived structures of being-embarrassed and being-ashamed-of-oneself: An empirical phenomenological study*. [Doctoral dissertation, Duquesne University]. Dissertation Information Service.
van den Berg, J. H. (1961). *The changing nature of man.* W. W. Norton & Company.
van den Berg, J. H. (1971). What is psychotherapy? *Humanitas, 7*(3), 321–370.
van den Berg, J. H. (1972). *A different existence*. Duquesne University Press.
van Kaam, A. (1966). *Existential foundations of psychology*. Duquesne University Press.
van Manen, M. (1990). *Researching lived experience: Human science for an action sensitive pedagogy*. SUNY.
van Manen, M. (2014). *Phenomenology of practice: Meaning-giving methods in phenomenological research and writing*. Left Coast Press, Inc.
van Manen, M. (2018). Rebuttal rejoinder: Present IPA for what it is—Interpretative psychological analysis. *Qualitative Health Research, 28*(12) 1959–1968. https://doi.org/10.1177/1049732318795474
Veliyannoor, P.V. (2011). *Transformation in "E": The structure and dynamics of the experience of the Eucharist.* [Doctoral Dissertation, Pacifica Graduate Institute]. #3500726 UMI Dissertation Publishing, Proquest.

von Eckartsberg, R. (1989). The unfolding meaning of intentionality and horizon in phenomenology. *The Humanistic Psychologist, 17*(2), 146–160. https://doi.org/10.1080/08873267.1989.9976848

von Eckartsberg, R. (1998). existential–phenomenological research. In R. S. Valle (Ed.), *Phenomenological inquiry in psychology: Existential and transpersonal dimensions* (pp. 21–61). Plenum Press. http://dx.doi.org/10.1007/978-1-4899-0125-5_2

von Eckartsberg, R. (2010). On the geography of human experience. *The Humanistic Psychologist, 38*(3), 255–266. https://doi.org/10.1080/08873261003635997

Wagemans J., van Lier, R., & Scholl, B. J. (2006). Introduction to Michotte's heritage in perception and cognition research. *Acta Psychologica, 123*(1–2), 1–19. https://doi.org/10.1016/j.actpsy.2006.06.003

Waldenfels, B. (1990). Experience of the alien in Husserl's phenomenology. *Research in Phenomenology, 20*, 19–33. https://www.jstor.org/stable/24654451

Waterman, A. S. (2013). The humanistic psychology-positive psychology divide: Contrasts in philosophical foundations. *American Psychologist, 68*(3), 124–133. https://doi.org/10.1037/a0032168

Weitkamp, K., Klein, E., & Midgley, N. (2016). The experience of depression: A qualitative study of adolescents with depression entering psychotherapy. *Global Qualitative Nursing Research, 3*, 1–12. https://doi.org/10.1177/2333393616649548

Wertz, F. J. (1983). Some constituents of descriptive psychological reflection. *Human Studies, 6*, 35–51, https://doi.org/10.1007/BF02127753

Wertz, F. J. (1986). Common methodological fundaments of the analytic procedures in phenomenological and psychoanalytic research. *Psychoanalysis & Contemporary Thought, 9*(4), 563–603.

Wertz, F. J. (1992). Representations of the "third force" in history of psychology textbooks. *The Humanistic Psychologist, 20*(2–3), 461–476. https://doi.org/10.1080/08873267.1992.9986810

Wertz, F. J. (2015). Phenomenology: Methods, historical development, and applications in psychology. In J. Martin, J. Sugarman, & K. L. Slaney (Eds.), *The Wiley handbook of theoretical and philosophical psychology: Methods, approaches, and new directions for social sciences* (pp. 85–101). Wiley Blackwell.

Wertz, F. J. (2023). Phenomenological methodology, methods, and procedures for research in psychology. In H. Cooper, M. N. Coutanche, L. M. McMullen, A. T. Panter, D. Rindskopf, & K. J. Sher (Eds.), *APA handbook of research methods in psychology: Research designs: Quantitative, qualitative, neuropsychological, and biological* (pp. 83–105). American Psychological Association. https://doi.org/10.1037/0000319-005

Willis, R. F. (1987). *Western civilization: A brief introduction*. Macmillan.

Wilshire, B. (1968). *William James and phenomenology: A study of the principles of psychology.* Indiana University Press.

Woodgate, R.L., Tennent, P., & Legras, N. (2021). Understanding youth's lived experience of anxiety through metaphors: A qualitative, arts-based study. *International Journal of Environmental Research and Public Health, 18,* 4315. https://doi.org/10.3390/ijerph18084315

Wertz, F. J. (2025a). A history of humanistic and existential psychology: The possibility and contexts of renewal in science. In Hoffman, L., Hocoy, D., & DeRobertis, E. M. (Eds.), *Handbook of humanistic and existential psychology* (Vol. 1, pp. 3–47. https://doi.org/10.1037/0000431-001

Wertz, F. J. (2025b). Phenomenological method in psychological science: A methodological retrospective. *Qualitative Psychology, 12*(3), 354–376. https://doi.org/10.1037/qup0000335

Wertz, F. J., Charmaz, K., McMullen, L. M., Josselson, R., Anderson, R., & McSpadden, E. (2011). *Five ways of doing qualitative analysis: Phenomenological psychology, grounded theory, discourse analysis, narrative research, and intuitive inquiry.* The Guilford Press.

Woody, W. D. & Viney, W. (2017). *A history of psychology: Emergence of science and applications* (2nd ed.). Routledge.

Wren, L. B. (1965). *The meaning of nothingness in the early philosophy of Martin Heidegger* [Master's thesis Loyola University, Chicago]. https://ecommons.luc.edu/luc_theses/2048

Wundt, W. (1917). *Völkerpsychologie: Eine untouching der entwicklungsgesetze von space, mythus und Sitte.* Alfred Kroner Verlag.

Yalom, I. D. (1980). *Existential psychotherapy.* Basic Books.

Young, L. (1992). Sexual abuse and the problem of embodiment. *Child Abuse & Neglect, 16,* 89–100.

Zahavi, D. (2021). Applied phenomenology: Why it is safe to ignore the epoché. *Continental Philosophy Review, 54,* 259–273. https://doi.org/10.1007/s11007-019-09463-y

Index

D

E

F

About the Author

Eugene Mario DeRobertis, PhD, is Professor of Psychology at Brookdale College in New Jersey. He also teaches part-time for Rutgers and Kean Universities. Dr. DeRobertis completed his education at Duquesne University, where he received his initial training in the phenomenological method as adapted for psychological research. Prior to committing himself to teaching full time in 1996, he worked as a developmentally oriented psychotherapist, an academic counselor, and an addictions counselor. He has published numerous peer-reviewed works in phenomenological psychology, existential–humanistic psychology, psychological theory, and developmental psychology with a particular emphasis on childhood. His books include *Humanizing Child Developmental Theory: A Holistic Approach* (2008); *The Whole Child: Selected Papers on Existential–Humanistic Child Psychology* (2012); *The Phenomenology of Learning and Becoming: Enthusiasm, Creativity, and Self-Development* (2017); and *Profiles of Personality: Integration, Paradox, and the Process of Becoming* (2021). He is a member of Divisions 32 (Society for Humanistic Psychology) and 5 (Society for Qualitative Inquiry) of the American Psychological Association and currently serves as Review Editor for the *Journal of Phenomenological Psychology*.

www.ingramcontent.com/pod-product-compliance
Lightning Source LLC
LaVergne TN
LVHW010641110826
845149LV00014B/2919

* 9 7 8 1 9 5 5 7 3 7 6 8 5 *